CHARTING LOVE WITH ASTROLOGY

About the Author

Tracy Quinlan is a Canadian astrologer who has been in love with astrology for more than forty years. After completing a bachelor of arts in sociology and psychology, she began her more formal astrology education in 2007 learning from Chris McRae. She went on to earn certificates from Kepler College and the School of Traditional Astrology (STA). She continues to learn, evolve, and develop her skills. "It is such an honor to be allowed to share people's natal promise and to step on their path with them, even for just a short time. The language of astrology is a gift." Tracy also contributes to Llewellyn's *Astrological Calendar.* You can find her at ConsultTheSky.com and TracyQuinlan.com and on Instagram, Threads, YouTube, and Facebook.

CHARTING LOVE WITH ASTROLOGY

UNLOCK THE RELATIONSHIP POTENTIAL IN YOUR BIRTH CHART

TRACY QUINLAN

WOODBURY, MINNESOTA

First Edition
First Printing, 2026

Cover design by Shira Atakpu
Interior art by the Llewellyn Art Department
Charts created using Solar Fire software, published by Astrolabe, Inc., www.alabe.com.

Library of Congress Cataloging-in-Publication Data (Pending)
ISBN: 978-0-7387-8118-1

Llewellyn Publications
A Division of Llewellyn Worldwide Ltd.
2143 Wooddale Drive
Woodbury, MN 55125-2989
www.llewellyn.com

Printed in the United States of America

GPSR Representation:
UPI-2M PLUS d.o.o., Medulićeva 20, 10000 Zagreb, Croatia
matt.parsons@upi2mbooks.hr

Other Works by Tracy Quinlan

Llewellyn's Astrological Calendar
(monthly forecasts)
Llewellyn, 2019–present

To the people who've stuck with me,
loved me for who I am,
and cheered me on.
This is not just for you…It's because of you.
Especially my PBC Darcy.

Contents

Tables

Charts

Introduction
What Is Your Love Story Made Of?

People usually come to astrology for two reasons: to understand why life unfolds the way it does and to get a glimpse into what the future might hold. Love and relationships are some of the most popular topics of exploration because, let's face it, they're one of the most complex parts of our lives. For most of us, the relationship story written in our chart is intricate, layered, and sometimes surprising.

When it comes to love in astrology, there's more to it than just the planets influencing our romantic tendencies or what we find emotionally safe. We also need to consider what we value in partners and, importantly, *where* we're most likely to find them. Every relationship I had before meeting my husband of twenty-plus years was through work. Astrology made that clear in hindsight, but at the time I had no idea why! If I had, would it have changed the way I approached dating? Maybe, maybe not. But it certainly would have given me some hints about where things were likely to go and what the *point* of those relationships was.

That's the heart of this book: showing you that your chart isn't just a map of personality traits or compatibility points. It's a tool for recognizing *how* you love, *who* you tend to attract, and *where* love might be waiting for you to show up.

This book is designed to help you explore your personal love story through the birth chart. Whether you're just starting to explore astrology or have been studying for years, this guide will help you connect the dots between Venus and Mars, the houses of love and intimacy, and the often overlooked clues about where relationship energy is most active in your life.

We'll start with Venus and Mars, the planets of attraction, connection, and desire. Then we'll look at the 5th, 7th, and 8th houses and how they shape your experiences of dating, commitment, and intimacy. From there, you'll learn how the signs on the cusps of these houses affect your approach to love, and how the planetary rulers of these houses tell their own story by where they show up in your chart. You'll also find a practical chapter that links all this to real-life locations and activities—yes, actual places to go and things to do—based on your chart. If that's what you're here for, skip ahead to chapter 8. I won't tell. (Appendix B has an even more detailed list of places to find love based on the houses.)

For those of you who want to understand the deeper themes, such as why certain patterns repeat in your relationships or why connection sometimes feels elusive, we'll also look at the aspects made to your house rulers and how timing matters. Transits, returns, progressions, profections, and eclipses can all play a role in when love enters (or exits) your life.

By the end, not only will you have a fuller picture of how love shows up in your chart, but you'll also have tools to work with your own timing, recognize recurring themes, and understand how your values, needs, and desires have shaped your past and present relationships.

No astrological background is required, though it helps if you've seen your birth chart before. If not, don't worry—I'll explain how to find what you need (so you can follow along) in the next section. This book is about *your* story. Astrology just happens to be one of the best tools I've found for reading between the lines.

So … Let's find your love story!

Finding Love in Your Birth Chart

To uncover where to find love in your birth chart (also called a natal chart), we need to go beyond those simplistic Sun sign compatibility lists you see everywhere. Love, like astrology, is layered, multidimensional, and deeply personal. It can't be boiled down to one or two planets; it's about how the entire chart works together (or not) to tell your personal story. To fully explore your relationship potential, we need to check out the planets *and* the houses most associated with love and relationships.

To help you get a deeper understanding of *your* personal love story, we'll first look at the roles of Mars and Venus—the planets of passion and romance—and how their placements affect the way you express and experience love. It's vital to understand the patterns in what you want (Venus) and how you go after it (Mars). You'll get the opportunity to self-reflect, with prompts and exercises to help you.

Then we'll look at the relationship houses in your birth chart. Since there are different types of relationships, there is more than one house to explore to get a full picture. The 5th house is the house of joy, romance, and creativity. It shows where you might find the spark of attraction and what brings you excitement in love. Then there's the 7th house of partnerships, which points to the qualities you seek in a significant other and what makes a relationship feel worthy of commitment. Finally, the 8th house takes us deeper—this is where we find intimacy, sex, and shared resources, the glue that can bind two people in a profound connection.

Since the houses are only the beginning, to get a fuller picture we'll look at the sign coloring each of these houses and how that describes who you're looking for. We'll examine where the rulers of those signs are in your chart, because these details provide clues about where love is more likely to show up in your life. You'll even find detailed lists of places and activities related to each of the twelve houses in your natal chart to help you zero in on the best places you might find your person.

Then we'll go a step deeper and look at how the planets involved are talking to each other (through aspects) and what that contributes to your love story.

In my experience working with clients over the years, I've seen over and over again how different our stories are. We are not all made to fit into the socially prescribed relationship picture. Just because everyone you know met their person through an app doesn't mean that's your best option. In my career, I've never seen two identical natal stories, yet we're often told that we're meant to want the same things and go after them in the same ways.

So whether you've been swiping left and right with no luck or just feeling unsure about where to direct your energy, this book is designed to help you stop wasting time on connections that don't align with your potential. Instead, I hope it guides you toward opportunities that fit with your chart and your distinct path.

Ready to uncover your story? Let's start exploring what your birth chart has to say about your relationship track.

A Quick Breakdown of Your Birth Chart

Your birth chart is a snapshot of the sky at the exact moment and location of your birth. It's like your personal blueprint, showing the positions of the planets, the twelve zodiac signs, and the twelve astrological houses. Together, these elements weave the story of your personality, life experiences, and relationships.

At first glance, a natal chart can look a bit overwhelming, like a wheel full of mysterious symbols and lines. But once you break it down, piece by piece, it becomes clearer. Here's what you're looking at:

The Planets: These represent different parts of your personality and life. The Sun and Moon form the core of who you are, while Mercury, Venus, and Mars add complexity, shaping how you think, connect, and act. Saturn and Jupiter reveal how you navigate social norms and expectations, while the outer planets (Uranus, Neptune, and Pluto) speak to influences beyond your immediate world, offering insight into broader social themes.

The Signs: Each planet sits in a zodiac sign, which adds its own flavor to how the planet's energy is expressed. Some signs make it easier for a planet to operate in its "natural" way, while others push the planet outside its comfort zone, creating challenges or new dynamics.

The Houses: The chart is divided into twelve sections, or houses, each representing a specific area of life, such as relationships, career, or home. A planet's placement in a house shows where its energy will show up most prominently in your life. The houses also have general themes that can be connected to places, people, and activities.

The Aspects: Aspects are the conversations that planets have with each other. The zodiac is a 360-degree circle, with each sign occupying 30 degrees. Aspects are determined by the angles that planets form with one another based on their positions in the circle. Each aspect carries its own energy. Some aspects create harmony and flow, while others bring tension and challenge, adding layers to how the planets work together in your chart.

A popular analogy of the birth chart and its components compares the chart to a play: The planets are the actors, the signs are their costumes, the houses are the stage/set, and the aspects are how the actors are interacting with each other.

Key Terms You'll See in This Book

This book assumes a basic understanding of astrology, but here's a quick rundown of terms that will help you get the most out of what's ahead:

Ascendant (Rising Sign): The Ascendant, also called the rising sign, is the sign on the eastern horizon at the time of your birth—the sign on your 1st house cusp. It starts the 1st house of your chart and represents how you meet the world.

Descendant: The Descendant sits directly opposite the Ascendant, starting the 7th house, and reflects how you approach relationships and what you seek in a partner. It is the sign on your 7th house cusp.

Midheaven (MC): The Midheaven (MC) is the highest point in the chart and represents your reputation, long-term goals, public life, and the dominant parent. It is the sign on your 10th house cusp.

IC (*Imum Coeli*): The IC (*Imum Coeli*) is opposite the MC and relates to your roots, family of origin, private life, sense of home, and the other (nondominant) parent. It is the sign on your 4th house cusp.

The chart is also divided into four **quadrants**, groupings of three houses each that carry a distinct energetic emphasis (personal, interpersonal, social, or transpersonal), which can offer added nuance to how relationship dynamics play out.

Each zodiac sign has a **planetary ruler**, a planet whose energy guides the themes of that sign. This book uses **traditional rulers** (see the next section) rather than the modern outer planets for clarity and consistency.

If your chart has a house cusp in a **late degree** (like 29° of a sign), the rulership is still attributed to the sign on the cusp, even if most of the house falls in the next sign. This can mean you come to understand that area of your life later—it can be an area of learning and personal growth.

Essential Dignities

In this book you will come across a concept known as a planet's **dignity**. This is what determines which planet is in charge of different areas of your life. In traditional forms of astrology, **essential dignity** describes whether a planet is in a sign that supports its natural expression. A planet in its own sign (like Venus in Libra) tends to act in ways that match its nature. But when a planet is in a sign ruled by a planet with a very different expression (like Venus in Aries, ruled by Mars), the planet will express itself differently—altered or at odds with the behavior we typically associate with it. The planet is not weaker; it's just not "at home," so how it functions will depend in part on the energy of the planet that rules the sign it's in. Planetary rulership becomes especially important when you start looking at which planets rule your relationship houses and what kinds of conditions those planets are working with.

Here are the four most commonly used traditional essential dignities: rulership, detriment, exaltation, and fall—tools that help us assess the *style* and *clarity* of a planet's expression.

Rulership: When a planet is in a sign it rules

Detriment: When a planet is in the sign opposite the one it rules

Exaltation: When a planet is in a sign where it functions like an honored guest

Fall: When a planet is in the sign opposite the sign of its exaltation

Traditional rulerships were established centuries ago, using only the planets visible to the naked eye. After Uranus, Neptune, and Pluto were discovered, modern astrologers assigned them rulerships as well. While I consider the outer planets important in interpretation, I don't use them as planetary rulers in this book. The concepts in this book are based on traditional rulerships.

Table of Planetary Rulers

Sign		Traditional Ruler (used in this book)		Modern Ruler	
Aries	♈	Mars	♂		
Taurus	♉	Venus	♀		
Gemini	♊	Mercury	☿		
Cancer	♋	Moon	☽		
Leo	♌	Sun	☉		
Virgo	♍	Mercury	☿		
Libra	♎	Venus	♀		
Scorpio	♏	Mars	♂	Pluto	♇
Sagittarius	♐	Jupiter	♃		
Capricorn	♑	Saturn	♄		
Aquarius	♒	Saturn	♄	Uranus	♅
Pisces	♓	Jupiter	♃	Neptune	♆

Your Love Story

In this book, we will focus on the areas of the chart most directly tied to love and relationships. By understanding your chart's dynamics, you'll gain insights into your romantic tendencies, the qualities you seek in a partner, and the best places to find love.

Don't worry if this feels like a lot at first. Take it one section at a time—you'll find plenty of guidance to help you along the way. If you want a clear breakdown of how to use this book, head to appendix A on page 293. You'll find everything you need there to help you navigate your way through this book with confidence.

Let's jump in!

1
Venus
Your Love Language

Venus is often called the planet of love, romance, and beauty, but its influence goes deeper than just relationships. Love, as Venus sees it, starts with how you feel about yourself. Self-love is the foundation—it shapes how you connect with others, what you're drawn to, and how you invite joy into your life.

In your chart, Venus shows what you find beautiful and appealing, both in yourself and in the world around you. It's about what makes *you* feel good, whether that's through relationships, creative outlets, or just soaking up life's simple pleasures. Venus reminds you to embrace what brings you joy and create a sense of harmony, starting from inside yourself.

Venus is considered the planet of attraction for a reason. It influences what we look for in all our social connections, including romantic relationships, and what makes us feel loved and appreciated. Venus is about our values, affection, sensuality, and the simple pleasures that make life feel good. It shapes how we express love, the art or styles we're attracted to, and what we find beautiful in anything, including a partner.

Venus also contributes to how you indulge. Whether it's a great meal shared with friends, a cozy night in on the couch, wrapped in a blanket and munching on your favorite chocolate while watching a murder show, or soaking up the little luxuries that bring you joy, Venus reminds us that life's pleasures aren't just big moments, but are meant to be enjoyed in everyday life.

Unlike Mars, which chases after what it wants, Venus draws things in. It works through attraction—subtle, magnetic, and often effortless. Venus doesn't push; it pulls. It's the longing that sets everything in motion. And perhaps most importantly, Venus answers the question "What do you truly want?"

When it comes to relationships, Venus is the key to understanding how we connect with others. At its best, Venus draws us toward partners who complement us, enrich our lives, and bring us joy. It highlights what makes us feel loved and appreciated, focusing on shared values, affection, pleasure, and emotional bonds—all the things that form a solid foundation for meaningful connections.

But Venus doesn't work alone. Its interaction with other planets—like Mars for passion or Saturn for commitment—adds layers to how we experience love. These connections can show where sparks fly, where we feel grounded, or even where challenges might come up in relationships. Not everyone is wired for romance, and Venus reflects that too. It's not just about romantic love; Venus speaks to all forms of connection. The sign that Venus occupies in your chart shows how you attract others, what you actually find *romantic* (beyond social or cultural norms), what you bring to relationships, and the values that guide the *way* you connect.

Venus has a youthful energy, especially in our earlier years, often centering on attraction, external beauty, and the thrill of being wanted. On some level, Venus wants to fit in. But over time, that changes. As we grow, so does Venus—its meaning deepens. What once revolved around getting love starts to revolve around *being* love. Healthy, fulfilling relationships are built on a foundation of self-love, and when we take the time to figure out what truly matters to us and learn to value who we are, something shifts. Venus reminds us that love doesn't just arrive from outside; it starts inside. And when you know your own worth, your relationships change. You attract connections that reflect who you are, not just what you offer someone else. Venus matures with us, showing us that the more we value ourselves, the more authentic, supportive, and meaningful our connections become.

Venus in Your Chart: Sign, House, and Aspects

Venus's placement in your birth chart—its sign, house, and aspects—tells a special story about how you connect with the world. The sign Venus is in shows your personal style when it comes to attraction, how you connect with others, and what makes you feel valued. The house it's in? That points to where you're most likely to find those connections: at work, through friends, in creative spaces, or somewhere else entirely. The aspects add another layer, showing how Venus gets along with the other planets in your chart. Sometimes it's smooth sailing and other times there's some tension or even conflict.

For example, if Venus is in your 5th house, you might feel most alive in relationships that are playful, creative, and full of fun. If Venus is in your 6th house, connection might feel more grounded, with love showing up through daily activities or your usual walk in the dog park.

When you put all these pieces together, you start to get a clearer picture of how Venus shows up for you. It's not just about love; it's about how you express yourself, what you're drawn to, and in what area of your life you're most able to feel valued by yourself and others.

Disruptive Venus: When Things Feel Off

Venus doesn't always shine as brightly as we'd like. When it's in a sign or house where it feels out of place or it's making tough aspects to other planets in your chart, that often shows up in your relationship patterns. Maybe you've found yourself dating the same type of person over and over, just in a different package, or dealing with the same issues that keep coming up in your connections. These patterns are a signal that Venus might need some attention. *You* might need some attention.

In that case, it's a good time to reflect on how self-love and self-worth are shaping your experiences. The quality of your relationships, whether with others or with yourself, can mirror how well Venus's energy is showing up for you. When things feel off, taking a closer look at what truly brings you joy and what you value most can help Venus find its balance again. This shift in perspective can help you break old cycles and open the door to deeper, more fulfilling connections.

Venus: More Than Love

Venus might get all the hype as the planet of love and attraction, but it's about so much more. Venus wants you to ask the real questions:

- What do I truly value?
- What actually makes me happy?
- How do I connect—not just with others, but with myself?

Venus is like your personal guide to understanding why you're drawn to certain relationships and experiences or even the way you treat yourself. It's not just telling your romance story; it's about figuring out what motivates you to chase the things that make life feel good.

Venus Through the Twelve Signs

What makes you feel loved and connected? Is it belly laughing over a shared joke, spending quiet time together, doing something creative, or showing and receiving kindness? The sign that Venus occupies in your chart holds some of the answers. It shows how you give and receive love, what you find beautiful, and the things that bring you joy.

The sign that Venus is in shapes your approach to relationships: how you attract others, what makes you feel valued, and the energy you bring to your connections. Each zodiac sign adds its own flavor, influencing everything from your taste in art and how you dress and decorate to how you navigate love and connection. Maybe Venus in Aries makes you bold and magnetic, Venus in Cancer brings out a nurturing and intuitive side, or Venus in Libra shines through with charm and sociability. Whatever the sign, it paints a vivid picture of your relationship style.

Before we get started, what sign is your Venus in? Go to the table of symbols in appendix A (page 298) and look for your Venus sign.

Venus in Aries

Venus in Aries has a fiery, passionate vibe that's hard to miss. Venus is considered to be in detriment in this sign, because Aries is the opposite sign to Libra, one of the signs Venus rules. (The word "detriment" is an old-timey label that, in modern language, sounds much more negative than it is. For our purposes, these traditional terms are used with a lot more nuance.) Venus simply operates very differently in Aries than it does in Libra. Venus in Aries is bold, direct, and driven by immediate desires.

When this Venus sets its sights on someone, the energy can feel *hot*. There's a Mars-like focus, with all attention zeroed in on the object of desire. Rejection? Let's just say it's not handled quietly. Passion and emotions run high with Venus in Aries, but the intensity will depend on which sign Mars occupies in your chart (since Mars rules Aries). A hot-headed Mars amplifies this energy, while a less direct Mars sign—like Mars in Pisces—will tone it down.

Once you've found someone who catches your eye, Venus in Aries doesn't hesitate, and you're not afraid to make the first move. Venus in Aries is direct and confident in its pursuit, and what you see is exactly what you get. However, one of the lessons for this Venus placement is learning that people—and relationships—are often more complex than they seem at first glance. Heartbreak can happen when those expectations don't align with reality.

Venus in Aries thrives on shared adventures. You want a partner who matches your zest for life and appreciates your need for independence, freedom, and spontaneity. Because you crave excitement, you can sometimes rush into love—and just as quickly rush back out if things get too dull.

In youth, if Mars is placed in a competitive sign or Venus is challenged by hard aspects, those with Venus in Aries might find themselves constantly chasing a challenge, always drawn to the thrill of the chase. With maturity, learning balance and understanding can bring a deeper, more rewarding connection and a realization that commitment doesn't necessarily equal boring.

Venus in Taurus

Venus feels right at home in Taurus, one of the signs it rules. This sign brings out this planet's most sensual and grounded qualities, emphasizing a deep connection to the physical pleasures of life. For Venus in Taurus, attraction isn't just a mental or emotional experience; it's something they feel in their body, a visceral reaction that resonates on a physical level.

Venus in Taurus thrives on slow, meaningful expressions of love. Life's pleasures—good food, beautiful surroundings, warm embraces—are meant to be savored, not rushed. Exploring the senses deeply and sharing those experiences with loved ones is essential for Venus in Taurus. You value comfort and often have a preference for quality over quantity, choosing well-made items and substance over anything cheap or fleeting.

In relationships, Venus in Taurus values affection, loyalty, stability, and consistency. You're willing to invest a lot in your partnerships, and you expect that investment to pay off in a secure and loving connection. But that level of commitment can come with a downside: You can be quite possessive, and due to the fixed nature of Taurus, you may struggle to let go of a relationship, even when it's no longer working.

With Venus in Taurus, once you make a decision—whether to stay or leave a relationship—it's hard to change your mind. Your unwavering nature can lead to incredible dedication, but it can also mean you hold on longer than you should.

Ultimately, Venus in Taurus reminds us of the beauty in slowing down, savoring love, and creating a life built on loyalty and shared comfort.

Venus in Gemini

Venus in Gemini brings a fun, social, and curious energy to relationships. As an air sign, Gemini thrives on communication, connection, and mental stimulation. This Venus is drawn to people who are easy to talk to and keep the conversation flowing. Friendship is key to all your connections, and you value a partner who feels like an intellectual equal.

Playful, witty, and sometimes a little scattered, Venus in Gemini needs variety and excitement to stay engaged. Predictability and routine won't cut it, and if things start feeling too stagnant, you're likely to move on in search of something more interesting. While some might call you fickle, it's really about your need for flexibility and mental engagement.

Attraction can make Venus in Gemini adorably awkward. You might stumble over your words, fidget, or get overly chatty when you're interested in someone. Since Gemini rules the nervous system, overstimulation in moments of attraction can lead to nervous energy—or even a preference for space to process your feelings.

For Venus in Gemini, communication is love. You mix connection with conversation and need a partner who is open to sharing their thoughts and feelings freely. That said, your values can change over time, so a partner who's adaptable and flexible is key. You need someone who gives you room to think, process, and even change your mind along the way. Commitment can't feel like pressure—it needs to be organic and easy.

Sometimes Venus in Gemini prefers a quick text over face time, especially when you're craving space to recharge or process. Your ideal relationship is one where you feel free to grow and adapt, knowing your partner supports your need for flexibility and exploration.

Ultimately, Venus in Gemini reminds us that love is a journey of discovery, filled with laughter, curiosity, and plenty of room to grow.

Venus in Cancer

For Venus in Cancer, love is all about nurturing, connection, and creating a sense of emotional safety. You show love by caring for others, whether through physical support, emotional warmth, or simply being there when someone needs you. Being needed makes this Venus feel valued, but the desire to care can sometimes come across as "mothering" in relationships. If this happens, turning that nurturing energy inward and prioritizing self-care/self-love can help balance the dynamic. Taking care of your own needs and valuing yourself brings a sense of calm to relationships.

Cancer is ruled by the Moon, and just like the Moon, Venus in Cancer's feelings ebb and flow like waves. This makes you deeply sensitive, and your emotional state can shift depending on the Moon's sign and phase. Love for this Venus is like an ocean wave: It needs to flow back with the same intensity with which it was given, or you risk feeling hurt or taken for granted.

Above all, Venus in Cancer craves comfort and safety in love. Kindness, tenderness, and empathy are vital for you to feel secure. You're naturally sentimental and nostalgic, often drawn to traditions and family values, which you find incredibly romantic. Whether it's your birth family, your chosen family, or both, family is at the heart of your idea of love. When you form a deep, soulful connection with someone, that person becomes part of your inner circle—your family.

This Venus places a high value on memories, traditions, and the small but meaningful gestures that build emotional intimacy. Your love is tender and often protective, creating a space where others feel seen, cared for, and cherished.

Ultimately, Venus in Cancer teaches us about the beauty of emotional connection, the importance of safety in love, and the deep romance found in kindness and shared history.

Venus in Leo

Venus in Leo is all about big, bold love. When this Venus feels appreciated and adored, you absolutely shine. Compliments, affection, and being noticed for your unique qualities make you light up like no other. While you might come across as reserved at first, feeling truly seen and valued by someone special helps you step into your full, vibrant self.

For Venus in Leo, love is meant to be sensational, not dull. You'd rather be remarkable than modest, and your love burns bright, full of passion and devotion. Leo rules the heart, so when you're attracted to someone, it can literally feel like a skipped heartbeat or a rush of warmth. You crave romance, excitement, and a connection that makes your heart come alive.

In relationships, you're loyal to the core, and you'll go above and beyond for the people you love. Praise, gifts, encouragement—you name it, you'll shower it on your partner. Venus in Leo is the ultimate cheerleader, always proud and supportive. But here's the catch: You need that same energy in return. If you feel unappreciated or—worse—taken for granted or—even worse—used, it's hard for you to bounce back.

Venus in Leo has a generous and bighearted nature, but there's a lesson here too. If you don't fully value yourself, you might end up putting all your worth into your partner instead. When that happens, you could underestimate your own value while inflating the other person's. Finding your own worth first is key to keeping your inner fire alive.

When Venus in Leo loves, you love fiercely. You're all about passion, loyalty, and a connection that feels exciting and meaningful. You need a partner who sees you for who you are, supports you just as much as you support others, and shares in your vision of love that's as bright and warm as the Sun itself.

Venus in Virgo

Venus in Virgo has a quiet, grounded beauty that's hard to pin down. There's a wildness here—a love of nature and the essence of things—that makes you both mysterious and alluring. At first you might seem aloof or even unapproachable, but that's because you value your privacy and need time alone to recharge.

This Venus takes comfort in the rituals and lifestyle you've carefully created, and you need others to respect and appreciate those things. You show love by being helpful, often going out of your way to be of service to the people you care about. Acts of service are also how you feel loved in return; it's a love language that speaks to your practical yet deeply caring nature—and your attention to details.

With Venus in Virgo, when you are attracted to someone, you can become adorably shy and self-deprecating, sometimes overthinking your feelings or how you come across. If you're unhappy or overwhelmed, though, your thoughtful nature can turn into being overly critical or analytical, of both yourself and others. Perfectionism is one of your biggest hurdles. You may focus so much on what could be improved that you miss the beauty in the imperfections that make love and life so meaningful.

That said, Venus in Virgo values putting real effort into relationships. You're willing to work to improve the quality of your time together and grow with your partner. With the right connection—someone who shares your values and appreciates the small, magical moments in everyday life—you feel deeply fulfilled.

Venus in Virgo has a subtle healing quality, a natural ability to create calm and harmony. You see the magic in simple things and have a way of grounding those you love. But for this Venus to truly thrive, you need to remember that love doesn't have to be perfect to be beautiful—and you don't have to be perfect to be loved.

Venus in Libra

Venus is at home in this sign because Venus rules Libra. This placement brings out the planet's airy qualities in their purest form; it's graceful, harmonious, and deeply connected to romantic ideals and beauty. Venus in

Libra loves to be surrounded by beautiful things, whether it's art, sculpture, or simply a perfectly arranged space. Aesthetic harmony feels essential, not just in your surroundings but also in your relationships.

Social by nature, Venus in Libra is a natural charmer, with excellent social skills. You thrive in relationships and are truly interested in other people, valuing connection and equality. However, there's a catch: Venus in Libra's desire to keep the peace can sometimes mean agreeing to things you don't actually want to do. Over time, learning to say no becomes an important lesson. For you to feel valued, it's vital to figure out what you truly want—and to say no to what you don't.

While Venus in Libra is incredibly romantic and thrives in relationships, you also need your own space. This helps you find the balance you crave, not just in your partnerships but also within yourself. Relationships are your natural habitat, but you flourish when you've cultivated equality and a deep connection with yourself first.

One of the challenges for Venus in Libra is understanding that people aren't always at their best. Even the "perfect" partner might need room to be messy, tired, or not so pulled together. Giving others (and yourself) grace helps you build deeper, more authentic connections.

When this Venus is under stress, such as through difficult aspects or transits, you might swing between being overly accommodating and unexpectedly antagonistic. It's part of your journey to find homeostasis again, and it's a skill you refine over time.

At its heart, Venus in Libra is all about creating harmony and connection. You're a romantic who values equality and meaningful relationships, and when you embrace your own needs as much as other people's, you'll attract and create a love that's both balanced and beautiful.

Venus in Scorpio

Venus in Scorpio craves a connection that's deep, restorative, and soul-stirring. Surface-level romance? Nope. This Venus values sincerity and honesty, and you need relationships that feel raw and real. But you don't open up easily. Trust takes time, and you often keep your feelings hidden until you feel completely safe. Even then, you may never fully share the depths of your emotions, preferring to keep parts of yourself private and protected.

Passion and intensity are at the heart of Venus in Scorpio. You're drawn to relationships that feel profound, gravitating toward people in emotional crisis. There's something about that vulnerability and openness that draws you in. While this can lead to transformative connections, it can also create a pattern. Without understanding what true, healthy love looks like, you may keep seeking out emotionally charged situations and damaged souls, mistaking the chaos for depth.

Known for your resilience, Venus in Scorpio is incredible in a crisis. You're the one we want around when the going gets tough, offering unwavering support and emotional strength. But you may also armor up, carrying layers of protection to guard your heart. Secretive by nature, you're a sucker for someone who shares their secrets, as it creates the sense of intimacy you crave.

Venus in Scorpio holds on to things—memories, feelings, even past relationships—long after the moment has passed. This can make moving on difficult. If you're fresh out of a relationship, potential lovers need to be cautious. They might find themselves in the rebound zone as you process what you've lost. For you, healing takes time, and the most important lesson you can learn is to let go and forgive (especially yourself).

This Venus placement has a reputation for traits like jealousy and possessiveness, but these tendencies often stem from the vulnerability you expose yourself to when you experience deep connection. Your ability to maintain emotional control protects you, but it can also attract jealousy and manipulation from others.

Venus in Scorpio is intense, passionate, and undeniably magnetic. For this Venus, a lasting, healthy relationship requires understanding the power of vulnerability, the strength in forgiveness, and the beauty of letting go.

Venus in Sagittarius

Venus in Sagittarius has a heart that longs for freedom, adventure, and endless possibilities. Love for this Venus isn't just about connection—it's about exploring the world together and growing through shared experiences. You're drawn to people who expand your horizons, whether that's a traveler, a teacher, a professor, or even a metaphysical guru. Anyone who can spark your curiosity and inspire your sense of wonder could win your heart.

This Venus thrives on the big picture. You value relationships that align with your philosophical outlook and desire to learn and experience new things. You're most open to love when you're on an adventure, whether that's a far-off journey or meeting someone with an adventurous spirit.

However, with Venus in Sagittarius, it's important for you to fulfill your need for exploration and discovery before committing to something serious. Without that, you may settle for someone who feels "exotic" or different, only to later resent them for what you didn't get to experience yourself. Freedom and space are nonnegotiable for this Venus, and a partner who encourages your wandering spirit will help you feel truly fulfilled.

Generosity and openness define your relationships, but your optimism can sometimes be a double-edged sword. Venus in Sagittarius is great at seeing the good in people, but sometimes you see potential where it doesn't exist. To find lasting love, you need to be as honest with yourself as you expect others to be with you.

A kindred spirit who supports your need for growth, exploration, and learning is key for this Venus. You want someone who's walking a spiritual path, someone who shares your thirst for adventure and understands your philosophical callings. With the right partner, Venus in Sagittarius thrives in a relationship that's expansive, exciting, and full of possibility.

Venus in Capricorn

For Venus in Capricorn, success, quality, and stability are the cornerstones of love and attraction. You're drawn to partners who are accomplished and skilled and have a solid reputation. A strong work ethic and clear goals are a must—you want someone who takes life seriously and values responsibility as much as you do.

This Venus has a deep appreciation for quality and is often drawn to things (and people) that exude sophistication and class. Expensive labels, timeless designs, and well-made everything hold a special appeal. But one of your biggest lessons is recognizing your own worth and value. With Venus in Capricorn, you are inherently capable, accomplished, and deserving of the rewards you seek, but if you haven't fully embraced this, you might project those qualities onto a partner. Instead of seeing yourself as the expert or the one who has it all together, you may elevate someone else, believing that person has the competence or status you lack. Owning your own accomplishments is key to building relationships that feel authentic.

Venus in Capricorn is all about tradition, commitment, and building something lasting. You're dependable, trustworthy, and incredibly dedicated to your relationships, and you expect this in return. If respect for your time and energy was a love language, it would be one of yours. You're highly self-reliant, which can make you miss romantic opportunities. Asking for help doesn't come easily and vulnerability can feel like a challenge. You often link affection to vulnerability, which means you might hold back or even try to "manage" your partner when you're feeling unsure.

Rules and structure are often part of your relationships. Whether it's spoken or unspoken, Venus in Capricorn likes clear boundaries and responsibilities within a partnership. While this creates stability, it can sometimes stifle spontaneity. You might also get hung up on status and wealth, mistaking them for true compatibility.

With Venus in Capricorn, what you ultimately need is a partner who matches your ambition and shares your desire for long-term success—someone who values hard work and responsibility but also understands the importance of emotional connection. When you find that balance, your dedication and dependability shine, creating a relationship that feels both secure and meaningful.

Venus in Aquarius

Venus in Aquarius brings a strange blend of freedom and commitment to relationships. As a sign traditionally ruled by Saturn, Aquarius has a deep respect for boundaries and structure, but it also craves independence and individuality. For Venus in Aquarius, the ideal relationship allows both partners to be completely themselves, with plenty of space to explore their own identities. Freedom is nonnegotiable, but so is the desire for a meaningful connection.

Attracted to partners who are unique, independent, and free-spirited, Venus in Aquarius values intellectual connection and shared ideals above all else. Friendship often forms the foundation of your relationships, and you might even blur the line between the two, confusing romantic feelings with platonic ones. With this Venus, you're likely the type to try to stay friends with your exes, believing the connection doesn't have to end just because the romance has.

While you might seem cool and aloof, this can often be a defense mechanism. Intimacy has the potential to stir up difficult emotions, and that can feel overwhelming for Venus in Aquarius. Learning that tough emotions pass and vulnerability is a strength is an important lesson for you.

With this Venus, you need a partner who shares your values about humanity, equality, and the big picture. You value honesty and open communication as well as a relationship dynamic where both people feel like equals. You're less interested in grand romantic gestures and more drawn to partners who engage their mind and share their vision for the world.

Ultimately, Venus in Aquarius thrives in relationships that balance closeness with freedom. When you feel safe to be your authentic self, your unique, progressive approach to love truly shines.

Venus in Pisces

Venus in Pisces is the ultimate dreamer. Pisces already sees no limits to the potential and beauty of connection, and with Venus exalted here, those qualities are taken to another level. This placement amplifies the longing for love to feel transcendent, spiritual, and deeply meaningful. With an exalted planet, there's often an added sense of expectation—almost an unconscious belief that love should unfold in an idealized way, aligning with your vision of romance and harmony.

This Venus craves a deep, almost mystical bond, where words and actions seem to fall short of capturing the vastness of your love. With Venus in Pisces, music, art, and acts of compassion often become powerful outlets for the overwhelming emotions you feel. There's a recognition that no single human connection may ever fully satisfy your longing, which is why channeling that energy into creativity or helping others can be so fulfilling.

However, the depth of your idealism can also create challenges. Venus in Pisces has a tendency to idealize partners, seeing them through rose-colored glasses or even trying to merge completely with them. If you're not careful, you may find yourself lost in a relationship, sacrificing too much of your own identity or self-worth in the process. Learning to create and maintain boundaries is crucial for you to find healthy, balanced love.

Another lesson for Venus in Pisces is staying grounded in reality. You're so good at imagining love's potential that you can build an entire relationship in your mind before it happens in real life. This can leave you further along the emotional commitment path than your partner, leading to heartache when reality doesn't match the dream.

You value the magical and the unseen in love, but you must also guard against martyring yourself for romance. When self-esteem is strong, Venus in Pisces becomes a true force of compassion and beauty, capable of creating connections that feel almost divine.

Venus in the Mirror

Grab a copy of your birth chart and locate the Venus symbol (♀) to find which sign it's in. Use the table of symbols in appendix A (page 298) if you need a refresher.

- In your journal, write down your Venus sign and a few key takeaways from this chapter.
- Have you noticed any difficult lessons in love or dating patterns that resonate with your Venus sign?
- Are there areas of self-love or self-worth that might still need some attention?

Take your time with this. Reflecting on your Venus placement is a great way to start connecting the dots between your chart and your experiences.

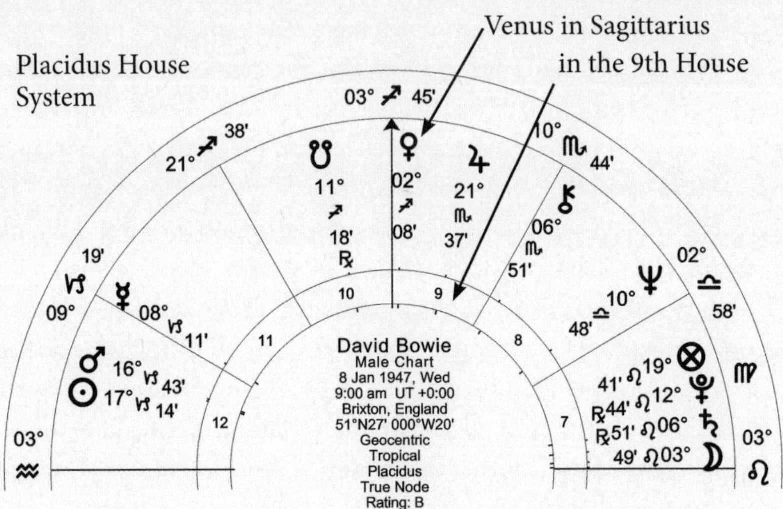

Chart 1: David Bowie, Venus Sign and House Placement

Which House Is Your Venus In?

In David Bowie's chart, Venus is in Sagittarius in the 9th house in the Placidus house system (chart 1). Which house is your Venus in?

Venus Through the Houses

If you've been learning about astrology, you might have come across books or articles that treat signs and houses as the same thing, but that's not my approach. Signs and houses are distinct, and blending them can make astrology feel way more confusing than it needs to be.

Think of it this way: The house a planet is in tells you where the planet's energy shows up in your life. The sign a planet is in, on the other hand, shows how that planet's energy is expressed. In the case of Venus, the house it occupies shows the area of your life where connection, pleasure, and beauty come most naturally to you.

In this section, we'll explore what Venus means in each of the twelve houses, helping you uncover the places in your life where its influence is strongest.

1st House Venus

With Venus in the 1st house, you have a natural charm that draws people in. Pleasant and easy to get along with, you're usually seen as attractive, with strong social skills, and maybe you're a bit of a flirt. Your sense of style is undeniable, and you know how to make a great first impression.

Relationships, however, can sometimes become a way to impress others or keep up appearances. Getting past this impulse and focusing on deeper, more meaningful connections is an important step for Venus in the 1st house. While you find it easy to make friends and social connections of all kinds, letting people see past the polished exterior can be tough.

You have a knack for smoothing things over and acting as a negotiator or diplomat, but this can sometimes backfire. Conflict makes you uncomfortable, and you might go out of your way to avoid it—even when addressing the issue head-on is what's really needed.

There's also a tendency to be overly concerned with looks, whether it's your own or your partner's. While there's nothing wrong with appreciating conventional beauty, it's important not to let it overshadow the deeper qualities that sustain a relationship.

At its best, Venus in the 1st house brings grace, charm, and an incredible ability to connect with others. When you learn to balance how you're perceived on the outside with who you truly are on the inside and embrace that authenticity, your relationships become even more rewarding.

2nd House Venus

With Venus in the 2nd house, you're happiest when surrounded by beauty, comfort, and the finer things. Status, money, and possessions matter to you, and you take pride in curating a life that feels both secure and aesthetically pleasing. This extends to your relationships too—you're just as selective about the people you keep close as you are about the things you treasure.

A small, trustworthy group of friends is essential, and while you're generous with your time and attention, you might find yourself holding back when it comes to money. Depending on the ruling planet of this house in your chart, there could even be a desire to be admired or worshipped for what you bring to the table.

Venus in the 2nd house values financial security in relationships. This isn't just a preference; it's nonnegotiable. You might make choices that aren't in your best interest if standing up for yourself feels like it could threaten that sense of stability.

This placement can also make you a bit status-conscious or materially driven, which might keep you from forming deeper, more meaningful connections with people who don't live up to those expectations. There's also a tendency to appreciate a well-timed gift. Yes, the right present at the perfect time can definitely win you over!

At its best, Venus in the 2nd house brings a grounded appreciation for the beauty and stability life has to offer. When you balance material desires with genuine connection and self-worth, your relationships—and your life—become much richer.

3rd House Venus

With Venus in the 3rd house, communication is everything. This placement values all forms of expression, whether it's talking, writing, texting, or emailing (sometimes all at once!). Venus here thrives on sharing perspectives, learning from others, and connecting through words. There's a natural charm in how you speak and write, making it easy for you to build friendships and social connections.

Venus in the 3rd tends to have a wide circle of friends and acquaintances, but those connections can sometimes stay on the surface. You're great at getting to know others, but you might avoid revealing too much about yourself, preferring to maintain appearances. This can lead to a lot of lighthearted relationships without much depth.

If other parts of the chart indicate a shy or reserved personality, Venus in the 3rd may feel more at home in the company of siblings or chosen family. You may play the role of peacekeeper or mediator among siblings, using your natural ability to smooth things over and keep everyone on good terms.

While you're an excellent talker with your Venus in the 3rd, you may need to practice the art of silence—learning to listen as much as you share. When you strike that balance, you can create more meaningful connections and foster deeper understanding with those around you.

At its best, Venus in the 3rd house brings people together through conversation, ideas, and a love of connection. It's a placement that thrives on curiosity and the joy of learning from others.

4th House Venus

Venus in the 4th house finds love and beauty in the comfort of home. You enjoy creating spaces that not only are beautiful but also feel inviting and peaceful. Hosting and entertaining loved ones is something you do with pride, and building a home with a significant other holds a special kind of magic for you.

Family is deeply important to Venus in the 4th—whether it's the family you're born into, the one you choose, or the one you create. Relationships serve as an anchor, giving you a sense of roots and stability. You're a homebody at heart, valuing the sense of safety and connection that comes from nurturing your inner world.

Because the 4th house is at the very bottom of the chart, Venus here can come across as shy or even aloof, especially in new situations. But this is often a defense mechanism, and once you feel comfortable, your warmth shines through. Bolder placements elsewhere in the chart might ease this reserved nature, helping you feel more comfortable opening up.

When it comes to love, Venus in the 4th doesn't take things lightly. You value emotional depth and may prefer committed relationships, often leaning toward serial monogamy. You bring people close who share your values, prioritizing quality connections over surface-level relationships.

At its best, Venus in the 4th creates a life filled with beauty, love, and a strong sense of belonging. Your relationships thrive when rooted in shared values and a mutual appreciation for the comforts of home.

5th House Venus

Venus in the 5th house thrives on romance, fun, and creativity. You love to play and flirt and enjoy the thrill of connection. Crushing hard and flirting harder might just be second nature. But while you're quick to dive into romance, you can sometimes confuse a light fling for true connection, which makes clear communication essential in your relationships.

The 5th house is a very creative placement for Venus, and having an outlet for that creativity is key to building self-worth and self-esteem. Whether it's art, dance, music, or any form of self-expression, creating is as vital as breathing for this Venus. You especially love collaborating with your partners, and a shared creative spark can keep romance alive.

Venus in the 5th loves excitement, which can sometimes lead to boredom if life feels too routine. Without enough romance, play, or creative outlets, you may lose interest. That said, you might need a little nudge to remember you can create these things for yourself instead of waiting for them to happen.

While you're fiercely protective of the friends you do have, there might be a phase where you prioritize romance and sex over meaningful friendships. Learning to invest time and energy in your friendships is an important lesson for this Venus.

At its heart, Venus in the 5th wants life to feel vibrant and alive, whether through love, creative pursuits, or joyful experiences. When you balance your love for fun with the effort it takes to build deeper connections, you truly shine.

6th House Venus

Venus in the 6th house finds connection in the little things—the routines, tasks, and day-to-day moments that make up life. For this Venus, love often looks like running errands together, sharing responsibilities, or even grocery shopping side by side. You thrive when your people are part of your everyday life, and you genuinely enjoy making the mundane feel meaningful.

With Venus in the 6th, you usually approach your work with pride, often deriving a lot of self-worth from what you do. Whether it's your job or your role in relationships, you feel best when you're contributing in a way that matters. That said, if you feel like you're being asked to work too hard without recognition, you might slip into a bit of self-pity.

Surrounding yourself with people who have healthy habits and routines is vital for your overall well-being. Venus in the 6th often gravitates toward careers or hobbies tied to beauty, decorating, or the arts. Even if you're not in those industries, you might approach your personal beauty regimen like it's a full-time job (depending on what sign Venus is in).

Romance for you might look a little different. A long walk with the dog or tackling a to-do list together could feel like the perfect date. If you're trying to get closer to someone with Venus in the 6th, finding a way to become part of their routine could be your secret weapon. On the flip side, a person with Venus in the 6th might feel like the whole "romance" thing is too much work and prefer to skip straight to the cohabitation stage.

When it comes to the practical side of relationships, Venus in the 6th is generally willing to compromise. You like to keep things running smoothly, but don't be surprised if you have strong opinions about how certain tasks should be done.

At its best, Venus in the 6th house creates connection through shared effort, mutual care, and a sense of partnership in everyday life. When you balance your work ethic with moments of joy, you shine in relationships that feel supportive and grounded.

7th House Venus

Venus in the 7th house can be in love with love. Relationships are central to your sense of self, and you thrive in one-on-one connections. However, this placement can bring a certain passivity—you may expect friends, lovers, or partners to magically appear without putting in the effort to actively connect.

If you have Venus in the 7th, you likely don't like to do things alone and often derive a lot of self-worth from having a partner. When your need for connection isn't met, you can feel deeply lonely, sometimes even desperate for companionship. Learning to nurture all one-on-one relationships—not just romantic ones—helps you build the fulfilling connections you crave.

Because of your strong desire for partnership, you might skip over the friendship or courting stage and jump straight into commitment. The risk here is putting your partner's needs ahead of your own, being overly passive, or losing yourself in the relationship. Autonomy and a strong sense of self are essential for those with Venus in the 7th to avoid codependency and create a healthier dynamic.

With Venus in the 7th, you value a romantic partner who brings a sense of security, but this can sometimes lead you to trade your own needs for what you perceive as a stable relationship. True relationship success comes when you understand your own worth and approach love from a place of balance.

At its best, Venus in the 7th house creates relationships that are harmonious, meaningful, and deeply fulfilling—when you remember that your most important relationship starts with yourself.

8th House Venus

Venus in the 8th house craves deep, transformative connections but needs to balance that intensity with time alone to process and recharge. Honest, open communication is crucial for you, even if it doesn't come naturally at first. Without it, relationships can feel murky, especially when boundaries aren't clearly defined.

The 8th is the house of sex, intimacy, and shared resources, so Venus here might have a tendency to blur the lines between friendship and romance. While you might be open to exploring sexually, allowing someone to truly know you on an emotional level can be much harder. Mixing sex and deeper relationships can feel complicated, and finding a balance is often a learning process.

There's a certain propriety with Venus, even when it's in the 8th house, but depending on the sign and other factors, this placement might also enjoy riskier sexual connections. It's important for you to check in with yourself to make sure those experiences are aligned with your values and self-worth.

When it comes to partnerships, shared resources and material comfort are significant factors. With Venus in the 8th, you value a partner who can contribute to creating a secure life together, and a fulfilling sexual relationship is a key part of your connection.

Before a truly healthy partnership can happen, you may need to do some deep inner work. With your Venus in the 8th house, understanding your own value—and learning to love yourself beyond sexual connection and physical expressions of love—is essential. Once you do, you can create connections that are as profound as they are life-changing.

9th House Venus

Venus in the 9th house thrives on adventure, learning, and connecting with people from different cultures, religions, and backgrounds. With this placement, you value knowledge and experience above all else, seeking relationships that expand your worldview or deepen your philosophical or religious understanding. Travel, higher learning, and big ideas light you up, and you're always on the lookout for the next opportunity to grow.

However, this constant search for "bigger and better" can sometimes lead to restlessness in those with Venus in the 9th. While you value honesty in your relationships, you may not always be forthcoming yourself, especially if it means avoiding conflict. Despite this, you have a knack for collecting a diverse array of friends, drawing people in with your superb social skills and the wealth of knowledge you bring to the table.

With Venus in the 9th, you often serve as a social cheerleader, encouraging the people in your life to grow and learn alongside you. You value the experiences and perspectives a person brings to a connection more than superficial qualities like appearance. That said, if Venus is challenged in the chart, there's a chance you might focus on collecting a diverse group of friends or connections as part of your worldly persona rather than forging deeper bonds.

This Venus placement can go one of two ways: You could embrace a free-spirited and open approach to life and love or you might lean toward being dogmatic and attached to tradition, especially if Venus is in a more traditional sign or is strongly influenced by Saturn.

At its best, Venus in the 9th house builds relationships rooted in curiosity, shared experiences, and a mutual love of growth. You remind us that connection isn't just about comfort—it's about broadening our perspective and finding meaning in the journey.

10th House Venus

Venus in the 10th house knows the power of being liked, especially in professional or public settings. This placement often comes with incredible social skills, making you an excellent diplomat and a natural networker. You tend to be entertaining, fun, and highly attuned to what's happening around you—skills you are likely to use to climb the social or professional ladder.

There's a chance, though, that Venus in the 10th might prioritize appearances over authenticity. You can focus on relationships that elevate your status or align with your ambitions, sometimes at the expense of true connection. What we see publicly might not fully reflect what's going on behind the curtain.

Learning your own worth is a crucial journey for this Venus placement. It might take a few "kissing rich frogs" experiences for you to realize status alone doesn't create happiness or fulfillment. Loyalty can come naturally to Venus in the 10th, but your relationships thrive when you involve your partner in your goals and dreams rather than leaving them out of the bigger picture. With this Venus placement, the worst thing anyone could do to you (unless it's part of the social climb) is to embarrass you publicly.

With Venus in the 10th, you can fall into the trap of using charm to smooth things over when relationships get tough. While your ability to disarm and persuade is impressive, true growth comes from addressing challenges head-on, instead of relying on charisma to sweep things under the rug.

At its best, Venus in the 10th house leads you to create relationships that are aligned with your ambitions while remaining grounded in authenticity and mutual respect. When you balance your drive for success with genuine connection, you're unstoppable.

11th House Venus

With Venus in the 11th house, you're a natural at making friends. You thrive in social settings, easily juggling multiple friend groups and memberships in clubs or organizations. Venus here loves talking to new people and might even take the prize over all other Venus placements for "Number of Friends Made in a Club Bathroom."

With Venus in the 11th, you have a knack for making people feel like you're their BFF from day one, but you're probably better at forming lighthearted, fun connections than the "share your deepest, darkest secrets" kind of friendships (unless there are other indicators for a need for depth in relationships in the chart). Group gatherings and social hangouts are your happy place, and you're likely to be the life of the party, whether in a small book club or at a massive community event.

With Venus in the 11th house, your sense of value and worth is often tied to your role in your social world. You feel most fulfilled when you're contributing to a community, connecting with people, or championing a cause you believe in. Knowing you're making an impact or being appreciated for your social skills gives you a sense of purpose.

However, with this Venus placement, if your self-worth isn't solid, you will be more vulnerable to relationships that isolate you from the very networks that bring you joy. Without a strong connection to your own values, you might prioritize a partner's needs over your own or allow yourself to be cut off from your social world to maintain a relationship. Recognizing your worth as an individual—and not just as part of a group—is key to avoiding these pitfalls.

With Venus in the 11th house, a partner who embraces and respects your need for connection is essential. Bonus points if that partner shares your passion for a cause—working together toward a shared goal might be the ultimate way to win your heart. Helping you champion your vision or making themselves a part of your mission isn't just a way to connect; it's how you know someone truly understands and values what drives you.

12th House Venus

Venus in the 12th house brings a deeply sensitive and soulful energy to love and relationships. You may long for a kind of soul connection, something transcendent, intuitive, and emotionally rich. You're likely highly empathic, with a psychic sensitivity to the emotional currents around you. This attunement can create incredible intimacy, but that same sensitivity can make it easy to absorb other people's feelings, expectations, or pain, especially when they're not being clearly expressed. Your gift, which can sometimes be your Achilles' heel, is the limitless love you have to share, combined with an incredible ability to see people's potential, often before they do.

The 12th house often describes parts of ourselves that operate out of our own line of sight—motivations or patterns that we don't always see clearly. That's why deep, honest friendships can be essential for those with this placement. Trusted people can reflect back what might be hard to recognize on your own, especially when emotions are heightened or attraction feels fated or overwhelming. There can be a tendency to idealize love.

You might be drawn to partners who are unavailable or situations that carry a sense of secrecy, sacrifice, or karmic pull. And yes, traditionally the 12th is called "the house of our undoing." But in modern interpretation, that usually points not to doom but rather to unconscious patterns that need gentle awareness. A strong spiritual practice, quiet time alone, or simply space to decompress can help you stay rooted in yourself. A strong sense of self-worth is key with this placement—not the kind that comes from being wanted, but the kind that grows from truly seeing and accepting yourself.

At its best, Venus in the 12th elevates love to a spiritual experience, blending deep emotional connection with imagination, intuition, and soul. Your capacity to love is infinite; just make sure to include yourself in that generosity.

Love Lives Here

Layering the pieces in our chart is how we start to get a full picture of our complex selves. Thinking about how the layers come together and what this may look like is how we begin to tell the story. Then we can make changes as we start to see the patterns.

In your journal, start by reviewing some key themes you discovered from your Venus sign and write them down. Add things that make you feel really good about yourself.

For example, I have Venus in Taurus, and I am affectionate and sensual and love to experience the physical side of love slowly and often. I prefer more traditional gifts and appreciate quality, handmade gifts. I am loyal and steady and don't like change, so in the past I have stayed in relationships way too long—past their expiration date. Someone who's loyal and affectionate makes me feel valued and seen.

Now consider which house your Venus is in and create some descriptions of the combination of the planet's sign and house.

For example, I have Venus in Leo in the 5th house, and I love to play and be creative. Making beautiful things makes me feel good about myself.

I love romance and grand gestures and expect the level of loyalty I express to be reciprocated. I love to dance and enjoy all forms of the performing arts. When I was younger, my self-worth was wrapped up in being adored and I tended to be attracted to people with star quality, but once I found that within myself, I was free to find a partner who offered me more substance.

Your Venus description doesn't have to look anything like mine. Think about the themes for your Venus sign and house—and write from your heart.

2
Mars
Planet of Passion and Desire

Venus is about what we want, and Mars is the energy that goes out and gets it. When you think of Mars, think *action*. This sexy planet represents the act of having sex or the thrill of the hunt to get it—or *anything* Venus wants.

Mars brings the heat, passion, and drive that fuel our desires, whether that's in love, work, or life in general. While Venus draws things toward it with a magnetic energy, Mars is all about action—it's the yang to Venus's yin, pushing energy outward and propelling us forward.

Mars also shows how you assert yourself and handle conflict. Its placement in the chart gives clues about how you pursue what you want, whether that's with boldness or patience or something in between. It's the spark that keeps the fire burning, but here's the thing: Mars doesn't filter or hold back. It is raw, unrestrained energy, and the way it shows up depends on the rest of your chart to shape and direct it.

Mars Through the Signs

The sign Mars is in describes your style of going after what you want. If Mars isn't sufficiently ignited, you might lack the energy to sustain the effort needed to reach your goals. But when it's activated, Mars is all about movement, competition, and passion. It's the force that keeps things alive and moving in relationships, helping you fight for what matters and bring your desires to life.

The sign Mars occupies in your chart shows your unique style of pursuit—how you go after what you want, express lust, and handle conflict.

What sign do you have Mars in?

Mars in Aries

Mars feels right at home in Aries—it's one of the signs Mars rules, embodying all the fiery, action-packed energy we associate with Martian principles. If you have Mars in Aries, you're a natural initiator, bursting with enthusiasm, independence, and a strong competitive streak. You're a warrior and a champion, ready to take on whatever challenges come your way.

With this Mars placement, you are bold and direct when going after what you want. You won't wait around patiently, and you're not likely to follow someone else's lead. Finding balance in relationships, especially when it comes to give-and-take, is a challenge. If you feel your freedom is being threatened, you'll get the urge to run. (This doesn't mean you'll act on the urge.)

Mars in Aries doesn't handle boredom or routine well. You crave excitement and thrive on energy and momentum. If someone needs to motivate you to do something you're not thrilled about, turning it into a competition is a surefire way to spark your interest. You might even approach romance with that same competitive edge, seeing it as a challenge to win someone over.

While this Mars placement is never short on enthusiasm and drive, learning patience and developing longevity are important lessons. Communicating feelings clearly and managing anger are also crucial, and looking to the Moon in your chart can offer insight into just how dramatic your emotional responses might be.

At its best, Mars in Aries is dynamic, passionate, and full of life—a natural cheerleader! When you balance your fiery energy with patience and emotional awareness, you can bring a sense of excitement and vitality to everything you do.

Mars in Taurus

Mars in Taurus is often underestimated. Mars is in detriment here, meaning it's in the opposite sign of one that it rules, and this sometimes gets misinterpreted as lacking drive. In reality, Mars in Taurus is one of the most tenacious placements. With Mars here, once you set your sights on something, you won't stop until you get there. Someone might not even notice you are in pursuit, because this Mars is slow, methodical, and relentless in its approach.

In Venus's sign of Taurus, Mars is sensual and deliberate, taking its time to enjoy the process. If you have Mars here, you're motivated by a prize, and while you can be stubborn and immovable, you're also deeply loyal. Taurus loves familiarity, but with Mars in the mix, there's a fine line between finding comfort in routine and falling into boredom.

Mars in Taurus doesn't get impatient—it gets frustrated. Your anger is a slow burn, simmering beneath the surface until it finally erupts, but it takes a lot for you to reach that point. You're grounded and steady, with an impressive amount of physical strength and endurance.

When it comes to love, you're all about sharing sensual experiences. Being in love can sneak up on you because your approach is slow and cautious. Trust takes time to build, but once it's there, your loyalty and commitment shine through.

At its best, Mars in Taurus is determined, steady, and full of sensual passion. With Mars here, you can teach the value of persistence and tenacity and the beauty of savoring life's pleasures along the way.

Mars in Gemini

Mars in Gemini thrives on mental stimulation. As an air sign, Gemini needs to think through its actions, and this Mars placement is quick, strategic, and constantly gathering information before making a move. However, like all planets in Gemini, Mars here can struggle with choosing a direction. With so many diverse interests, you often lose interest just as quickly as you gain it.

Commitment can feel tricky for Mars in Gemini—you're more likely to settle down when you know there's room for flexibility or a way out if needed. Your moods can swing unpredictably, and you tend to get caught up in your own head, overthinking every move. Witty banter and verbal sparring are big turn-ons for you, and you'll gravitate toward someone who can keep up with your mental energy.

If Mercury, Gemini's ruler, is in a thinking sign (Virgo, Aquarius, Gemini, or Libra) in your chart, you'll crave a partner who can provide consistent intellectual engagement. Mars in Gemini doesn't handle boredom well, and a lack of mental stimulation is a fast track to losing your interest.

While you don't like to lose, this aversion can sometimes hold you back from taking risks. In order to build a deeper, lasting connection, you need someone you can talk to—someone who helps you work through your options and concerns without rushing you or making you feel your way is wrong. In relationships, you may even feel like you're searching for your "missing twin," someone who truly gets you.

With Mars in Gemini, when you feel safe and secure, you are youthful, playful, and full of curiosity. At its best, this placement brings energy, adaptability, and a sharp mind to all pursuits, keeping life interesting and engaging.

Mars in Cancer

Mars in Cancer may be in its fall (opposite its sign of exaltation), but that doesn't mean it lacks power. Cancer is a cardinal sign, meaning this Mars is driven and capable of decisive action. However, its energy ebbs and flows and is strongly influenced by emotions, since Cancer is ruled by the Moon. Tracking the Moon's sign and phase can be especially helpful when you have this placement—to help you navigate life's highs and lows.

With this Mars, you are tenacious, often pursuing goals with a fierce determination rooted in emotional satisfaction. Your actions are driven by your feelings—the full range of feelings. You're fiercely protective of those you love, whether they're family by birth or by choice, and you have a natural instinct to save, nurture, and protect those who are vulnerable, people and animals alike.

However, this deep focus on others can sometimes cause you to lose sight of your own needs and desires. With this Mars, you can struggle with expressing your feelings and asking for what you want, which can lead to frustration or burnout. The Cancerian instinct to protect yourself emotionally can also hold you back from forming deeper connections, even though you have a remarkable capacity for intimacy.

Rejection can hit this Mars hard, given your emotional depth and brooding intensity. Yet that same intensity can be magnetic to others, adding a mysterious, sexy edge to your personality. Learning to communicate openly—sharing how you're feeling and what you need—is the key to building fulfilling relationships and avoiding misunderstandings.

At its best, Mars in Cancer combines passion, emotional depth, and a protective nature to create meaningful connections and pursue goals that resonate deeply with your heart.

Mars in Leo

Mars in Leo is fueled by the Sun, drawing energy from an inner light and fire that shines brightly. If you have this placement, you thrive on inspiration and, as with any personal planet in a fire sign, you need to feel a spark to take action. However, unlike the quick bursts of Mars in Aries, Mars in Leo burns with a slower, steadier flame—it's fixed fire, constant and determined.

This Mars loves to be desired and often brings play, drama, and flair to romance. You're naturally good at highlighting your strengths, which helps you move forward swiftly in life. But you're also highly sensitive to feedback, and when threatened or feeling insecure, you can protect yourself behind stubbornness or even arrogance.

"Pride goeth before the fall" could have been written for Mars in Leo. Managing your pride is key to unlocking the fullness of what this Mars can achieve. With age and experience, you learn to move beyond ego-driven pursuits and focus on authentic desires that feed the very best side of this placement.

When it comes to relationships, Mars in Leo brings grand gestures, passion, and a touch of drama. You can be playful and even a little mischievous with the objects of your desire, but once you've decided someone is worth it, your loyalty is unwavering. However, you need a partner who is completely faithful and generous with praise—applauding your efforts is the way to keep you fully committed.

At its best, Mars in Leo is dynamic, bold, and filled with creative energy. When you align your actions with your deepest passions and manage your pride, you can light up the world around you with your beautiful inner flame.

Mars in Virgo

When you need a project polished to an impeccable shine, Mars in Virgo is your go-to. But here's the trick: You might need a hard deadline. This Mars thrives on preparation, analysis, and refining things until they're as flawless as possible—but without clear boundaries, you can get lost in the details and miss the bigger picture.

Mars in Virgo is methodical, rational, and highly organized (or at least is always striving to be). You have an unmatched talent for detecting patterns, solving problems, and improving systems. However, since no organizing system is ever *truly* perfect, you can find yourself in a lifelong pursuit of order.

This Mars shines in work or any structured setting where your discriminating eye and drive for progress are appreciated. But when it comes to relationships, things can get trickier. People aren't perfect, and most don't respond well to constant criticism, even if it comes from a well-meaning place. With Mars in Virgo, the key to relationship happiness is focusing on improving yourself and the relationship rather than the people you let into your life.

Mars in Virgo craves steady progress and thrives when things are showing improvement, no matter how small the steps. Creating healthy routines is very helpful for your well-being, and having a partner who shares your love for self-improvement is a dream match. You work best within well-organized systems, so bringing order to your world helps you feel grounded and productive.

In love, you value someone who listens and lets you work through obstacles in your own methodical way. As an earth sign Mars, you're sensual and physical, often using physical outlets such as exercise or other hands-on activities to work out your frustrations. But here's a pro tip: If you're with a Mars in Virgo and you want to be on the receiving end of that physical passion, you might need to take a shower first! Good hygiene might even be a turn-on for this Mars.

At its best, Mars in Virgo brings precision, dedication, and a desire for growth to every aspect of life, creating relationships and projects that are always improving and evolving.

Mars in Libra

Mars in Libra finds itself in detriment, as Libra is opposite to Aries, the sign that Mars rules. This means its usual boldness and directness are somewhat muted. Instead of charging forward, you tend to focus on others' wants and desires, often to your own detriment. You're great at negotiation and diplomacy, but sometimes your need to please others comes across as indecisive.

As the warrior planet, Mars's role in our charts is to go after and—if necessary—fight for what we want. But in Libra, it trades armor for tact. Libra's preference for diplomacy means this Mars takes a more strategic approach to conflict. When you feel threatened or vulnerable, you're unlikely to confront the issue head-on. Instead, you might resort to passive-aggressive tactics to let those closest to you know you're not happy. While this indirect approach can feel safer in the moment, it often leads to confusion or frustration in your relationships, making open and honest communication a vital skill to develop.

One challenge for Mars in Libra is the fear of making the wrong choice. This can lead to hesitation or actions that contradict your words, leaving others confused—especially if the other person has been clear about their needs. With this Mars, when you're really into someone, you might avoid being forthright about what you want out of fear it'll conflict with what the other person desires.

Mars in Libra craves smooth give-and-take, harmony, and balance, sometimes at all costs. You are a natural at casual social interactions and are sometimes accused of being nicer to strangers than to the people you love. This tendency comes from your skill in keeping things light and pleasant, but it's also why learning to assert your wishes is such an important life lesson.

In relationships, Mars in Libra is unmatched (but don't tell Mars in Leo) at the game of romance. You're skilled at wooing, bringing charm and thoughtfulness to the early stages of relationships. This is the gift of getting to know what the other person *really* wants. However, the deeper, messier aspects of love—where things get real—can feel much harder to navigate.

At its best, Mars in Libra brings grace, charm, and a deep desire for mutual respect to all relationships. By learning to balance your need for harmony with the courage to express your own wants, you can create connections that are as authentic as they are beautiful.

Mars in Scorpio

Mars in Scorpio brings together the tenacity of a fixed sign, the emotional depth of a water sign, and the raw, unrelenting power of Mars in a sign it rules. This placement is the truest expression of Mars's passion and drive, creating an intensity that's hard to match. If you're the object of this Mars's attention, resistance might be futile—they have the focus and determination to win you over.

With Mars in Scorpio, you approach life with power and intensity in everything you pursue. Trust is everything for you, and when it's broken, the fallout will be ice-cold. You may expect full disclosure from others while keeping your own cards close to the chest—a strategy that allows you to maintain control and emotional safety. Honesty, loyalty, and integrity are nonnegotiables, and you have a deep need to share at the most intimate levels with a partner.

That said, you can sometimes expect partners to read your mind instead of being straightforward about your needs. And there's nothing more disappointing for you than dipping your toes into the pool of romance only to find the waters aren't as deep as you'd hoped. When you commit, it's meant to be long-term, but if the relationship ends, there's no going back.

This Mars loves a conquest, whether in love or in other areas of life, and you're willing to put in the time and effort to get what you want. If Mars is challenged in your chart, this can lead to pursuing unattainable romantic interests, which is a way to avoid vulnerability while still having something to work toward.

But when Mars in Scorpio is all in, you bring 100 percent of your energy and passion—and you expect the same in return. At its best, this placement creates deep, transformative connections built on trust and intensity, reminding us that true power lies in the willingness to be vulnerable with the right person.

Mars in Sagittarius

Mars in Sagittarius is impulsive, adventurous, and always searching for the next great quest. In a mutable fire sign, this Mars thrives on optimism and far-off dreams, bringing enthusiasm, warmth, and excitement to every pursuit. However, your big-picture thinking can sometimes lead to trouble, as you often see the end goal clearly but overlook the steps it takes to get there.

This placement is all about possibilities. With Mars in Sagittarius, you're often more motivated by the thrill of seeing if you *can* accomplish something than by the task itself. But because your energy is tied to inspiration, your focus can wane when the excitement fades. Without the fixed determination to push through, you may abandon projects before they're finished, leaving a trail of half-realized dreams behind.

With this Mars placement, freedom is essential. Feeling stuck or trapped can sap your energy and dampen your mood, making you restless and uninspired. You are driven by a desire to express your ideas and opinions openly and need a partner who won't judge you for your bold, expansive views.

Mars in Sagittarius is passionate about philosophy, culture, and learning. You're always searching for deeper meaning, and the best partner for you is a fellow adventurer—someone who shares your love of exploration, both physical and intellectual. Together you can embark on meaningful quests that satisfy your shared hunger for growth and discovery.

At its best, Mars in Sagittarius channels its impulsive energy into inspiring adventures and connections. When you balance your enthusiasm with follow-through, you can create a life filled with passion, purpose, and endless possibilities.

Mars in Capricorn

Mars is exalted in Capricorn, meaning that, with this placement, you likely have the discipline, determination, and willpower to achieve almost anything you set your sights on. Mars here is a master at knowing what it wants, creating a plan, and following through. Hard work is king for Mars in Capricorn, and you have little patience for laziness or indecisiveness.

Status and achievements are big motivators, and you're willing to be frugal and resourceful if that's what it takes to succeed.

But what happens when this energy is channeled into relationships? Mars in Capricorn approaches intimacy much like everything else in life: with a practical, goal-oriented mindset. A partner who supports your ambitions—or, even better, someone who can contribute to your success—will win your heart. You excel at creating structure and stability in your connections, bringing reliability and commitment to the table.

That said, Capricorn placements often feel compelled to *manage* situations, and romance is no exception. You can come across as authoritarian or controlling, especially if you see your partner as a challenge to "fix." While you thrive on overcoming obstacles, extending this approach to people can backfire, especially if your partner feels more judged than loved.

Mars in Capricorn's strengths shine when you focus on building something meaningful with your partner. You are steadfast, dependable, and incredibly loyal. This Mars placement brings consistency and security to relationships, qualities that create a strong foundation for love. A partner who is equally ambitious—but not in competition with you—will thrive alongside you, especially when you share a common vision or goals.

At its best, Mars in Capricorn combines ambition with a deep sense of responsibility and care, creating relationships that feel solid, supportive, and long-lasting. While you may need to soften your tendency to control, your drive and determination can inspire your partner to grow and build a life of mutual success and achievement.

Mars in Aquarius

Mars in Aquarius brings a blend of intellectual energy and independence to the way you take action. As with Mars in the other air signs, you can get stuck in your head, overthinking how to move forward. But as a fixed sign, Aquarius adds a layer of stubbornness, sometimes clinging to specific ideas or expectations that can make flexibility a challenge.

Even with a love for the weird and wonderful, Mars in Aquarius doesn't always stray far from traditional expectations. You thrive when working with others on projects or in groups that are aligned with what's important to you, where your innovative and forward-thinking energy can shine.

When it comes to romance, Mars in Aquarius values mental stimulation above physical or emotional closeness. Both Mars and Venus in this sign can be content with relationships that play out in their minds, sometimes preferring the safety of online or long-distance connections—or even choosing celibacy to avoid the messiness of ongoing, in-person connections. With Mars here, you're great at rationalizing how you feel, sometimes convincing yourself you're "above" romance or attachment—but this might be more about self-protection than actual clarity.

With Mars in Aquarius, you have a strong need for individuality and independence. Finding a balance between partnership and personal freedom can take time, age, and experience. You often keep at least one toe out the door in relationships, not because you don't care, but to avoid feeling trapped or losing your sense of self.

At its best, Mars in Aquarius uses its sharp intellect, unique perspective, and drive for independence to create relationships and projects that push boundaries and inspire others. With time, you can find the sweet spot where both freedom and connection thrive.

Mars in Pisces

Mars in Pisces is all about navigating action through intuition and empathy. My favorite moment of understanding this placement came from a student who, when asked how she takes action, paused, sputtered a bit, and finally said, "I don't know, I just do what feels right." That's the beauty of Mars in Pisces—it moves with what feels right, guided by a spiritual and emotional compass that doesn't follow logic but usually lands exactly where it needs to.

This is the placement of the spiritual warrior, someone who acts on an energetic level and connects deeply with the world around them. Mars in Pisces is incredibly creative and can process negative emotions beautifully through dance, music, or other artistic outlets. However, your deep empathy can sometimes hold you back—you may struggle to stand your ground for fear of hurting others, especially if you feel those emotions as your own.

When it comes to love and sex, Mars in Pisces has a tendency to idealize partners, often blurring boundaries and projecting fantasies onto them. While this can create magical, romantic moments, it can also lead to disappointment when reality doesn't match the dream. Learning to tap into your intuition while staying grounded in your own needs and desires is a pivotal lesson for this Mars.

Because you're the least direct of any Mars placement, a firm understanding of your own desires is essential. Without it, you risk losing yourself in your relationships, becoming selfless to the point of self-sacrifice. With this Mars placement, you may even rationalize bad behavior from others, putting a positive spin on it until the emotions inevitably bubble over and need to get out.

At its best, Mars in Pisces brings selflessness, compassion, and creative energy to all pursuits. With a strong sense of boundaries and a balance between intuition and self-care, you can inspire others and create deeply meaningful connections.

Explore Your Action Style

In your journal, write down the qualities of your Mars sign that speak to you. What might you still need to work on to be better able to go after what you want?

For example, I have Mars in Sagittarius and I'm definitely a big dreamer/big-picture person who will fight over ideology. I can get bored once the beginning phase of something is realized and the hard work needs to begin. I continue to work on this, making sure to finish things I start and not starting things that I'm pretty sure won't hold my attention through to completion. Having a partner who cheers me on and lets me share my big dreams without ridicule is very important to me.

Mars Through the Houses

The house Mars occupies in the chart shows where we take action, which areas of our lives drive us, and where we assert ourselves—and reveals where that energy is most visible or accessible. Whether it's in relationships, career, or personal growth, Mars lights a fire under us, pushing us toward what we want and where we plan to get it. Each house gives Mars a unique stage to perform on, shaping how we pursue our goals, handle challenges, and express passion.

Mars in the 1st

Mars in the 1st house is bold, direct, and ready to dive headfirst into life. With this placement, you are sexually magnetic and often jump into action without overthinking—which can make you a great initiator but sometimes leads to decisions made without fully considering the consequences. You're motivated, competitive, and driven to go after what you want, often setting things in motion wherever you go.

This Mars placement isn't one for subtlety. Emotional reactions are hard to hide, and you're likely to wear your feelings on your sleeve. You might blush or feel heat rise to your face when Mars energy is activated, whether from excitement, anger, or embarrassment.

While Mars in the 1st is passionate and full of energy, your lack of patience can sometimes work against you. You might not give situations or relationships enough time to develop, missing out on what could be. You're not big on small talk, preferring action and directness over idle chatter (unless you have an air sign Ascendant with Mars in the same sign: Libra, Aquarius, and especially Gemini—who all enjoy talking).

Mars in the 1st can also attract aggression, or it can make you seem more intense than you intend to be. Your natural Mars energy is magnetic, but it can sometimes come across as confrontational. Finding a balance between expressing yourself and giving others space to engage is key to navigating relationships and social dynamics.

At its best, Mars in the 1st house is dynamic, enthusiastic, and a natural leader. With a little patience and mindfulness, you can channel your energy into creating bold and exciting opportunities in life and love.

Mars in the 2nd

Mars in the 2nd house is driven by the tangible: security, rewards, and material goals. With this placement, you thrive when there's something to build or achieve, and your motivation often centers around creating and protecting what you value, whether that's financial stability, personal belongings, or meaningful relationships.

In relationships, shared goals and values are essential for this Mars placement. You often need some form of guarantee, whether that's emotional, financial, or practical, to feel secure in your connections. You're driven to create stability and may work hard to build a strong foundation before fully committing.

With Mars in the 2nd, learning your own values—what you bring to a relationship and what you truly want in return—can lead to more balanced and lasting connections. Building personal financial security is also key to feeling safe and confident when entering into partnerships, as it reduces the need to rely on someone else for stability.

With this Mars placement, you can be a little defensive about your "stuff," whether that's material possessions or emotional investments. You're likely to appreciate valuable or meaningful gifts as part of your love language—it's a tangible expression of care and commitment that resonates with your values.

At its best, Mars in the 2nd house uses drive and determination to create a life filled with stability, shared goals, and a sense of mutual support.

Mars in the 3rd

Mars in the 3rd house is all about communication. This placement thrives on verbal sparring, whether it's playful banter, debates, or even a bit of flirty sexting. You are driven to express yourself and are likely motivated by pursuits such as writing, learning, or engaging with your community.

Speed and action are key themes for this Mars. You might have a soft spot for fast cars or adrenaline-filled experiences, but your real thrill comes from the quick exchange of ideas. In relationships, you're often most comfortable in the early stages, where witty conversation and sexy banter take center stage. The deeper, more emotional bonding can feel less natural to you, but you're willing to learn when the connection feels worth it. (The extent of the discomfort in going deeper will be determined by the sign Mars is in.)

With Mars in the 3rd house, you may be motivated to create a podcast, blog, or other platform where you can share your ideas, grievances, or passions. Protecting or advocating for your community might also be a driving force for you, giving you a sense of purpose and connection.

At its best, Mars in the 3rd house is sharp, engaging, and full of curiosity. You bring energy and enthusiasm to your connections, keeping relationships interesting with your clever words and dynamic approach to life.

Mars in the 4th

Mars in the 4th house operates beneath the surface but is anything but inactive. This house, being the lowest and darkest part of the chart, can sometimes bury the planet's energy, but Mars is angular here, which means it is active—others just might not be privileged enough to see it.

This placement is deeply tied to home, family, and security. With Mars in the 4th house, you will fight fiercely for your sense of home and the people you consider family, whether that's your birth family, your chosen family, or even your country. However, if the fight happens *with* family, then building and maintaining a chosen family becomes even more critical for your sense of belonging.

You're passionate about 4th house matters, driven to create a home that feels secure and is aligned with your needs. Sharing a home with the right person is an important goal for you, as it fulfills both your emotional and your practical desire for connection and stability. You go so far as to feel like you can't really know someone until you've lived together.

While Mars in the 4th may seem subdued at first glance, it's quietly powerful. Your energy operates at a foundational level, influencing your actions in deeply personal and meaningful ways. When you channel your drive into building a stable home life, you create a secure base from which you can thrive.

Mars in the 5th

You can't avoid talking about sex with this Mars placement. The 5th is the house of casual sex, romance, children, and play, and Mars is the sex planet—so, depending on the chart and Mars's sign, this placement for Mars might be insatiable.

With Mars in the 5th house, you thrive on fun, creativity, and passion. Here, Mars brings a playful and competitive energy to life, whether it's through sports, dancing, or viewing sex as a form of recreation. You're motivated by enjoyment and need a partner in crime who's just as eager to suck the marrow out of life as you are.

Romance is a theme for this Mars, but you might approach it as a game—one filled with theatrics and excitement. It's important for the people in your orbit to understand the rules of your game, as Mars in the 5th can sometimes come off as carefree to the point of not recognizing when "fun" might hurt others. To you, it's all in good fun, but not everyone sees things the same way.

This Mars placement is passionate about creativity. You may channel your energy into working on artistic projects, creating something meaningful, or simply expressing yourself physically with friends, lovers, and partners. You may be inclined to risk-taking, including in all things romance and sex.

At its best, Mars in the 5th house infuses life with passion, excitement, and creativity. When you balance your playful nature with awareness of others' feelings, you can create vibrant and fulfilling relationships filled with joy and shared adventures.

Mars in the 6th

Mars in the 6th house thrives on routine and purpose, pouring energy into work, health, and daily life. With this Mars placement, you benefit greatly from having a disciplined exercise routine, as it helps balance your drive to put so much energy into your tasks. Whether it's health, fitness, or work, Mars in the 6th is motivated by progress and a desire to make things better.

This Mars placement can bring a strong passion for animals. You might become a fierce protector of furry friends or find yourself advocating for animal rights. Whether it's through volunteering, work, or simply a deep connection to your pets, this placement often ties Mars's energy to caring for and defending the vulnerable.

In relationships, you value partners who can align with your love of routine and a healthy lifestyle. This Mars placement thrives on shared goals and structure, so a partner who can appreciate or even join in your routines is ideal. You might also bring your natural sense of guardianship to your connections, acting as a protector or anchor for those you care about.

At its best, Mars in the 6th house combines productivity, passion, and a sense of purpose. By channeling your energy into meaningful routines and habits—whether related to health, fitness, or the welfare of animals—you can create a life filled with both structure and heart.

Mars in the 7th

Mars in the 7th house of partnerships brings intensity and passion to one-on-one connections, but it also has a knack for attracting conflict or even aggression in relationships. This placement often draws in "Marsy" folks—partners who are bold, assertive, or competitive—which can lead to dynamic connections but also requires careful navigation to avoid power struggles.

For Mars in the 7th, relationships are a key source of motivation. In romantic, professional, or platonic partnerships, you thrive when you have a partner who can match your energy and join you in active interests. Whether it's hitting the gym together or collaborating on a project, having someone to share your drive with is essential.

However, this placement comes with a lesson in balance. With Mars in the 7th, you need to be mindful of not attracting bullies—or becoming one yourself. Your strong will and assertive nature can sometimes overshadow the need for compromise and give-and-take, which are vital for building healthy, lasting relationships.

At its best, Mars in the 7th house brings passion, energy, and drive to partnerships, creating dynamic and engaging connections. By learning to balance your intensity with collaboration and compromise, you can create partnerships that are both fiery and harmonious.

Mars in the 8th

Mars in the 8th house dives deep into the murky, transformative waters of intimacy, passion, and power. This placement craves a connection that intertwines sex and intimacy, often feeling unfulfilled if the relationship lacks emotional and physical depth. Surface-level connections simply won't do—this Mars is all or nothing, seeking a bond that goes straight to the soul.

With Mars in the 8th, sex is rarely just about pleasure for you—it's about vulnerability, trust, and the merging of two (or more) people on every level. True intimacy is the ultimate goal, but getting there can be a complicated process. You can struggle with fears of betrayal or rejection, which may lead to protective or even possessive tendencies. You can become fiercely attached not only to your partner but also to your partner's resources, whether financial, emotional, or otherwise.

Jealousy can be a shadow side of this Mars placement, fueled by an intense need to feel secure in your connections. But when you channel this passion into building trust and mutual support, you can create bonds that are deeply transformative for both you and your partner.

Mars in the 8th isn't afraid to confront the darker, messier aspects of love and desire. Power struggles can come up, especially if you feel you're not being met with the same level of intensity that you bring to the table. The lesson here is to balance the need for control with vulnerability, allowing space for true connection without losing yourself in the process.

At its best, Mars in the 8th house brings incredible depth and transformation to relationships. When you learn to trust both yourself and your partners, you create connections that are as profound as they are passionate.

Mars in the 9th

Mars in the 9th house is the ultimate adventurer, driven by a hunger to explore, learn, and expand horizons. Whether it's through physical travel, intellectual pursuits, or spiritual journeys, this Mars thrives on the excitement of discovery. Fighting for principles, ideals, and philosophies is second nature, and you're passionate about sharing your beliefs with others.

With Mars in the 9th, knowledge can be a major turn-on for you. You're drawn to partners and connections that challenge your mind and worldview, ignite curiosity, and engage in big-picture conversations. Rituals, traditions, or even a shared religious or spiritual practice might hold special meaning for you, as you're often motivated by a desire to connect to something greater than yourself.

With this Mars placement, promises of adventure and experience are the keys to your heart. Whether it's traveling to distant lands, taking a risk on a new idea, or diving into an unexplored philosophy, you're all in when your spirit feels inspired.

At its best, Mars in the 9th house fuels a life filled with passion, purpose, and exploration. You bring enthusiasm and energy to your relationships, especially when those connections align with your ideals and thirst for adventure.

Mars in the 10th

Mars in the 10th house is fueled by ambition and a drive to succeed. Career and public image are top priorities, and you often find yourself drawn to Martian professions—anything from athlete to agent (fighting for their high-profile clients), bodyguard, or even sex worker. You want to be seen as strong, dynamic, and sexy in the eyes of the world, often crafting a public persona that reflects your power and determination.

With Mars here, you can sometimes put ambition ahead of relationships, focusing more on reaching the top than nurturing personal connections. You may even seek a partner who enhances your image, someone who adds to your sense of virility, strength, or sex appeal. Public perception matters to you, and being seen with someone who aligns with your vision of success can be as important as the relationship itself.

That said, with this Mars placement, a partner who supports your goals while also encouraging you to step away from the spotlight now and then is ideal. Balancing your public drive with private intimacy is key to maintaining both your professional and your personal well-being.

At its best, Mars in the 10th house inspires others with its determination, showcasing what's possible when passion meets hard work. When you channel that energy into relationships as well as career, you can create a dynamic life that's both fulfilling and impactful.

Mars in the 11th

Mars in the 11th house is socially driven and thrives on the energy of groups, organizations, and shared aspirations. This placement often finds motivation in fighting for a cause or championing a collective vision, whether that's through activism, leadership, or simply being the person who rallies others to take action.

You may take on a leadership role within groups, using your drive to push shared goals forward. However, your intensity and assertiveness can sometimes come across as socially aggressive or even create conflict within the group dynamic. Finding clarity about what truly motivates you and understanding your deeper priorities is key to balancing your strong presence with harmony in your social circles.

This Mars placement may also bring a unique flair to how you connect with others, possibly even in the realm of romance or sexuality. You are energized by being around people and might find group dynamics particularly stimulating, but this can sometimes blur boundaries or lead to challenges if you don't navigate it thoughtfully.

At its best, Mars in the 11th house is a dynamic force for collective progress. You inspire others with your passion and ability to turn ideas into action. When you balance your personal drive with the needs of the group, you can create powerful and lasting connections.

Mars in the 12th

Planets in the 12th house often operate behind the scenes, sometimes even hidden from your own conscious awareness. Mars in the 12th gives you a rich inner life, but it can take time to understand what really motivates you or what you're reacting to. Learning these things about yourself is an important part of your process in building relationships.

Mars here moves in subtle, emotional ways. Your drive might surface through intuition, dreams, or quiet but powerful convictions. You may act instinctively and only later realize what was fueling you underneath. That can lead to moments of self-sabotage, but it can also lead to incredible spiritual breakthroughs and emotional clarity, especially when you take the time to reflect.

When you're triggered or overwhelmed, solitude is vital. You often need peace, quiet, or time alone to recharge and reconnect with your deeper motivations. Mars in the 12th can draw you toward private or deeply intimate relationships—sometimes hidden, sometimes spiritual, often transformative. The physical side of your energy may ebb and flow, but that doesn't make you less capable; it just means you have your own rhythm.

With Mars in the 12th, it's important to find safe, supportive people who can help you recognize your patterns without judgment. With reflection and care, this placement can become a quiet superpower: a source of profound creativity, empathy, and healing. You don't have to be loud to be powerful. Mars in the 12th teaches you to trust your inner fire—because once it's aligned with your purpose, your ability to channel that energy makes you unstoppable.

What Lights Your Fire?

In your journal, review some key themes you discovered from the description of your Mars sign and write them down. Add some things that you're passionate about and that really heat you up. This can include actual physical/sexual passion and issues, projects, or just about anything that gets you going!

For example, I have Mars in Gemini, and I cannot consume enough information. I *love* to gather and share opinions. There's nothing like a little dirty talk to heat me up. Someone I can talk to and who can keep up with conversations and shares my interests is hotter than anything.

Now consider which house Mars occupies in your chart and create some descriptions of the combination of its sign and house.

For example, With my Mars in Gemini in the 9th house, I have strong opinions and a love of philosophy. My search for information and desire to expand my worldview are very important and can sometimes be all-consuming. I'm a total sucker for witty banter and someone who wants to hear all about what I've been discovering. I love travel, but sometimes the idea of travel is enough—deciding where to go and committing to the time can get in the way of me actually exploring the world.

Your turn! Think about the themes for your Mars sign and house, and write from your solar plexus—that's where the Mars fire burns.

3

The Places of Love in Astrology

Houses That Hold Relationship Clues

The answer to *where* in astrology lies in the houses. To find love in your natal chart, we need to look beyond Mars and Venus or those overly simple (and honestly ineffective) Sun sign compatibility ideas. This means diving into the houses connected to romance, partnership, and deep intimacy. The places of love are the 5th house of joy, creativity, and love affairs, the 7th house of committed partnerships, and the 8th house of deep sexual connection and shared resources. These houses, along with the ruler of each house and where those rulers are in your chart, offer detailed clues about where you might meet potential partners and what to look for.

In this chapter we'll explore these houses and their rulers to look at where love might be waiting for you. By the end, you'll have a clearer map to help you navigate your relationship potential—whether that means giving online dating a try or letting your mom set you up with the neighbor next door. This is about finding the most direct and meaningful path to the connections you're looking for.

Keep in mind that most natal relationship stories aren't linear. We don't all have love planets neatly placed in relationship houses or planetary rulers in the signs they rule. Real charts, like real lives, are full of complexity, detours, and contradictions. That's why this process is about gathering clues and connecting patterns, not looking for a straight path from dating to "happily ever after."

The Role of the 5th House: Social and Self-Discovery

The 5th house is where we step out of the safety of family and start connecting in new ways. It's a space of social discovery—and self-discovery through those interactions. Relationships here are about exploring, having fun, and finding joy in experiences. They're not about deep commitment or long-term connection. Instead, they're meant to draw us out of our comfort zones and into a world where we can learn more about ourselves by how we interact with others.

Depending on the rest of your chart, these 5th house experiences can feel amazing and exciting or intimidating and overwhelming—but they're rarely boring. If your early home life didn't feel safe or secure, the pleasure found in the 5th house can sometimes become a place to hide. In these cases, moving toward deeper, more meaningful connections (like those of the 7th and 8th houses) may feel like a huge leap.

The 5th house is also about self-expression and creativity, which ties into its connection with children—not just literal ones, but also the things we "birth" creatively. Sharing connection here comes through what we create, whether it's art, passion projects, or romantic experiences.

The 5th house carries themes of competition and gambling, adding a playful or even daring edge to romance. This energy can show up as a love of the thrill of the chase or the excitement of "winning" someone's attention. In dating, this might mean enjoying a little competition, testing boundaries, or even viewing romance as a gamble worth taking. The highs and lows of this house can be a rush, but they also teach us important lessons about what actually fulfills us versus what's only a brief thrill.

Without a strong sense of self-worth (a lesson from the 2nd house), the relationships we attract through the 5th house can sometimes reflect our own insecurities. Love here can become self-serving or indulgent, feeding a fragile ego instead of helping us grow. But when we use the energy of the 5th house to explore who we are through self-awareness, we open the door to joy-filled experiences that can help us develop and share our true selves with others.

The Role of the 7th House: Partnerships and One-on-One Connections

The 7th house, starting at the Descendant (the cusp of the 7th house), is where "I" becomes "we." Often described as a reflection of ourselves, this house can be the shadow of the Ascendant (the cusp of the 1st house)—where our mask comes off and the true work of relationships begins. (We'll talk more about house cusps in the next chapter.) It's here that we explore the give-and-take dynamic, balancing our needs with the needs of another.

The 7th house is all about relationships defined by commitment or contracts. Romantic partnerships, business collaborations, and even professional relationships—like those with doctors, lawyers, clients, or patients—all fall under the domain of the 7th house. It's also where we find open enemies, those whose opposition forces us to see things from another perspective.

Relationships in the 7th house help us grow. These are the connections that challenge and change us, or vice versa. They're marked by a sense of mutual dependency, where we can rely on someone or they can rely on us, for better or worse. The 7th is the house of negotiation, where we learn to balance what we want with what the other person needs, creating space for a shared path forward.

The sign on the 7th house cusp gives clues to what we seek in partnerships, from personality traits to the energy we're drawn to in others. For example, a fire sign on this cusp might signal a desire for a bold, creative partner, while a water sign on the cusp might suggest a need for emotional depth and connection. Planets in the 7th house bring even more details. Each planet tells a story about how we approach commitment, how we navigate one-on-one connections, and what we can learn about ourselves through the relationships we form.

The 7th house teaches us about shared responsibility, collaboration, and the beauty—and sometimes the challenge—of seeing ourselves through the eyes of another.

The Role of the 8th House: Intimacy, Shared Resources, and What Transforms Us

The 8th house is where we move beyond the surface of relationships and dive into the depths of intimacy, vulnerability, and transformation. While the 7th house focuses on partnerships and agreements, the 8th is about what happens when those bonds deepen—when we share not just our lives but also our resources, secrets, and even fears. The 8th house is—on some level—what scares us.

This house governs the profound connections that ask us to trust completely. It's where we navigate shared finances, inheritances, and the merging of energy with another. The 8th house is also tied to sex—not the playful, romantic side we find in the 5th house, but the kind of intimacy that comes with emotional exposure and shared vulnerability.

The 8th house is often described as the house of transformation, because relationships here have the power to fundamentally change us—or to be changed by us. It's where we confront power dynamics, learn to navigate control, and face the deeper truths about ourselves and others. It's here that we can access our unconscious.

The 8th house is also where we encounter loss, fear, and the things we try to keep hidden. This house reminds us that intimacy is as much about letting go as it is about holding on. This can manifest as learning to trust another person with what's most private to us—or letting go of old patterns that keep us from fully connecting.

The sign on the cusp of the 8th house gives insight into how we approach these deep themes, while planets *in* the 8th house reveal even more. Each planet adds a layer of complexity, showing how we navigate the deeper, darker, transformative aspects of life and love.

The 8th house teaches us that intimacy and trust aren't just given—they're earned. When we embrace the lessons of this house, we can build relationships that are profoundly transformative, rooted in vulnerability, and capable of weathering life's biggest challenges.

What If a House Is Empty?

If you notice that a house (or several houses) in your chart is empty, don't panic! An empty house doesn't mean that area of life is unimportant or nothing will happen there. It simply means there weren't any planets actively influencing that house at the time of your birth.

Instead, the sign on the cusp of a house (the sign that starts the house) and its ruling planet tell the story. For example, if your 8th house is empty but starts in Scorpio, you'd look to where Mars (Scorpio's traditional ruler) is in your chart to understand how you approach intimacy, trust, and shared resources and where you might look for them.

Empty houses usually function more quietly or neutrally compared to houses with planets, where the energy is more active or dynamic. It's like a room in your house that doesn't have furniture yet: It's still part of your life and can be filled as needed, but it doesn't have a permanent occupant shaping its vibe and you likely don't spend a lot of time there.

And here's the thing: Those houses *do* get "filled" as we move through life. Transits (the current movements of planets in the sky) and progressions (your chart's gradual unfolding over time) can activate empty houses, bringing fresh energy and focus to those areas. The Moon races through all twelve houses every month! The people we bring into our lives also reflect the energy of these houses, helping us learn and grow in those areas. For example, say you have Gemini on the cusp of your 4th house of family and it's empty. But when you think about it, you realize that you have several people in your life who are Geminis—you've filled that house through your connections. Life has a way of filling in the blanks, ensuring that every house plays its part in your journey.

Tracking How Life Activates Your Empty Houses

Do you have empty houses in your chart? If you do, which ones are empty? Is there a specific one you've filled with people of that Sun sign? Which one? What sign is it?

Where the Story Unfolds: Hemispheres and Quadrants

As you move through the relationship houses, and the rest of your chart, it helps to understand the layout of the birth chart as a whole. Each chart is divided into hemispheres and quadrants, and these larger zones offer another layer of meaning for how the houses express themselves.

Eastern Hemisphere (Houses 10–3): The eastern hemisphere, on the *left-hand side* of the chart, reflects how we initiate, act independently, and shape our lives from the inside out.

Western Hemisphere (Houses 4–9): The western hemisphere, on the *right-hand side* of the chart, highlights how we engage with others, respond to the world, and grow through relationships.

We also divide the chart into northern and southern hemispheres—the lower and upper halves of the chart:

Northern Hemisphere (Houses 1–6): The northern hemisphere, in the *bottom half* of the chart, centers on private, personal development. These houses describe our inner world, what lies beneath the surface.

Southern Hemisphere (Houses 7–12): The southern hemisphere, in the *top half* of the chart, focuses on how we show up in the outer world—through career, community, and shared experience. These houses describe what we want to share with the world.

On top of that, the chart is divided into four quadrants:

1st Quadrant (Houses 1–3): The 1st quadrant is all about self-discovery and early development.

2nd Quadrant (Houses 4–6): The 2nd quadrant explores how we build stability, routines, and emotional foundations.

3rd Quadrant (Houses 7–9): The 3rd quadrant is where relationships come into focus. This is where “me” becomes “we.”

4th Quadrant (Houses 10–12): The 4th quadrant turns our attention toward legacy, visibility, and spiritual integration.

The farther we move around the chart from the Ascendant (the self), the more outward-facing the focus becomes. Understanding these zones gives you context for *where* your relationship story is unfolding.

Further Reflections: Who You Invite into Your Life

Think about the signs that seem to show up most often in your friendships, partnerships, family, or even the people you feel naturally drawn to. This is another way we activate and work with parts of our chart, often without even realizing it.

- Are there certain signs you notice over and over again?
- Where do those signs show up in your birth chart?
- Which house (or houses) are they connected to?
- What part of yourself do you think you're stimulating or exploring by bringing these people into your life?

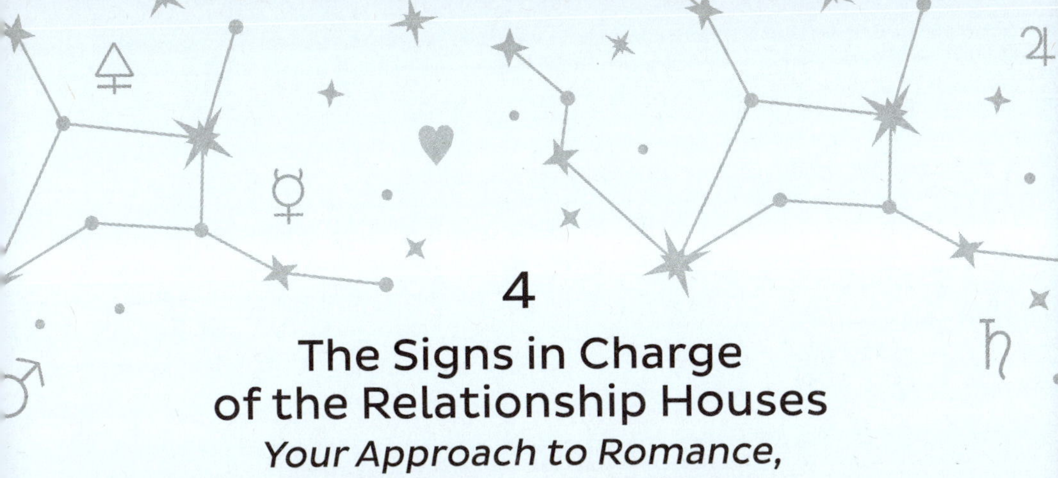

4
The Signs in Charge of the Relationship Houses
Your Approach to Romance, Partnership, and Intimacy

Each house in your chart is like a room in your astrological home, and the zodiac sign on the cusp of each house is the color palette giving it character. The sign sets the tone for how you express yourself in that area of your life, what you're looking for, and how you approach the themes of that house. Whether it's bold and fiery or calm and earthy, the sign on the cusp flavors the house with its specific energy and character.

Understanding the signs in charge of each house gives you insights into the *how* and *who* of different areas of your life. How do you approach romance, partnerships, and intimacy? What kind of person do you want to share these types of experiences with? Where do you find joy or build trust? These are just some of the questions the zodiac signs can answer. The sign tells us the tone and style of the house, revealing the kind of energy you bring to it and what you're most likely to attract and be drawn to.

This chapter explores each zodiac sign's influence on the 5th, 7th, and 8th houses—the houses of romance, relationships, and intimacy. I've included a table of symbols (glyphs) on page 298 and an example chart here to show you where to look to find which sign is on the house cusp.

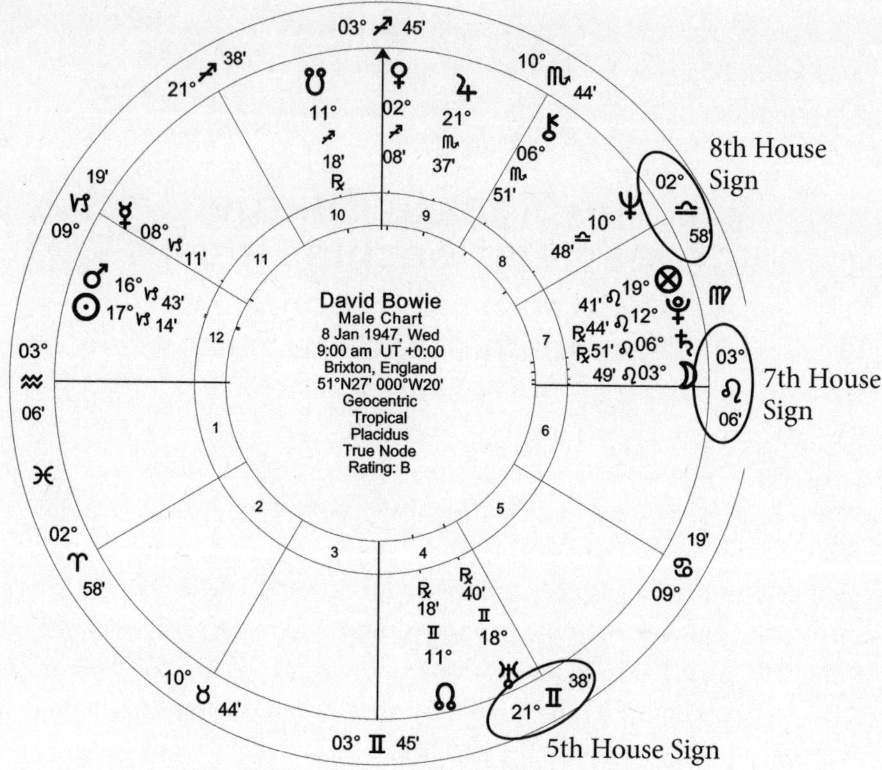

Chart 2: David Bowie, Signs on Relationship Houses

In David Bowie's chart, Gemini rules his 5th house, Leo rules his 7th house, and Libra rules his 8th house (chart 2).

Have a look at the signs influencing your relationship houses and what they can tell you about how you express and attract romance, joy, and creativity. Whether your energy is fiery, earthy, airy, or watery, the sign on the cusp will begin to guide you toward deeper understanding—and you might even have a few aha moments about your approach to these parts of your life. Before you get started, find which signs rule the 5th, 7th, and 8th houses in your chart.

The Sign on the 5th House

Which sign do you have on the cusp of your 5th house?

Aries on the 5th: How You Approach Joy and Play

With Aries ruling your 5th house, you bring bold, fearless energy to joy and play. Spontaneity and adventure drive your sense of fun and you're naturally drawn to activities that challenge and excite you. Play for you isn't just lighthearted—it's a way to channel your fiery enthusiasm, explore new passions, and discover more about yourself.

What You Bring to Romance and Dating

In romance, your directness and passion are unmistakable. With Aries on your 5th house, you approach dating with initiative and excitement, often diving headfirst into making new connections. You know how to generate excitement, and your self-assurance can be charming—though it might sometimes come across as a little intense! You're not afraid to take the lead in romance, and your enthusiasm is usually contagious. If this doesn't describe you, then these qualities are likely what you're looking for.

What You Want from Romance and Dating

With Aries here, you're drawn to people who are confident, adventurous, and independent. You want a relationship that feels alive, with someone who can keep up with your energy and share in your excitement for life. Aries energy here means you value passion, spontaneity, and a sense of play in romantic connections. Predictability or routine can leave you bored, so you'll thrive with a partner who can surprise and inspire you. And let's not forget independence! You thrive when you maintain your own sense of independence and give that same space to your romantic connections. You expect partners to have their own life outside of the relationship, just as you do.

Which Forms of Creativity and Expression Best Suit Your 5th House

Your creativity is fueled by short bursts of fiery intensity. You're happiest when you can express yourself boldly and take risks in your creative pursuits. However, your energy isn't always sustained and you can lose interest in things quickly. Physical activities like dance, sports, or action-oriented hobbies might feel especially satisfying, but any project that lets you lead, innovate, or dive headfirst into an exciting idea will light you up. Turning a 5th house project into a competition can help you stay interested and pull you through to the finish line.

Taurus on the 5th: How You Approach Joy and Play

With Taurus ruling your 5th house, your approach to joy and play is sensual and grounded. You find joy in simple, earthly pleasures, whether it's savoring good food, enjoying music, or soaking up nature's splendor. For you, play isn't about rushing or chasing thrills; it's about slowing down, indulging *all* your senses, and savoring the moment. Stability and comfort are key—you're probably not into chaotic or high-voltage hobbies.

What You Bring to Romance and Dating

When it comes to romance, you bring a steady and devoted energy to the situation. Taurus here means you're naturally affectionate, loyal, and deeply committed once you decide to pursue romance. You're not one to rush into relationships; you take your time to assess whether the other person shares your values. You're warm and patient, but your need for security can sometimes come across as cautious. Your sensual nature ensures you know how to create a traditionally romantic atmosphere.

What You Want from Romance and Dating

You're drawn to people who are steady and grounded and share your appreciation for life's simple pleasures. Stability is important—you crave a connection that feels secure and enduring. Predictability and consistency are important, but not at the expense of romance and beauty. Taurus ruling the 5th house means you value physical affection and shared sensual experiences, whether that's cooking together, relaxing in a beautiful space, or simply enjoying each other's presence. You thrive with a partner who can match your steady energy and isn't afraid to savor life with you.

Which Forms of Creativity and Expression Best Suit Your 5th House

Your creativity is fueled by a love of beauty and a desire to create something lasting. Whether it's gardening, cooking, crafting, or any artistic pursuit that allows you to work with your hands, you excel in projects that engage your senses and let you take your time. Taurus energy thrives on tangible results, so you're likely drawn to projects that produce something you can touch, see, or share. Music and singing might also resonate with you, as Taurus energy has a natural affinity for rhythm and harmony.

Gemini on the 5th: How You Approach Joy and Play

With Gemini ruling your 5th house, your approach to joy and play is lively, curious, and full of variety. You thrive on mental stimulation and love activities that challenge your mind, spark conversation, or introduce you to something new to learn. Play for you usually involves socializing, whether that's chatting with friends, exploring new ideas, or enjoying some quick banter with someone who can keep up. Fun isn't just about action; it's about keeping your mind engaged and entertained.

What You Bring to Romance and Dating

In romance, you bring wit, charm, and an undeniable spark. Gemini energy here means you're a natural flirt, and your quick sense of humor can easily draw people in. You're curious and fun, often more interested in getting to know someone's mind than their looks. While your enthusiasm for new social connections is infectious, your tendency to hop from one interest to the next can sometimes make you seem less serious. Your adaptability and casual nature are your strengths, but you might need to be aware of your restlessness or lack of focus in relationships.

What You Want from Romance and Dating

You're drawn to people who are clever and communicative. For you, connection starts with exchanging words—you need someone who can keep up with your mental energy and isn't afraid to discuss ideas. Routine or predictability can feel suffocating; you want a relationship that keeps you on your toes, with a partner in crime who is just as curious and adaptable as you are. Gemini on the 5th house cusp means you value humor, spontaneity, and a sense of exploration in your romantic connections, and you want someone who enjoys your mischievous side.

Which Forms of Creativity and Expression Best Suit Your 5th House

Your creativity thrives on diversity and versatility. Writing, journaling, or storytelling might come naturally to you, as Gemini energy loves to put thoughts into words. Social activities such as theater, improvisation, or group brainstorming sessions can also ignite your creativity. You're happiest when your creative outlets allow you to experiment, communicate, and explore multiple ideas at once. Learning something new that captivates your interest is a happy place for you! Whether it's dabbling in different writing or art mediums or switching projects frequently, you need variety to keep your inspiration flowing.

Cancer on the 5th: How You Approach Joy and Play

With Cancer ruling your 5th house, your approach to joy and play is emotional, nurturing, and personal. You find happiness in meaningful connections, sentimental experiences, and moments that feel close to the heart. Play for you isn't just about having fun; it's about creating memories and building bonds. You're drawn to activities that bring comfort, whether that's spending time with loved ones, indulging in creative hobbies, or enjoying the simple pleasures of home life.

What You Bring to Romance and Dating

In romance, you bring tenderness, sensitivity, and a nurturing style. Cancer energy here means you approach dating with a strong desire to care for and connect with others on an emotional level. You are intuitive and can easily sense the needs and feelings of the object of your affection, regularly offering support and comfort. While your warmth is a gift, your vulnerability can make you hesitant to open up until you feel safe. Once you do, your loyalty and devotion shine.

What You Want from Romance and Dating

You're drawn to partners who are caring, empathetic, and emotionally available. In romance, you want a relationship that feels like home—one that offers safety, comfort, and emotional connection. Cancer energy in the 5th house means you crave romance that's heartfelt and meaningful, where both people feel seen and valued. Predictability and reliability in romance are important to you, as is someone who can appreciate your sentimental side. You're likely to feel most fulfilled in a relationship where vulnerability is met with understanding and love. Cancer is not a sign that is good at casual dating, so having it in charge of your 5th house likely means you don't take romance lightly.

Which Forms of Creativity and Expression Best Suit Your 5th House

Your creativity is fueled by emotion and nostalgia. Artistic pursuits that allow you to express your feelings, like painting, writing, or crafting, can feel especially rewarding. You may also find joy in creating things that nurture others, such as cooking, home design, or making gifts for loved ones. Cancer energy here ties creativity to the heart, so your best work often comes from personal inspiration or experiences that hold deep meaning. As the 5th is the house of children, you might even be called to share and teach creative hobbies to kids. Family-oriented projects or anything that celebrates traditions can also be beautiful outlets for you.

Leo on the 5th: How You Approach Joy and Play

With Leo on this cusp, you bring a bold, vibrant, and radiant energy to 5th house matters. You approach fun as an opportunity to shine, express yourself, and take center stage. You love being surrounded by laughter, attention, and applause, thriving in situations where you can entertain, create, and inspire. For you, play isn't just lighthearted—it's a chance to show the world your special spark. If the rest of your chart indicates shyness instead of seeking attention, you'll thrive on projects you can take pride in, even if only those nearest and dearest get to you see what you've created.

What You Bring to Romance and Dating

In romance, you're magnetic, passionate, and unforgettable. You approach dating with flair, bringing excitement and warmth to your connections. Leo energy here means you naturally draw people in with your confidence and generosity. You're the romantic who pulls out all the stops, from grand gestures to heartfelt compliments. Your enthusiasm can light up any relationship, and your loyalty and devotion are hard to beat. However, you might occasionally (or regularly) expect the same level of effort and attention in return, which can lead to disappointment if it's not met.

What You Want from Romance and Dating

You're drawn to partners who recognize your worth, celebrate your successes, and match your level of enthusiasm. Leo energy in the 5th house means you want a relationship that feels exciting, romantic, and special. You thrive with someone who makes you feel adored and valued but also respects your independence and ambition. You're looking for a partner who brings their own sense of flair and confidence, someone who can shine alongside you and keep the energy alive. Loyalty, admiration, and shared fun are nonnegotiables in your romantic connections.

Which Forms of Creativity and Expression Best Suit Your 5th House

Your creativity is fueled by your natural charisma and need for self-expression. Anything creative that puts you in the spotlight will feel deeply fulfilling. You love creating things that inspire and bring joy to others, whether it's art, music, or even planning memorable events. Leo energy thrives on recognition, so you're happiest when your creative efforts are seen, appreciated, and celebrated. If you're ever feeling stuck, tap into your playful side—fun and spontaneity often unlock your best ideas.

Virgo on the 5th: How You Approach Joy and Play

With Virgo ruling your 5th house, you approach joy and play with a practical, thoughtful, and deliberate energy. For you, fun often has a purpose, whether it's improving a skill, learning something new, or creating order out of chaos. You enjoy activities that feel productive or serve a greater goal, and you may find joy in hobbies that require precision and focus. Play might not feel like an immediate priority, but when you let yourself relax, you discover the simple pleasures in small, meaningful moments.

What You Bring to Romance and Dating

In romance, you bring thoughtfulness, care, and an eye for the little details that make a person special. You're observant and intuitive about your person's needs, often expressing love through acts of service or practical support. Virgo energy here means you approach dating with a discerning eye, looking for someone who meets your high standards. While you may initially seem reserved, you have a quiet charm and genuine warmth that make you endearing to those who take the time to get to know you.

What You Want from Romance and Dating

You're drawn to partners who value reliability, thoughtfulness, and self-improvement. Virgo energy in the 5th house means you want a relationship that feels grounded, practical, and mutually supportive. Grand gestures might not impress you as much as small, meaningful actions that show care and commitment. You thrive with someone who respects your need for order and shares your passion for growth and refinement. While romance might feel like a puzzle you're trying to solve, finding someone who appreciates your efforts will bring you the most joy.

Which Forms of Creativity and Expression Best Suit Your 5th House

Your creativity shines in pursuits that require precision, focus, and attention to detail. Virgo energy thrives in crafts, writing, or projects where you can analyze, improve, and perfect. You might enjoy creating systems, organizing spaces, or doing anything that combines beauty with function. Your work often carries an understated elegance, reflecting your meticulous nature. If you find yourself overthinking, try letting go of perfection and embracing the imperfections—sometimes the most authentic creations come from moments of spontaneity. Someone with a creative chart and earthy Virgo energy here would get great satisfaction and joy out of making tangible things—the more detailed, the better!

Libra on the 5th: How You Approach Joy and Play

With Libra ruling your 5th house, you approach joy and play with a sense of grace and beauty. You're drawn to activities that let you connect with others, especially in beautiful and calm environments. Whether it's a gallery opening, a dinner party, or a shared creative project, you find joy in experiences that blend social connection with artful expression. Play for you likely involves collaboration, and even though you can easily get things done on your own, you shine when you get to share these moments with others.

What You Bring to Romance and Dating

In romance, you bring charm, elegance, flirtation, and a natural ability to make your partner feel special. Libra energy here means you approach dating with a refined sense of courtship, valuing mutual respect and shared interests. You're a skilled conversationalist and have a knack for making others feel comfortable and appreciated. However, your desire for harmony might lead you to avoid conflict, which can sometimes keep relationships on a surface level. When you lean into vulnerability, your connections deepen, becoming more meaningful and lasting.

What You Want from Romance and Dating

You're drawn to partners who are charming, kind, and considerate and appreciate beauty and balance as much as you do. Libra energy in the 5th house means you value partnerships that feel equal and fair and match your energy. You thrive in relationships where there's mutual support and a shared sense of aesthetics or values. While you enjoy being courted, you also love creating a romantic atmosphere for your partner. A relationship that feels like an ongoing dance of give-and-take filled with shared experiences will appeal to you the most.

Which Forms of Creativity and Expression Best Suit Your 5th House

Your creativity thrives in areas that emphasize beauty, cohesion, and collaboration. Libra energy loves design, whether it's fashion, decorating, or creating balanced and beautiful spaces. You might also find joy in music, painting, or anything that allows you to work with others on a shared vision. You have a natural eye for aesthetics and are skilled at bringing people together through your creative pursuits. Whatever you do, your creative expression will often reflect your desire to bring harmony and beauty into the world.

Scorpio on the 5th: How You Approach Joy and Play

With Scorpio ruling your 5th house, your approach to joy and play is anything but superficial. You're drawn to experiences that feel intense, transformative, and deeply meaningful. You may not take to whimsical fun, preferring activities that challenge your emotions or provoke a sense of mystery and intrigue. If you do partake in frivolity, it might be something to do with being scared or scaring others. For you, play often doubles as a way to explore the depths of yourself and others, uncovering truths and embracing vulnerability. Scorpio loves secrets, so something you get to keep all to yourself would be special to you.

What You Bring to Romance and Dating

In romance, you bring intensity, passion, and a magnetic energy that others can't help but notice. Scorpio energy here means you can be deeply committed when you invest in someone, and you expect the same in return. You might approach dating cautiously at first, preferring to understand someone's true nature before fully opening up. Or, to avoid the emotional side all together, you could just bring a lot of sex to romance. However, once you're in, you're all in. You're not afraid to delve into the deeper, more complex aspects of relationships, and your loyalty runs deep. That said, your powerful emotions can sometimes come across as possessive or overly intense, so finding balance is key.

What You Want from Romance and Dating

You're drawn to partners who are authentic and willing to explore the raw, unfiltered aspects of connection. Surface-level relationships won't do it for you—you crave a bond that's intimate and full of trust and has emotional depth. Vulnerability is a must, and you want a partner who's unafraid to bare their soul. Scorpio energy in the 5th house means you value loyalty and emotional honesty and you seek someone who can match your depth and passion. Power dynamics can come into play, so finding a partner who values equality is important.

Which Forms of Creativity and Expression Best Suit Your 5th House

Your creativity thrives in transformative, emotionally charged expressions. Scorpio energy loves to dive deep, so you may be drawn to art, writing, or music that explores themes of rebirth, mystery, or any kind of emotional intensity. (Stephen King has Scorpio here.) You might also find fulfillment in psychology, healing practices, or any creative outlet that helps others face their shadow side. Passion projects that let you channel your intensity into something meaningful will resonate the most. You're at your best when your creative pursuits help you uncover hidden truths, bring out intense emotions, or foster deep connections with others.

Sagittarius on the 5th: How You Approach Joy and Play

With Sagittarius ruling your 5th house, your approach to joy and play is adventurous, optimistic, and limitless. You seek experiences that expand your life in some way, whether that's through travel, learning, or exploring new philosophies. Fun for you often involves a sense of freedom, and you're most alive when you're discovering something new. Spontaneous trips, cultural experiences, and outdoor adventures are your idea of a good time.

What You Bring to Romance and Dating

You bring excitement, energy, and a sense of adventure to romance. Sagittarius energy here means you approach dating with curiosity and openness, often seeing each connection as an opportunity to learn and grow. Your charm lies in your enthusiasm and the joy you bring to those around you. However, your free-spirited nature can sometimes make you seem noncommittal, especially if a relationship feels too restrictive. You thrive in connections that allow you to explore and grow, and your natural optimism can be a breath of fresh air to those you date.

What You Want from Romance and Dating

You're drawn to partners who share your love for adventure and thirst for knowledge. Intellectual stimulation is a must, and you're likely to be captivated by someone who can challenge your worldview or introduce you to new ideas. Predictability or monotony (or, in some cases, monogamy) can feel stifling, so you crave relationships that offer excitement, exploration, and growth. Sagittarius energy in the 5th house values honesty, but it also needs flexibility—rigid expectations or rules won't work for you.

Which Forms of Creativity and Expression Best Suit Your 5th House

Your creativity thrives in projects that involve exploration, education, or big ideas. Writing, teaching, or creating content about your travels, philosophies, or cultural experiences might feel especially fulfilling. You're also drawn to creative expressions that involve movement, like dance or sports, as they let you channel your boundless energy. Sagittarius rules the hips, and you might love to shake yours! Projects that let you share your optimism and inspire others to expand their worldview fit perfectly with your 5th house Sagittarius energy.

Capricorn on the 5th: How You Approach Joy and Play

This placement always has me imagining a child dressed in business attire running their own lemonade stand and, at the end of the sale, teaching their parents about margins and sales projections! Because with Capricorn ruling your 5th house, you bring a structured and a goal-oriented approach to joy and play. Fun for you often involves something productive or meaningful—you might prefer hobbies that lead to tangible results or allow you to develop a skill. While you may not be the most spontaneous person, you take your leisure seriously, planning activities that align with your plans and ambitions. There's a quiet satisfaction in working toward something, even in your downtime. Fun for you is likely tied to a challenge that allows you to reach a goal. Someone with a chart emphasizing business and Capricorn here might even find a way to monetize fun.

What You Bring to Romance and Dating

You approach romance with seriousness and intentionality, often taking your time to build a connection. You are a realist and a pragmatic when it comes to romance. Capricorn energy in the 5th house means you're not one to rush into love; instead, you're deliberate about who you let into your life. When you do commit, your loyalty and dedication shine. Your steady presence can feel grounding to partners, but your reserved nature might come off as aloof until trust is established.

What You Want from Romance and Dating

With Capricorn energy here, you're drawn to relationships that feel stable and dependable and are aligned with your long-term goals. A partner who shares your ambition or appreciates your disciplined approach to life will capture your heart. While you value tradition and commitment, you also need someone who respects your independence and understands your drive. Predictability is a comfort, not a hindrance, and you find satisfaction in building something lasting.

Which Forms of Creativity and Expression Best Suit Your 5th House

Your creativity is best expressed through projects that involve planning, discipline, and tangible results. You might excel in pursuits such as design, architecture, or any art form that combines beauty and function. Creative outlets that allow you to showcase your leadership skills or work toward a long-term goal, like writing a book or organizing a large event, can feel especially rewarding. While your approach to creativity might lean toward the serious, it also carries a quiet, understated elegance that speaks volumes.

Aquarius on the 5th: How You Approach Joy and Play

With Aquarius ruling your 5th house, you approach joy and play with a sense of curiosity and individuality. Fun for you often involves breaking away from the norm, trying something unconventional, or engaging in activities that align with your ideals and engage your mind. You thrive in group settings and enjoy connecting with like-minded individuals who share your vision. Play isn't just about fun—it's also an opportunity to explore new ideas and express your unique personality.

What You Bring to Romance and Dating

Your approach to romance is quirky, open-minded, and often intellectual. With Aquarius energy in the 5th house, you might prefer relationships that feel like friendships, valuing connection and mutual respect above all else. You bring a sense of excitement and unpredictability to dating, keeping things fresh and engaging. However, you may also seem aloof or detached at times, preferring to keep intense emotions out of it until you feel truly comfortable.

What You Want from Romance and Dating

You're drawn to people who value independence, intelligence, and shared ideals. A relationship that feels free yet connected is perfect for you. Predictability or overly traditional dynamics might leave you restless—you need a partner who can embrace your unconventional nature and join you on your adventures. Above all, you want someone who respects your need for autonomy while sharing a deep intellectual connection.

Which Forms of Creativity and Expression Best Suit Your 5th House

Your creativity thrives in innovative and collaborative environments. You might excel in technology, social activism, or any field that allows you to push boundaries and think outside the box. With airy Aquarius energy here, writing, social media, or sci-fi might be ways to connect to your creative side. Group projects or creative endeavors that connect you with a community can be especially fulfilling. Whether you're designing something cutting-edge or using your artistic talents to promote a cause, your 5th house Aquarius energy shines brightest when it's tied to something bigger than yourself.

Pisces on the 5th: How You Approach Joy and Play

With Pisces ruling your 5th house, you approach joy and play with imagination, sensitivity, and a touch of magic. Play for you isn't just about fun—it's a way to connect with the intangible, express your emotions, and escape into a world of possibility. You're naturally drawn to creative and spiritual activities, finding joy in art, music, or anything that stirs your soul. Your sense of play often has a dreamy, otherworldly quality, making even ordinary experiences feel extraordinary.

What You Bring to Romance and Dating

You bring a romantic, almost ethereal energy to dating. With Pisces on the cusp of your 5th house, you approach romance with a sense of wonder and idealism, often seeing the best in people and situations. You have a natural ability to make others feel deeply understood and cherished, and your empathetic nature can be incredibly magnetic. However, your romantic style might sometimes lean toward fantasy, leaving you vulnerable to disappointment if reality doesn't match your dreams.

What You Want from Romance and Dating

You're drawn to connections that feel spiritual, emotional, and transcendent. Superficial connections won't do—you crave something deeper, something that feels like it was written in the stars. You want a romantic partner who can share in your dreams, support your creative pursuits, and offer a safe space for your emotions. However, learning to balance your idealism with practicality is key to finding fulfillment in love. You thrive with a partner who respects your sensitivity while grounding you when it's needed.

Which Forms of Creativity and Expression Best Suit Your 5th House

Your creativity is limitless, flourishing in anything that allows you to tap into your imagination and emotions. Whether it's painting, writing, music, or dance, your artistic expression is often infused with a sense of spirituality and transcendence. You may also find joy in the healing arts or activities that connect you to the collective, such as meditation, yoga, or volunteering. Your 5th house Pisces energy thrives when it's channeled into something meaningful, helping you create beauty that stirs something in people and touches their hearts.

How You Love, Play, and Create

What sign do you have on the cusp of your 5th house? This part of the chart speaks to the pursuit of pleasure, joy, romance and describes where creative expression begins to take shape. What lights you up and how do you chase fun or flirt with risk? The following questions will help you explore how this energy shows up for you and how you might work with it more intentionally.

- What does the sign on the cusp of *your* 5th house say about your approach to romance? Which parts of the description speak to you? What would you add?
- Is traditional romance how your relationships typically start?
- How do you express joy and creativity in your life, and does it align with the qualities of your 5th house ruling sign?
- How do you take risks or pursue fun and pleasure in your life? Do you feel a connection to the energy of the sign on your 5th house cusp, or are there opportunities for growth?
- What hobbies, projects, or events aligned with your 5th house would you like to get involved in that could connect you with this house?

The Sign on the 7th House

Which sign do you have on the cusp of your 7th house?

When we step from the playful discovery of the 5th house into the realm of partnership and commitment in the 7th house, the energy shifts from "me" to "we." The 7th house marks the point in the chart where relationships become a mirror, showing us who we are through the connections we form. Here, partnerships aren't just about excitement or attraction; they're about creating something mutual, something lasting.

The sign on your 7th house cusp gives big clues to the kinds of partnerships you seek, the qualities you're drawn to, and the patterns you're likely to encounter in close relationships. Planets that fall in your 7th house add even more dimension, highlighting both what you naturally bring to relationships and what you're learning through them. This house isn't just about romance; it covers business partners, best friends, counselors, consulting professionals (doctors, lawyers etc.), and even the people you clash with—anyone who calls you into a deeper awareness of yourself.

Next we'll explore what the sign on your 7th house cusp says about how you relate, how you connect, and what you need for true partnership. Whether you're hoping for deeper romantic connections or just want to understand your relationship patterns better, the 7th house offers important clues.

Aries on the 7th: What You're Looking For in a Partner

With Aries on the cusp of your 7th house, you're drawn to partners who are bold, independent, and willing to take the initiative. You appreciate someone who is confident and assertive and knows what they want. A partner with a sense of adventure and fire in their personality and approach to life will keep you engaged.

What You Bring to Committed Relationships

Aries on the 7th usually brings a direct, action-oriented approach to relationships. You will fight for a partnership and aren't afraid to take charge when needed. You can be fiercely loyal but may need to work on balancing your own needs with your partner's.

Partnership Themes

With Aries on the 7th house cusp, relationships can be passionate, dynamic, and sometimes fiery. You need to feel a sense of excitement and movement in a relationship. You may attract partners who challenge you or push you out of your comfort zone.

Balancing the Libra Ascendant

For someone with a Libra Ascendant, Aries on the 7th house offers a powerful lesson in asserting yourself and embracing your own desires. While Libra can be overly accommodating or focused on keeping the peace, Aries teaches you the value of standing up for what you want and pursuing it directly. This dynamic helps balance your natural tendency to prioritize others over yourself, showing you the importance of individuality within a partnership.

Taurus on the 7th: What You're Looking For in a Partner

With Taurus on the 7th house, you're drawn to partners who offer stability, loyalty, and sensuality. You want someone dependable who can provide a sense of grounding and security. A partner who appreciates life's pleasures, such as good food, comfortable (even luxurious) surroundings, and meaningful connection, will capture your heart.

What You Bring to Committed Relationships

You bring a steady, devoted energy to partnerships. Once committed, you are deeply loyal and dependable and value consistency and reliability. However, you may need to work on potential stubbornness or a reluctance to compromise.

Partnership Themes

With Taurus on the 7th, relationships are often focused on building something stable and lasting. Shared values, physical connection, and a sense of comfort are key themes. You seek a partner who values quality over quantity and is willing to invest in a long-lasting connection.

Balancing the Scorpio Ascendant

For someone with Scorpio rising, Taurus energy on the 7th offers lessons in trust, sharing, and opening up. While Scorpio's instinct is to hold their cards close and keep things private, Taurus encourages you to share your resources, emotions, and vulnerabilities more freely. It also reminds you to find joy in the simple, sensual pleasures in life—balancing Scorpio's intensity with Taurus's steady, grounding energy.

Gemini on the 7th: What You're Looking For in a Partner

With Gemini ruling your 7th house, you're drawn to partners who are curious, communicative, and mentally stimulating. You want someone who keeps things interesting, whether through witty banter or shared experiences or by constantly introducing you to new ideas. A partner who values open dialogue and adaptability is especially attractive to you.

What You Bring to Committed Relationships

You bring an engaging, playful energy to partnership. You love to share ideas, information, and experiences, and you excel at keeping things light and fun. However, you may need to work on staying focused and following through, as your Gemini energy can make you prone to distractions or restlessness in long-term commitments.

Partnership Themes

With Gemini on the 7th house, relationships often emphasize communication, intellectual connection, and shared learning. You thrive in partnerships where both parties feel free to express themselves and explore new possibilities together. A sense of humor and a willingness to grow mentally and emotionally are key ingredients for a lasting commitment.

Balancing the Sagittarius Ascendant

For someone with a Sagittarius Ascendant, Gemini energy on the 7th house helps you balance your bold, exploratory quality with the intellectual and adaptable curiosity of Gemini. While your Sagittarius side seeks big-picture meaning and grand adventures, Gemini reminds you of the importance of staying curious, listening closely, and embracing a lighter, more flexible approach to relationships. Learning when to employ intellect and communication can be just as vital to a partnership as passion and ideals.

Cancer on the 7th: What You're Looking For in a Partner

With Cancer ruling your 7th house, you're drawn to partners who are caring, emotionally available, and connected to their feelings. You want someone who creates a sense of home and emotional safety in the relationship—a partner who isn't afraid to show their softer, more vulnerable side.

What You Bring to Committed Relationships

You bring a steady, dependable energy to your relationships. While your Capricorn Ascendant gives you a practical and goal-oriented approach to life, Cancer on the 7th house allows you to open up to emotional connection and prioritize care and comfort in partnership. You may initially approach relationships cautiously, but once committed, you're loyal and deeply invested.

Partnership Themes

With Cancer on the 7th house cusp, relationships often emphasize emotional intimacy, caregiving, and shared nurturing. You thrive in partnerships where there's a strong sense of mutual support and understanding, and you're especially drawn to partners who value family and traditions. However, you may need to avoid overmanaging or trying to "fix" emotions within the relationship.

Balancing the Capricorn Ascendant

Your Capricorn Ascendant can sometimes lead you to separate from your emotions or approach relationships from a practical, managerial perspective. You're learning that nurturing does not have to equal smothering. Cancer energy on the 7th house teaches you to embrace care and compassion, reminding you that vulnerability and emotional connection are strengths, not weaknesses. By learning to lean into your softer side, you can build partnerships that are deeply fulfilling and emotionally supportive.

Leo on the 7th: What You're Looking For in a Partner

With Leo ruling your 7th house, you're drawn to partners who are confident, charismatic, and expressive. You're looking for someone who shines brightly, is warm and affectionate, and knows how to make you feel special. A Leo-influenced partner is likely to bring a sense of fun, drama, romance, and creativity into your life, making you feel celebrated and loved. When you have Leo here, you may be looking for someone who's a "star" in some way.

What You Bring to Committed Relationships

You bring an openness to connection and a desire to create something meaningful together. Your Aquarius Ascendant may make you naturally independent and focused on the big picture, but Leo on the 7th house brings warmth and passion to your partnerships. You're learning to prioritize the individuality and emotional richness of a partner rather than getting stuck in purely intellectual connections.

Partnership Themes

With Leo on the 7th house cusp, relationships are often characterized by passion, admiration, and mutual support. You're drawn to partners who inspire confidence and encourage you to step into the spotlight. However, it's important to make sure the admiration and attention flow both ways—balance is key in relationships.

Balancing the Aquarius Ascendant

Your Aquarius Ascendant can make you focused on the collective or external achievements, sometimes pulling you away from your personal creative expression. Leo energy on the 7th house encourages you to embrace individuality and self-confidence. By learning to put yourself out there and express your own creative genius, you can find fulfillment not only in your partnerships but also in how you relate to the world. A Leo partner helps you connect with your inner fire, teaching you how to shine unapologetically and take pride in who you are.

Virgo on the 7th: What You're Looking For in a Partner

With Virgo ruling your 7th house, you're drawn to partners who are practical, grounded, smart, and reliable. You value someone who can bring order to chaos, who is attentive to detail, and who supports you with a thoughtful, down-to-earth approach. A Virgo-influenced partner often prioritizes acts of service and is someone you can depend on, especially when life feels overwhelming.

What You Bring to Committed Relationships

Your Pisces Ascendant gives you a deep sense of empathy and intuition, allowing you to "feel" your way through life and anticipate a partner's needs. This can sometimes leave you struggling to communicate your own needs clearly. Virgo energy on the 7th house helps you develop tools for clearer communication and brings a partner who values clarity and honesty in relationships. You, in turn, bring emotional depth and creativity, offering a sense of magic and wonder that complements Virgo's practicality. Together, the two of you create a blend of heart and head, ensuring that both emotional and practical needs are met.

Partnership Themes

With Virgo on the 7th house cusp, relationships are often about finding a balance between practicality and idealism, from the smallest details to the *biggest* picture. You may need to navigate moments where your partner's attention to detail or critique feels like a harsh contrast to your sensitivity. However, this dynamic can help you stay grounded while also teaching your partner to appreciate imperfection and the beauty in vulnerability.

Balancing the Pisces Ascendant

Your Pisces Ascendant thrives on emotion and intuition, sometimes preferring to idealize or romanticize relationships. Virgo energy on the

7th house brings a reality check, encouraging you to accept that imperfection is part of every relationship. While your natural empathy helps you sense what others feel, Virgo energy aids in learning to communicate more clearly and effectively. A Virgo partner teaches you how to balance your dreamy tendencies with practical action, creating a relationship built on mutual understanding, trust, and growth.

Libra on the 7th: What You're Looking For in a Partner

With Libra ruling your 7th house, you're drawn to partners who radiate charm, fairness, and social grace. You seek someone who values equality and brings a sense of grace and symmetry to your life. A Libra partner can teach you the art of compromise, showing you how to create relationships that are balanced, collaborative, and mutually fulfilling.

What You Bring to Committed Relationships

As an Aries Ascendant, you bring boldness, passion, and a sense of adventure to your relationships. You have a natural ability to take charge and add a spark to your relationships, keeping things exciting. While your assertiveness can sometimes overshadow more sensitive dynamics, it also guarantees that your relationships remain lively and vital. You thrive on passion and intensity, but learning to temper these qualities with Libra's diplomacy can create a beautifully balanced interaction.

Partnership Themes

Libra on the 7th brings themes of collaboration, equality, and mutual respect to partnerships. The focus here is on creating a relationship that feels balanced, where both partners' needs and perspectives are honored and there is a generally equal amount of give-and-take. Decision-making, compromise, and cultivating harmony are key themes that come with Libra here. This placement highlights pursuing shared goals and ensuring both individuals feel seen and valued in the relationship.

Balancing the Aries Ascendant

Your Aries Ascendant thrives on independence and taking action, usually propelling you forward without waiting for much input. Libra on the 7th house serves as a counterbalance, teaching you the value of slowing down and engaging with others on an equal footing—it's okay to collaborate. While Aries pushes you to prioritize your needs, Libra reminds you of the importance of considering your partner's needs and helps create a sense of teamwork. Together, these themes help you establish relationships that blend passion and calm, which ensures both enthusiasm and stability.

Scorpio on the 7th: What You're Looking For in a Partner

With Scorpio ruling your 7th house, you're drawn to partners who exude intensity, depth, and passion. You crave a connection that feels profound, even soul-stirring, with someone who isn't afraid to dive into the deeper, more vulnerable aspects of life and love. Trust, devotion, and emotional honesty are essential in your partnerships, and you're looking for someone who values these as much as you do.

What You Bring to Committed Relationships

As a Taurus Ascendant, you bring loyalty, stability, and a strong sense of grounding to your relationships. You're deeply committed and reliable, offering a sense of comfort and security to your partner. However, your attachment to the material world and love of the familiar can sometimes make it hard for you to welcome the emotional depth and power that a Scorpio partnership commands.

Partnership Themes

Scorpio on the 7th brings themes of emotional excavation, intimacy, and trust to relationships. This placement highlights the need to confront your fear of being vulnerable and can help you learn to navigate power struggles/dynamics in partnerships. Relationships challenge you to let go of a need for surface-level security and step into deeper emotional waters, where true connection and growth live.

Balancing the Taurus Ascendant

Your Taurus Ascendant loves the steady and tangible, whether that's a home, a routine, or the comfort of accumulating material wealth. Whatever it is, this attachment to security can sometimes create stagnation or a reluctance to let go of what feels safe. Scorpio energy on the 7th house pushes you to let go of these attachments and accept the transformative potential of your relationships. It teaches you that real value isn't just about what you own or hold on to, but also the deep emotional bonds you create with others. Together, Taurus and Scorpio energies can balance stability with depth, building partnerships that are solid *and* soul-stirring.

Sagittarius on the 7th: What You're Looking For in a Partner

With Sagittarius ruling your 7th house, you're drawn to partners who bring adventure, optimism, and an open-minded perspective on life. A sense of humor and a thirst for exploration are especially appealing. You admire those who expand your worldview and share a passion for knowledge, travel, and big ideas, so you may be drawn to people who are exotic to you. This energy keeps your relationships lively and interesting, but make sure they're grounded enough to build a sustainable connection.

What You Bring to Partnerships

Your Gemini Ascendant gives you a quick wit and a knack for communication, making you engaging and endlessly curious in partnerships. You thrive on mental stimulation and bring a fun lightheartedness to partnerships. Your ability to adapt and keep things fresh helps your relationships stay dynamic, but your tendency to spread yourself too thin can leave some relationships lacking any depth.

Partnership Themes

The Sagittarius influence brings a sense of freedom and expansion to your relationships. You seek a partnership that feels like an adventure, where experiencing and learning new things happen together. Themes of exploring, philosophy, and shared curiosity dominate. You may also find that partnerships teach you to expand your horizons, let go of rigid expectations, and embrace the unknown. Finding a balance between freedom and commitment will be the key to thriving partnerships.

Balancing the Gemini Ascendant

As a Gemini rising, your quick mind and love for chatter can sometimes leave no room for deeper bonding. Sagittarius on the 7th house cusp can teach you the value of listening—not just hearing words, but *really* understanding and considering your partner's perspective. Where your Gemini Ascendant may have you flitting from one topic to another, Sagittarius wants you to focus on the big picture. By learning to integrate your mental agility with a sense of purpose and direction, you can create partnerships that are both interesting and meaningful.

Capricorn on the 7th: What You're Looking For in a Partner

With Capricorn ruling your 7th house, you're drawn to partners who are stable, responsible, and ambitious. You value people who are goal-oriented and capable of building a secure future, both financially and emotionally. Their ability to offer structure and dependability appeals to your Cancer Ascendant's need for security and protection. A partner with a strong work ethic and a clear vision of their goals will hold your interest, but be careful not to sacrifice what you really want and need for a potential partner's social status and success.

What You Bring to Partnerships

Your Cancer Ascendant gives you a nurturing and empathetic energy that complements Capricorn's steadiness. You bring emotional connection, warmth, and a strong sense of loyalty to partnerships. While your instinct may be to protect and care for others, Capricorn energy in your relationships encourages you to balance giving with receiving. You offer a safe emotional space, while your partner provides the practical grounding and direction. Together, you can create a partnership that thrives on emotional support and shared aspirations.

Partnership Themes

Capricorn in the 7th house emphasizes relationships that feel purposeful and long-term. You're likely to seek partnerships built on mutual respect, shared goals, and a commitment to building something lasting. This placement usually brings partnerships that involve lessons about patience, perseverance, and the balance between work and love. You may find yourself drawn to partners whose accomplishments inspire you, but it's crucial to also seek emotional depth and an alignment of values to guarantee a well-rounded connection.

Balancing the Cancer Ascendant

With a Cancer Ascendant, you're deeply tuned into your emotions and the emotions of others, but it can sometimes lead to a tendency to overnurture or depend too heavily on relationships for emotional fulfillment and security. Capricorn on the 7th house encourages you to step into a more balanced dynamic, teaching you to create healthy boundaries and rely on your own sense of inner stability. Whereas Cancer is on the hunt for emotional safety, Capricorn helps you see the value of structure and practicality in partnerships. Together, these energies draw you toward relationships that combine heart and ambition and offer both emotional and material security.

Aquarius on the 7th: What You're Looking For in a Partner

With Aquarius on the cusp of your 7th house, you're drawn to partners who are open, independent, and forward-thinking. You admire people who aren't afraid to march to the beat of their own drum and are willing to challenge social norms. Intellectual stimulation and shared ideals are often more important to you than traditional romantic gestures. A partner who values individuality and shares your vision for the future will spark your interest and keep you engaged.

What You Bring to Partnerships

Your Leo Ascendant brings warmth, charisma, and a natural confidence to your relationships. You're vibrant and expressive, which can balance the cool, intellectual energy of Aquarius. While your partner may be more focused on ideas and the collective good, you bring passion, creativity, and a sense of fun to the connection. Together, you can inspire each other, blending your bold, heart-centered approach with their progressive, big-picture thinking.

Partnership Themes

Aquarius energy in the 7th house emphasizes the importance of equality and freedom in relationships. You're likely to look for partners who feel more like a friend, where mutual respect and autonomy are key. This placement can bring relationships that challenge traditional definitions of commitment, encouraging you to think beyond social norms about what partnership means to you. Themes of collaboration, shared ideals, and progressive thinking often feature in your one-on-one connections.

Balancing the Leo Ascendant

Your Leo Ascendant craves attention, admiration, and validation, but Aquarius on the 7th house cusp pushes you to focus on partnership as a meeting of equals. While Leo energy might initially seek the spotlight in a relationship, Aquarius teaches the importance of stepping back and considering the needs of the "we" over the "me." By welcoming Aquarius's values of autonomy and innovation, you'll learn how to share the stage in your relationships while still expressing your own unique light. A partner who challenges your ideas and encourages your growth will help you strike this balance beautifully.

Pisces on the 7th: What You're Looking For in a Partner

With Pisces on the cusp of your 7th house, you're drawn to partners who are empathetic, imaginative, and in tune with their emotions. You value people who can tap into the intangible and bring a sense of magic or spiritual connection to your life. Idealism plays a big role in your view of partnership, and you may look for someone who embodies your dreams or inspires you in some way. You're likely to be attracted to partners who are nurturing and understanding, even if they bring some chaos and confusion with them.

What You Bring to Partnerships

Your Virgo Ascendant gives you a practical approach to life, but in relationships, you bring a quiet sense of devotion and a willingness to help your partner thrive. You're great at offering support and keeping things grounded, balancing Pisces' desire to be untethered. Your ability to see flaws and improve things can be a gift when you use it with care in a partnership. You bring stability and a strong work ethic, guaranteeing even the most whimsical relationship goals can become a reality.

Partnership Themes

Pisces on the 7th house emphasizes a need for an emotional and even spiritual connection, compassion, and the blending—and sometimes blurring—of boundaries in relationships. This placement can bring partnerships that challenge you to open your heart fully while also teaching you the importance of maintaining clear boundaries. Themes of sacrifice and selflessness can come up, but learning when to give and when to hold back is crucial to avoid losing your sense of self. The Virgo/Pisces axis highlights the potential for healing in partnerships, where the practical and emotional come together to promote growth and mutual care. Navigating the balance between helping and enabling is one of the key lessons this placement offers.

Balancing the Virgo Ascendant

Your Virgo Ascendant thrives on order and practical solutions, but Pisces on the 7th house cusp asks you to soften your rigid edges and accept the messy, unpredictable flow of emotions in relationships. While Virgo can focus on fixing or perfecting, Pisces urges you to approach love with acceptance and trust. The healing energy of the Virgo/Pisces axis asks you to balance your tendency to solve problems with the ability to simply hold space for your partner's emotional needs. By integrating Virgo's discernment with Pisces's empathy, you'll create partnerships that are both stabilizing and spiritually enriching.

Your Partnership Blueprint

Use the following prompts to explore how your 7th house sign influences your approach to committed relationships and what that means for the kind of connection you're really looking for.

- How does the sign on your 7th house cusp shape your approach to partnerships and one-on-one relationships? Consider how this sign reflects the qualities you look for in a committed partnership as well as what you bring to the table in relationships.
- What patterns or themes do you notice in your close relationships and how do they reflect the energy of your 7th house sign? Think about whether your partnerships mirror the traits, strengths, or challenges associated with this sign.
- Which 7th house sign traits do you embody? Which traits would you like to embody? Reflect on how acknowledging these qualities might help you form fulfilling and meaningful partnerships.
- What patterns or themes do you notice in your close relationships and how do they reflect the energy of your 7th house sign? Think about whether your partnerships mirror the traits, strengths, or challenges associated with this sign.

The Sign on the 8th House

Which sign is on the cusp of your 8th house?

The 8th house is where relationships deepen—or unravel. It's not about surface connections or casual fun; this is the house where you decide if someone can be trusted with your truest self. Vulnerability lives here, along with the fear of betrayal, rejection, or loss. Letting someone into your 8th house means exposing the parts of you that are raw and real, the parts you might otherwise keep hidden.

Often called the house of death and rebirth, the 8th house symbolizes endings, transformations, and what manifests after we face our fears. It's tied to intimacy, not just physical but also emotional and energetic. While the 5th house may flirt with sex as pleasure, the 8th house views it as a profound connection, carrying themes of power, trust, and surrender.

The 8th is also the house of shared resources: money, inheritances, and everything we pool together in deep partnership. It's where we learn the complexities of merging lives, from joint bank accounts to the unspoken power dynamics that can surface. Breakups play out here too, highlighting the struggles of control and the pain of letting go.

Ultimately, the 8th house is a testing place for partnerships. It's where trust is tested and the foundations of connection are either strengthened or crumble. Relationships that survive the trials of the 8th house have the potential to reach the expansive understanding of the 9th house, but getting there requires you to confront your fears, embrace vulnerability, and find the power in mutual transformation.

Aries on the 8th: How You Approach Intimacy

With Aries on the cusp of your 8th house, you bring a bold, passionate energy to intimacy and trust. You plunge headfirst into emotional depth, craving intense, daring connections. You're drawn to people who share your courage and willingness to explore life's deeper layers. While your confidence is appealing, it's important to recognize that true connection often takes patience—something Aries energy isn't naturally wired for.

What You Seek in Deep Connection

One of the biggest challenges with Aries here is a tendency to act impulsively, especially in areas like shared resources or emotional exchanges. Power struggles can surface if you're too quick to take charge. Learning to balance action with reflection will help you avoid unnecessary conflict.

Navigating Vulnerability

Aries on the 8th craves intensity but can be sensitive to issues of control and betrayal. You're fiercely protective of your emotional boundaries, but lasting intimacy requires you to share power and build trust. Letting go of the need to always be in control is the key to unlocking deeper connections.

Taurus on the 8th: How You Approach Intimacy

With Taurus ruling your 8th house, you manage intimacy with a grounded, steady energy. You crave stability and comfort in your deeper connections and value trust and loyalty above all else. You're drawn to relationships that feel secure and dependable and thrive when there's a sense of shared emotional and material resources. However, you can be quite protective of what you consider "yours," whether that's emotional space, material possessions, or shared finances.

What You Seek in Deep Connection

Taurus energy here can sometimes resist change, making it difficult to navigate the transformative nature of the 8th house. This might show up as possessiveness or an unwillingness to let go of control, whether it's over shared resources, a partner's attention, or even past wounds. Building deeper connections means accepting the discomfort of change and learning to trust others, even when it feels risky.

Navigating Vulnerability

For you, the 8th house is a space to cultivate trust and harmony in relationships, but it also challenges your attachment to material security and control. The vulnerability of this house asks you to release your possessive tendencies and welcome the unpredictable aspects of intimacy. By finding a balance between your need for stability and the emotional risks of connecting, you can form stronger, more meaningful bonds.

Gemini on the 8th: How You Approach Intimacy

With Gemini on the cusp of your 8th house, you navigate intimate connections through curiosity and communication. You're fascinated by the emotional and intellectual layers of others, though you might avoid full emotional immersion by keeping things light or analytical. Vulnerability for you often starts with words. Talking through feelings feels safer than diving straight into them, and you may need to write things out before you share them with anyone.

What You Seek in Deep Connection

While your curiosity keeps things interesting, your tendency to overthink emotions can make it harder to fully commit to intimacy. You might avoid getting too close for fear of losing your sense of freedom or becoming trapped in someone else's emotional baggage. Finding a balance between staying mentally engaged and emotionally present is the key.

Navigating Vulnerability

In deep connections, you're drawn to partners who stimulate your mind and are willing to talk about feelings and deeper issues. You value open, honest communication and someone who's willing to explore both ideas and emotions with you. A relationship that lets you share power and resources while keeping your independence feels most fulfilling.

Cancer on the 8th: How You Approach Intimacy

With Cancer ruling your 8th house, you bring a deeply caring and protective energy to intimate relationships. You naturally create a safe emotional space, helping your partner feel seen, valued, and secure. Your capacity for care runs deep, and you offer loyalty and emotional warmth once trust is built. However, your protectiveness can sometimes veer into possessiveness if you feel your vulnerability isn't being respected.

What You Seek in Deep Connection

You crave a bond that feels safe, tender, and deeply emotional. You're looking for a partner who understands and appreciates your emotional complexity, someone who can honor your vulnerability and meet you on a soul level. Casual or surface connections won't fill your intense need for trust and intimacy.

Navigating Vulnerability

For you, emotional openness means that betrayal or rejection can cut deep, so you're cautious about letting someone into your inner world. Cancer's connection to family will add intricate layers to navigating shared resources and emotional ties, especially when you're dealing with inheritances or financial matters. You're learning how to balance your instinct to protect and nurture a partner with the need to shield yourself, making sure your emotional generosity isn't taken for granted.

Leo on the 8th: How You Approach Intimacy

With Leo ruling your 8th house, you bring warmth and passion to deep connections. Your presence in intimate relationships feels larger than life since you're naturally warm and generous with your emotions, but are you being authentic? You want your partner to feel adored and valued, and you're not afraid to go all in when the connection feels right. However, your pride may sometimes make it hard to admit when you're feeling vulnerable.

What You Seek in Deep Connection

You're drawn to partners who make you feel admired and special—someone who reflects your inner light and treats you like royalty. Deep intimacy for you requires a partner who values loyalty, respect, and mutual admiration. Superficial connections won't cut it; you're looking for a relationship that allows your inner fire to burn brightly and unapologetically.

Navigating Vulnerability

Trust and vulnerability can be a challenge for Leo energy, especially when betrayal threatens your pride. Relinquishing control—whether over shared resources or emotional matters—might feel daunting, but once trust is established, your fierce loyalty and protectiveness shine. Intimacy for you is about balancing your desire for admiration with the courage to let your guard down and reveal your softer side. This dynamic can sometimes create a flair for psychodrama, which is powerful for self-discovery but potentially overwhelming for a partner. True connection happens when you learn to share the spotlight rather than demand it, creating space for mutual growth and authenticity.

Virgo on the 8th
How You Approach Intimacy

With Virgo ruling your 8th house, you bring a practical approach to intimate relationships. You're observant and thoughtful, always looking for ways to improve the connection and provide meaningful support. Your grounded energy can help create a safe space for intimacy to flourish. You're a problem-solver, always ready to analyze emotional dynamics and find ways to keep things running smoothly.

What You Seek in Deep Connection

You crave a connection built on trust, reliability, and mutual effort. You'll want a partner who's dependable and willing to put in the work of maintaining a relationship. Emotional vulnerability can feel daunting, so you seek someone who values honesty and clarity as much as you do. Although diving deep into the depths of emotion isn't a natural place for you, if it leads to healing, you're willing to do this work. Practical expressions of love, like shared tasks or acts of service, speak deeply to your heart.

Navigating Vulnerability

Being vulnerable isn't easy for Virgo energy, especially the 8th house kind. You might overanalyze emotional situations, looking for flaws or problems that don't exist, which can create distance instead of closeness. There's also a tendency to focus on "fixing" your partner or the relationship, which can be counterproductive. True intimacy for you comes when you accept imperfection—in both yourself and others—and learn to let go of control. By focusing on the bigger picture and not the tiny details, you can open yourself up to a transformative, meaningful partnership.

Libra on the 8th:
How You Approach Intimacy

With Libra on the cusp of your 8th house, you bring diplomacy and a strong desire for harmony to your most intimate connections. You're naturally skilled at creating a sense of balance in relationships, striving to ensure both partners feel seen and valued. At its best, Libra here can help you excel at promoting an environment where emotional depth and vulnerability can thrive without losing a sense of fairness or equality.

What You Seek in Deep Connection

You're drawn to partners who bring grace, sophistication, and emotional intelligence to the relationship. While the *idea* of emotional depth appeals to you, you may struggle with the messiness that often comes with it. Instead, you might focus on finding balance, beauty, and shared ideals in your partners, trying to find the harmony instead of exploring uncomfortable truths. With Libra on the 8th house, you will need to step outside your comfort zone and embrace the imperfect and raw aspects of love and vulnerability to find true intimacy.

Navigating Vulnerability

Being vulnerable can be hard for Libra energy because it often means disrupting the composure you hold dear. You may struggle with avoiding difficult emotions or smoothing over conflicts instead of plunging into the raw truth of the situation. True intimacy requires you to lean into discomfort and allow flaws—and sometimes imbalances—into a relationship. Learning to adjust your desire for harmony with the reality of messy emotions can unlock a deeper, potentially transformative connection. Sharing power in relationships, rather than striving for control or equality at all times, is key to building trust.

Scorpio on the 8th: How You Approach Intimacy

With Scorpio on the 8th house cusp, you bring a magnetic intensity to your connections. You're unafraid to confront the raw, unfiltered truths that others might shy away from, and you have an innate understanding of and attraction to complex emotions. Your loyalty runs deep, but so does your need for trust—this placement demands honesty and authenticity in relationships.

What You Seek in Deep Connection

You're drawn to partners who can match your depth and are willing to share their inner world without hesitation. Emotional honesty is crucial, and you're looking for someone you can share a profound connection with—where secrets and vulnerabilities are shared freely. You want a relationship that allows you to go beneath the surface, exploring the hidden layers of yourself and your partner.

Navigating Vulnerability

A potential danger of this combination is secrets that become a form of currency. Vulnerability can feel both enticing and threatening with Scorpio on the 8th. Few understand better than you the kind of power that comes from holding others' secrets. The intensity of the 8th house, combined with Scorpio's energy, means you may instinctively hold back until you're certain your trust won't be betrayed. Power dynamics often play a significant role here, as you navigate how much of yourself to reveal and how much control to relinquish. Letting go of the need to shield yourself completely—and accepting that true intimacy requires risk—can help you build the deep, meaningful relationships you crave.

Sagittarius on the 8th: How You Approach Intimacy

With Sagittarius on the 8th house cusp, you bring a sense of optimism, adventure, and expansiveness to your intimate connections. You're naturally open-minded and willing to explore the deeper aspects of relationships with curiosity and enthusiasm. Your free-spirited nature can make emotional depth less intimidating for both you and your partner, as you approach even serious matters with a sense of possibility and hope.

What You Seek in Deep Connection

You seek a partner who shares your thirst for knowledge, exploration, and growth. Intimacy for you isn't just about emotional vulnerability—it's about expanding your understanding of the world through a shared journey (literal or figurative). Whether it's exploring different philosophies, diving into metaphysical discussions, or embarking on literal adventures to help you discover your psychological depths, you need a partner who's willing to grow with you. Emotional stagnation or a partner who isn't curious about life can leave you feeling detached.

Navigating Vulnerability

Sagittarius energy here can make you hesitant to stay in one emotional place for too long. Vulnerability might feel like a trap, especially if it seems to limit your freedom. You're more likely to open up when trust is established gradually and when the relationship feels like an adventure worth taking. However, you sometimes avoid emotional depth in favor of keeping things positive, which can leave your relationships feeling shallow. With Sagittarius on the 8th house, the challenge is to balance your need for independence with the willingness to engage in the messy, life-changing work of deep intimacy. Trusting that vulnerability doesn't have to come at the cost of your freedom will help you create relationships that feel both expansive and grounding.

Capricorn on the 8th: How You Approach Intimacy

With Capricorn on the 8th house cusp, you're drawn to relationships where trust and accountability are paramount. In matters of intimacy, you seek a partner who is dependable, steady, and willing to put in the effort to build something meaningful over time. Emotional or financial frivolity is a turn-off, as you value a partnership that feels structured and mutually supportive.

What You Seek in Deep Connection

Capricorn on the 8th house can make it challenging to let your guard down. You may instinctively build walls around your emotions, fearing the loss of control that comes with true vulnerability. While you might be willing to share resources or responsibilities, exposing your deeper feelings can feel like a risk you're reluctant to take. Learning to trust your partner with the softer, more sensitive parts of yourself is vital. There's a tendency here to equate intimacy with duty or obligation, which can make emotional depth feel like a task rather than a natural unfolding. Once you begin to brave the emotional work of the 8th house, you discover that vulnerability can lead to the type of enduring and transformative (or deeply impactful) relationship you're ultimately looking for.

Navigating Vulnerability

Capricorn's influence here often brings a focus on financial or material stability within partnerships. You may feel strongly about managing shared resources and ensuring they're used responsibly. This can lead to a need for control over finances or a tendency to take on the "provider" role in the relationship. You can neutralize this dynamic by allowing your partner to share in the responsibility, which can create a healthier sense of mutual investment.

Aquarius on the 8th: How You Approach Intimacy

With Aquarius on the 8th house cusp, you bring an inventive, open-minded, and forward-thinking approach to intimacy. You thrive when your relationships foster individuality and encourage discovery. Your willingness to explore unconventional relationship dynamics can inspire a partner to open their mind, but your tendency to intellectualize emotions can keep others guessing about your true feelings. In shared resources, you value fairness and equality and strive to keep things balanced and objective.

What You Seek in Deep Connection

With Aquarius here, you're drawn to partners who value their independence as much as you do. Emotional intimacy for you is less about merging completely and more about creating a bond where all parties can express their individuality. A partner who brings originality and intellectual stimulation will ignite your interest, while someone overly traditional or emotionally needy may leave you feeling boxed in. You want fairness and collaboration in your relationships, preferring to keep things transparent and balanced.

Navigating Vulnerability

Aquarius on the 8th house can make vulnerability a complicated expedition toward wholeness. While you value emotional honesty, you instinctively keep your feelings at a distance, choosing to analyze rather than fully experience them. Power dynamics in relationships can come up as you work to maintain your independence while sharing your life with someone else. True connection comes when you accept the idea that trust and openness don't threaten your autonomy—they can actually enhance it. Balancing your need for freedom with a willingness to risk emotional exposure is key to building meaningful intimacy.

Pisces on the 8th: How You Approach Intimacy

With Pisces on your 8th house cusp, you bring deep empathy and a natural sense of compassion to your intimate connections. You have a special ability to sense unspoken emotions, creating a safe space for others to open up. Your approach to intimacy is spiritual and intuitive, often blurring the lines between emotional and physical connection. This sensitivity helps you to form profound bonds, but it can also open you up to losing yourself in the process—especially if you're not careful to maintain your boundaries.

What You Seek in Deep Connection

You crave a connection that goes far beyond the physical, looking for a partner who can meet you on a soulful level. For you, intimacy isn't just about trust—it's about a merging of energies where both people feel deeply seen and understood. You're drawn to people who are compassionate, emotionally attuned, and capable of engaging in the same, almost otherworldly connection you seek. Someone who values spirituality or shares your creative interests will resonate with your 8th house needs.

Navigating Vulnerability

With Pisces here, vulnerability can be both your strength and your challenge. On one hand, you're willing to dive into emotional depths that others might avoid. On the other, your tendency to idealize partners or situations can leave you blindsided when reality doesn't match your dreams. This placement can also leave you susceptible to feeling overwhelmed or drained by others' emotional baggage. Learning to set clear boundaries and distinguish between what's yours to carry and what belongs to others is crucial for maintaining healthy, balanced relationships.

Into the Deep: Exploring Your Intimate Bonds

Take some time to reflect on how the sign on your 8th house cusp shapes your experiences with intimacy, vulnerability, and shared emotional or material resources. Use the prompts below to explore how this energy shows up in your closest bonds—and where there may be room for growth or deeper connection.

- How does the sign on your 8th house cusp shape your approach to your most intimate relationships? Consider how this sign reflects the qualities you look for in an intimate partner, as well as what you bring to the table in this area.
- What patterns or themes do you notice in the area of intimacy and shared resources and how do they reflect the energy of your 8th house sign? Think about whether these relationships mirror the traits, strengths, or challenges associated with this sign.
- Which 8th house sign traits do you embody? Which traits would you like to explore? How might working on expressing the positive expression of this house/sign combination improve intimacy in your relationships?
- What patterns or themes do you notice in your intimate relationships and how do they reflect the qualities of your 8th house sign? Think about whether your intimate relationships display the traits, strengths, or challenges associated with this sign.

5
The Relationship House Rulers Through the Zodiac
How Your Love Story Speaks Through the Signs

Now that you've explored the signs on the cusps of your relationship houses, it's time to add another layer to the story: the planetary rulers of those houses. *The planets in charge of the signs on the cusps of your relationship houses* give you even more insight into how your relationship themes come to life—where you're most likely to find love, how you connect, and what makes your partnerships tick.

In this chapter we'll break each planetary ruler down by the element of the sign it's in: fire, earth, air, or water. Each element brings its own energy and expression to your chart. Fire is bold and passionate, earth is steady and practical, air is social and communicative, and water is deep and emotional. By looking at the sign your house ruler is in, you'll see how these qualities influence the energy of that planet in your chart.

We'll also look at blending the ruler's planetary energy with the sign's elemental flavor. It's like finding the key to how each planet expresses in its sign, and reveals the feeling it brings to your relationship houses. Whether it's the bold confidence of fire, the steady reliability of earth, the curious mental energy of air, or the deep emotional pull of water, these combinations will help you understand how the way you express and attract romance, connection, and intimacy is symbolized in your chart.

Grab your chart and use the table of symbols (glyphs) on page 298 to find the signs of the ruling planets of your relationship houses:

5th house ruler is _________ (planet) in _________ (sign)

7th house ruler is _________ (planet) in _________ (sign)

8th house ruler is _________ (planet) in _________ (sign)

The Planets in Fire Signs (Aries, Leo, and Sagittarius)

Fire always brings warmth, creativity, and a spark of inspiration to whatever it touches. In astrology, fire is an element that needs connection—it can't exist on its own. This dependence gives fire a unique energy, infusing planets and houses with a sense of interdependence and vitality. Some planets flourish in fire, radiating confidence and charisma, while others might struggle to express their true gifts in an outward-expressing sign. As we look at how fire signs influence the planetary rulers of your relationship houses, you'll see how fire's passion, boldness, and need for connection may be playing out in your chart.

The Sun (Leo on the House Cusp)

The Sun feels right at home in fire signs, as it shares their vibrance, warmth, and vitality. Fire fuels the Sun's natural radiance, amplifying its ability to express enthusiasm, confidence, and creativity. When the Sun rules one of your relationship houses and is in a fire sign, expect themes of passion, excitement, and boldness to be a big part of who you attract and what you're looking for. However, the mode of each fire sign (cardinal, fixed, mutable) adds layers to the story, shifting the way this energy is expressed.

For instance, when the Sun is in Aries, the cardinal quality leads to independence, action, and spontaneity. While Leo's fixed nature thrives on commitment and consistency, Aries can bring a focus on individuality and immediate gratification. Relationships may become a journey of self-discovery before deeper connections can fully develop.

When the Sun is in Leo, it's in rulership, expressing its most authentic solar qualities. The description of Leo on the cusp of the house remains consistent, and this placement underscores loyalty, creativity, and the desire for admiration in partnerships. Leo's fixed quality supports long-term connections that shine with mutual respect and appreciation.

In Sagittarius, the Sun's fire blends with the mutable mode, adding a love for freedom, exploration, and adventure. Unlike Leo's steady commitment, Sagittarius energy may lead you to resist traditional partnerships until you find a way to balance your desire for independence with the stability needed for meaningful connections.

The Moon (Cancer on the House Cusp)

The Moon in fire signs brings emotional intensity, passion, and a need for self-expression. While the Moon is typically associated with nurturing, introspection, and emotional safety, fire signs are action-oriented and external, which can create tension between emotional needs and how we satisfy them. When the Moon rules one of your relationship houses and is in a fire sign, emotions are likely to be bold, immediate, and sometimes overwhelming. While the warmth and excitement of fire energize the Moon, these placements can struggle with patience, self-care, and emotional vulnerability and might need a few (or many) practice relationships to learn what they need.

With the Moon in Aries, the emotional, nurturing energy of Cancer becomes bolder and more independent. Whereas Cancer typically seeks emotional safety and comfort, Aries energizes this area with a desire for action and immediate gratification. The changeable nature of Cancer on the cusp is still present; it just might show up in more impulsive or unpredictable ways. The house with Cancer on the cusp still craves emotional connection, but the Moon in Aries might rush to resolve conflicts or act impulsively. Emotional care becomes direct and action-oriented, though learning patience and empathy will help balance these tendencies.

When the Moon is in Leo, the nurturing qualities of Cancer become less fluctuating. Cancer's instinct to protect and care might become more dramatic. In the house with Cancer on the cusp, emotional expression is warm, generous, and creative, but there might be a need for external validation for its efforts. The Leo Moon adds playfulness and joy to Cancer's caretaking nature, but there's a risk of neglecting deeper emotional needs in favor of being admired.

With the Moon in Sagittarius, Cancer's emotional energy takes on a philosophical tone. The house with Cancer on the cusp is still about nurturing and connection, but the Sagittarius Moon brings a need for freedom and exploration. This can lead to relationships in this area feeling freer and full of learning and growth but occasionally distant or inconsistent. Emotional care can be expressed through shared adventures or encouraging a partner's independence, but grounding the energy will be the key to developing closer bonds.

Mercury in Fire Signs (Gemini or Virgo on the House Cusp)

When Gemini or Virgo is on the cusp of one of your relationship houses, Mercury's placement adds a mental, communicative, and analytical lens to that area of your life. But when Mercury finds itself in a fire sign—Aries, Leo, or Sagittarius—its expression becomes bold, spontaneous, and passionate. Fire's warmth and intensity can greatly affect the natural adaptability and tendency to intellectualize that Gemini and Virgo display.

With Mercury in Aries, Gemini's curiosity and playfulness take on a more assertive, fast-paced energy. Whereas Gemini typically skips from idea to idea, Mercury in Aries demands action and directness. This can make communication in relationships quick, bold, and to the point, as the combination of Mercury and Aries does not indicate patience for long, involved conversations. For Virgo, Mercury in Aries brings an edge of impatience to its natural precision and organization. Rather than taking time to perfect every detail, this placement favors bold decisions and quick solutions, sometimes at the expense of long-term planning and details.

When Mercury is in Leo, Gemini's communicative style becomes dramatic and expressive. This adds flair to how you approach relationships ruled by Gemini. While Gemini is typically more detached, Leo's influence makes you more emotionally invested in conversations, and the fixed nature of Leo calms the fickleness that comes with Gemini energy. For Virgo, Mercury in Leo can introduce creativity and confidence into your typically practical way of thinking. Relationships governed by Virgo gain warmth and a sense of purpose, but there's a risk of focusing too much on "performing" in interactions instead of developing genuine connection.

Mercury in Sagittarius adds to Gemini's natural curiosity, with a love for big ideas and philosophical study. In relationships ruled by Gemini, this combination changes the focus from small talk to meaningful conversations about beliefs and ideals. But Mercury's restlessness in Sagittarius can make consistency a challenge, as you can find yourself constantly needing new mental stimulation. For Virgo, Mercury in Sagittarius broadens your typically detail-focused approach, encouraging you to think bigger about relationships and shared goals. While this adds optimism and vision, it may come at the cost of losing sight of the practical steps needed to build lasting partnerships.

Venus in Fire Signs (Taurus or Libra on the House Cusp)

When Libra or Taurus rules one of your relationship houses, Venus sets the tone with themes of love, beauty, harmony, and values. But when Venus is in a fire sign—Aries, Leo, or Sagittarius—it can ignite a bold, passionate energy that reshapes the way the Venus-ruled signs express themselves in your chart.

Venus in Aries brings an impatient and independent vibe to Libra's usual focus on maintaining harmony and diplomacy. Relationships ruled by Libra can take on a more impulsive and assertive quality, choosing excitement over balance. You may find yourself or your partners acting boldly and with a desire for immediate gratification, which can disrupt Libra's usual give-and-take dynamic. As Aries is Libra's opposite, there will be important relationship lessons to learn from the opposite house. For Taurus, Venus in Aries shifts the steady, grounded affection to a fiery need for action and adventure. Taurus's usual desire for stability is challenged by Venus in Aries's impulsive, independent streak, making relationships feel like a thrilling pursuit instead of a calm, comfortable space.

Venus in Leo adds drama and flair to Libra's refined, social energy. Relationships ruled by Libra gain a dose of romantic grandiosity, with a focus on admiration. You might attract partners who crave attention, or you might find yourself wanting to "perform" in relationships to feel validated. The fixed fire of Leo helps counter the tendencies of codependence or people-pleasing often seen in relationships influenced by Libra on the house cusp. For Taurus, Venus in Leo introduces a playful, creative energy that adds warmth and vitality to its steady approach to love. While Taurus's groundedness gives a solid foundation, Venus in Leo pushes for more creativity and a touch of extravagance, making material indulgence or generous displays of affection a likely theme.

Venus in Sagittarius infuses Libra's need to connect socially with a sense of adventure and exploration. Relationships ruled by Libra might be freer and less defined, with a focus on shared experiences and growth instead of strict commitment and social convention. This placement encourages you to find partners who share your love for discovery, travel, and personal freedom. For Taurus, Venus in Sagittarius challenges the sign's usual attachment to routine and stability. Venus here encourages you to broaden your horizons in relationships, seeking partners who stimulate curiosity and bring new experiences into your life. The Sagittarius energy can push you to reassess how much freedom you're comfortable giving—or receiving—in different types of love.

Mars in Fire Signs (Aries or Scorpio on the House Cusp)

When Aries or Scorpio rules one of your relationship houses, Mars takes charge, emphasizing action, passion, and drive. Both signs are already fueled by Mars's assertive energy, but when Mars itself lands in a fire sign—Aries, Leo, or Sagittarius—it amplifies the intensity and introduces bravery, spontaneity, and an extra spark of creativity.

Mars in Aries doubles down on Aries's raw, unfiltered quality. You're likely to look for partners who are equally dynamic and assertive, with relationships that are fiery and full of action. With Scorpio on the cusp, Aries shifts the emotional intensity and fixed energy of Scorpio into having a more immediate, direct approach. While Scorpio tends to hold back and assess, Mars in Aries pushes for quick action, perhaps skipping the deeper side of Scorpio energy in favor of straightforward tactics. The intensity is still there, but it's more external and impatient, which could make you more prone to impulsive moments in relationships.

Mars in Leo adds a charismatic edge to Aries's natural dynamism. If Aries is on the cusp of a relationship house, Mars in Leo adds a desire for creativity and an appreciation for grand gestures. You may be drawn to partners who crave admiration or enjoy the spotlight. There may be some difficult lessons around ego through the relationships you have. This placement tempers Aries's spontaneity with Leo's fixed nature, making it more focused and stable for your Aries house. For Scorpio, Mars in Leo softens Scorpio's brooding intensity, introducing warmth and a need for mutual recognition. While Scorpio is often concerned with control and power dynamics, Mars in Leo prioritizes loyalty and expression. You're still looking for passion and depth, but there's a need to be seen and/or find someone you are proud to be with.

Mars in Sagittarius brings an adventurous, freedom-loving energy to Aries's bold drive. If Aries is on the cusp of a relationship house, Mars in Sagittarius shifts the focus from immediate action to exploring the big picture. The Aries tendency is less direct and more flexible, with a strong emphasis on growth and shared experiences. For Scorpio, Mars in Sagittarius lightens the intensity and focus associated with Scorpio. Instead of being preoccupied with issues of power and control, this placement invites exploration and optimism into these houses. There's still a drive for deep connection, but it's found through shared adventures and intellectual or spiritual pursuits, making your connections feel more expansive and rooted in discovery.

Jupiter in Fire Signs (Sagittarius or Pisces on the House Cusp)

When Sagittarius or Pisces rules one of your relationship houses, Jupiter takes the lead, bringing expansion, optimism, and a need for growth. But when Jupiter itself is in a fire sign—Aries, Leo, or Sagittarius—it adds a layer of fiery energy, amplifying the bold, passionate, and adventurous qualities of those houses. Here's how fire influences these two Jupiter-ruled signs.

When Jupiter is in Aries, Sagittarius on the cusp of a relationship house takes on an even more dynamic and action-oriented vibe. Relationships become about new adventures, taking risks, and diving headfirst into shared experiences. You're likely drawn to partners who inspire you to grow through daring actions and independent pursuits. But Jupiter in Aries can also magnify impatience, making it harder to stick with relationships when challenges arise. For Pisces on the cusp, Jupiter in Aries shifts the dreamy, idealistic nature of Pisces into something more assertive and energized. While Pisces typically approaches relationships with gentleness and compassion, Jupiter in Aries introduces a more active pursuit of connection and spiritual growth. This could make your relationships feel more like a journey of discovery and less like an emotional escape. Just watch out for idealizing partners who match your adventurous spirit but lack depth.

Jupiter in Leo adds a layer of grandeur and generosity to Sagittarius on the cusp. Relationships are seen as opportunities to celebrate life, share joy, and create lasting memories. You're likely drawn to partners who are confident, creative, and passionate, valuing a sense of drama and flair in your relationships. However, this placement can sometimes lead to inflated expectations, especially if you're looking for someone who constantly admires or praises you. With Pisces on the cusp, Jupiter in Leo brightens Pisces's often understated and subtle approach to making connections. There's a stronger focus on self-expression, creativity, and sharing your feelings in bold, noticeable ways. This can help you build relationships that feel more balanced, as your partners see and appreciate the full scope of who you are. However, the Leo energy might also make you prone to seeking validation in relationships, so it's important to cultivate self-confidence outside of partnerships.

Jupiter in Sagittarius stays true to the sign's adventurous, optimistic energy to its fullest expression. You're drawn to people who expand your worldview, whether it's through travel, philosophy, or shared aspirations. While this energy can be incredibly inspiring, the restlessness or unwillingness to settle down when a relationship feels too limiting might feel justified, leaving you uncompromising. With Pisces on the house cusp and Jupiter in Sagittarius, the idealistic nature of Pisces becomes more dynamic and outwardly focused. Jupiter in this sign brings optimism and a desire to have experiences. The need for merging is dulled by a Sagittarian craving for freedom and individuality within relationships. This combination shifts the focus from emotional merging and martyrdom to shared adventures and personal growth. While the desire for a soul connection of Pisces remains, it's more likely to be found in an open and adventurous approach or partner.

Saturn in Fire Signs (Capricorn or Aquarius on the House Cusp)

When Capricorn or Aquarius rules one of your relationship houses, Saturn is the planet in charge, bringing structure, discipline, and a need for responsibility and stability from your connections. But when Saturn itself is in a fire sign—Aries, Leo, or Sagittarius—it adds a fiery edge to Saturn's usual pragmatic and reserved nature.

When Saturn is in Aries, Capricorn on the cusp of a relationship house takes on a more assertive and impatient approach. While Capricorn typically prefers careful planning and steady progress, Saturn in Aries (its sign of detriment) adds a sense of impatience and maybe frustration to this house. Relationships can feel like a challenge you need to conquer and may also bring a tendency to push too hard that can clash with Capricorn's preferred methodical pace. For Aquarius on the cusp, Saturn in Aries makes your typically intellectual approach to relationships more aggressive. You may be drawn to people who challenge you to take risks. Just be mindful of a preoccupation with independence or impulsivity.

Saturn in Leo might be drawn to dramatic and confident energy with Capricorn on the cusp. You might be interested in partners who share your ambitions but are also able to bring creativity and open expression to a relationship. Saturn in Leo can highlight your insecurities, leading to a need for external validation. Finding a balance between self-assurance and collaboration can help you build stronger partnerships. For Aquarius on the cusp, Saturn in Leo shifts your focus from overintellectualizing to creativity and self-expression within a partnership. You're likely drawn to people who celebrate your unique qualities and inspire you to shine. However, this combination can also create power struggles if one partner's need for attention overshadows the other's contributions. Learning to share the spotlight and value each other's individual gifts is key to creating a fulfilling connection.

When Saturn is in Sagittarius, Capricorn on the cusp of a relationship house takes on a more adventurous and freedom-loving energy. While

Capricorn usually needs stability and structure, Saturn in Sagittarius encourages you to explore different ways to be in relationship and embrace a broader perspective in connecting. You may be drawn to partners who share your thirst for knowledge and adventure, but the challenge lies in balancing Capricorn's grounded nature with Sagittarius's restless spirit. For Aquarius on the cusp, Saturn in Sagittarius injects a need for philosophy and big-picture thinking into your desire for an intellectual connection. This placement encourages you to seek people who inspire you to grow your worldview. Saturn in Sagittarius demands a balance between freedom and commitment. Navigating this interaction will help you build partnerships that are both inspiring and enduring.

The Planets in Earth Signs (Taurus, Virgo, and Capricorn)

Earth provides a steady groundedness to everything it touches. It's the element that keeps us practical, focused, and rooted in reality. Earth energy is all about building something real and tangible, but it can also slow things down or lead us to want to play it safe. Some planets thrive in earth signs, finding focus and stability, while others can feel a little too tied down by the need for structure. As we dive into how the earth element influences the signs on the cusps of your relationship houses, you'll see how this down-to-earth, patient energy shapes how you connect and commit, as well as what you're looking for in your relationships and what you bring to them.

The Sun in Earth Signs

When you have Leo on the cusp of a relationship house and the Sun is in an earth sign, it takes on a grounded, practical, and reliable tone. Earth signs add stability and focus to the Sun's expressiveness and creativity, building a dynamic that's less about bold theatrics and more about tangible results. When the Sun rules a relationship house and is in earth, you're likely looking for relationships that feel steady, supportive, and built to last. Each earth sign (Taurus, Virgo, Capricorn) shapes this energy in its own special way, influencing how you shine and who you are in the particular house's kind of love.

With the Sun in Taurus, Leo's radiant energy is infused with a need for comfort, beauty, and consistency. While Leo craves admiration and dramatic expression, Taurus grounds this energy, bringing more of a focus on loyalty and permanence. With the Sun here, there's a strong appreciation for creature comforts in life, and you may seek partners who share your values around stability, sensuality, and building something meaningful together. However, the fixed nature is a part of both Leo and Taurus, so flexibility will likely be a relationship lesson.

When the Sun is in Virgo, Leo's boldness is dampened by practicality and attention to detail. Acts of service come to be important, where taking care and thoughtfulness become *the* expressions of love. Instead of grand romantic gestures, you're more likely to show love through supportive actions and shared routines. Virgo's mutable energy introduces a need to improve and grow within relationships, balancing Leo's natural flair with a focus on meaningful connection. Just be conscious of overcriticism or striving for or expecting perfection. Relationships thrive when you embrace both your and your partner's special imperfections.

With the Sun in Capricorn, Leo's warmth and creativity are channeled into ambition and long-term goals. This placement adds a focus on building partnerships that support shared aspirations, with a deep appreciation for loyalty and mutual respect. Capricorn's cardinal energy drives you to take the lead in relationships, setting clear expectations and working toward a stable future together. While Leo loves the spotlight, Capricorn's influence brings a quiet confidence and an emphasis on achievements and shared accomplishments. Just remember to balance work with play—relationships need moments of joy and spontaneity too!

The Moon in Earth Signs

When Cancer is on the cusp of a relationship house and the Moon is in an earth sign, it brings a steadiness, practicality, and nurturing to your emotional world. Earth signs help ground the Moon's natural sensitivity, creating a balance between deep, changeable feelings and tangible actions. If the Moon rules one of your relationship houses and is in an earth sign, you may find yourself looking for relationships that provide security, stability, and a sense of grounded connection. Each earth sign shapes the Moon's expression differently, influencing how you nurture and connect with others.

The Moon is exalted in Taurus, meaning it expresses its nurturing qualities easily here. Cancer's emotional depth and Taurus's steady reliability combine to create a profound need for comfort and security in relationships. You may seek partners who make you feel safe and grounded, sharing your love for cozy routines, physical affection, and creating a beautiful home environment. With Taurus's fixed nature, your emotional connections run deep and are hard to shake, but it's essential to guard against possessiveness or resistance to change.

When the Moon is in Virgo, Cancer's emotional intuition is complemented by Virgo's analytical and service-oriented energy. You likely express love through acts of care, like helping your partner organize their life or offering practical solutions to problems. This placement often seeks relationships that feel purposeful and supportive, where mutual growth is a shared goal. Virgo brings flexibility, but its mutable nature can lead to overthinking or striving for perfection. Learning to embrace emotional vulnerability and let go of a tendency to focus on emotional micro-details will help to make and keep connections alive.

The Moon in Capricorn is in detriment, and its emotional qualities can feel restricted by Capricorn's practical approach to emotions. However, this combination creates a strong sense of responsibility and commitment in relationships. You may seek partners who share your focus on long-term goals and value loyalty and structure. While Cancer thrives on emotional closeness, Capricorn's cardinal energy channels those feelings into building a strong foundation. It's important to balance emotional vulnerability with your natural tendency to manage anything that has the potential to get messy.

Mercury in Earth Signs

When Gemini or Virgo rules one of your relationship houses, Mercury brings a focus on communication, thought processes, and adaptability to that area of your life. But when Mercury is in an earth sign—Taurus, Virgo, or Capricorn—its expression becomes more grounded, steady, and practical. Here's how earth influences the analytical and communicative tendencies of Mercury.

For Gemini on the cusp, Mercury in Taurus slows Gemini's usual quicksilver energy, adding patience and a focus on practical communication. This placement encourages meaningful conversations rooted in shared values and physical presence, making relationships feel more stable and secure. While Gemini usually loves variety, Mercury in Taurus brings an appreciation for consistency and loyalty in partnerships.

For Virgo on the cusp, Mercury in Taurus amplifies the earthy, detail-oriented nature of Virgo's energy. You may approach relationships with a strong sense of purpose, valuing clear boundaries and tangible goals. Communication becomes more deliberate, with an emphasis on resolving issues practically rather than getting bogged down by emotional analysis.

When Mercury is in Virgo, it's in rulership, expressing its sharpest analytical qualities. For Gemini on the cusp, this placement adds precision and focus to your natural curiosity, helping you engage in meaningful, thoughtful conversations that have real impact. Relationships feel like an opportunity to learn and grow, with a focus on improving communication and understanding.

For Virgo on the cusp, Mercury in its home sign doubles down on its organizational powers. You may approach relationships with an eye for improvement, wanting to build something practical and beneficial for both parties. But sometimes this placement can fall into overthinking or nitpicking, so it's crucial to balance practicality with emotional warmth.

For Gemini on the cusp, Mercury in Capricorn tempers Gemini's free-spirited curiosity with a more goal-oriented mindset. Communication becomes deliberate and strategic, focusing on long-term plans rather than fleeting ideas. You might be drawn to partners who bring structure and ambition to your life. While this adds depth and reliability to relationships, it may also make casual connections feel too trivial.

For Virgo on the cusp, Mercury in Capricorn adds a layer of discipline and determination to your naturally precise nature. Relationships ruled by Virgo gain a sense of purpose and direction, with communication prioritizing shared goals and mutual respect. However, there's a risk of becoming overly rigid or formal, so allowing space to be spontaneous is important to keep connections thriving.

Venus in Earth Signs

When Libra or Taurus rules one of your relationship houses, Venus takes the stage, bringing themes of love, beauty, and diplomacy into focus. When Venus finds itself in an earth sign—Taurus, Virgo, or Capricorn—it expresses these qualities with grounded, practical energy. Let's look at how the steady, reliable nature of earth influences these Venus-ruled houses.

For Libra on the cusp, Venus in Taurus emphasizes the steady, sensual qualities of Venus's rulership, grounding Libra's sociable charm in the physical world. Relationships feel secure and comforting, with a focus on shared pleasures like physical affection or indulging in good food. This placement encourages patience in building trust and creating long-lasting connections, but it may also bring a tendency toward possessiveness or stagnation, which can feel restrictive for Libra's forward-moving energy.

If you have Taurus on the cusp, Venus in Taurus amplifies Taurus's natural love of comfort and security. You likely approach relationships with a steady, deliberate energy, valuing loyalty and shared values above all. This placement reinforces your preference for tangible expressions of love and physical comfort. However, it's important to avoid getting stuck in routines or becoming overly reliant on material stability in partnerships.

With Libra on the cusp, Venus in Virgo brings a practical and thoughtful approach to relationships, tempering Libra's charm with Virgo's focus on service and mutual progress. You may be drawn to partners who appreciate meaningful gestures and are committed to growth. While Venus in Virgo adds a nurturing energy to relationships, it also introduces a tendency toward self-criticism or being overly critical of your partner. It's important to balance this analytical nature with emotional warmth, creating a connection that feels sincere and supportive.

For Taurus on the cusp, Venus in Virgo enhances your natural attention to detail and preference for steady partnerships. Relationships feel purposeful, with a focus on shared values and mutual improvement. This placement encourages finding joy in small, everyday moments and approaching love with care and thoughtfulness. However, it's important to avoid nitpicking or focusing on flaws, as this can undermine the stability and comfort you crave in partnerships.

With Libra on the cusp, Venus in Capricorn brings ambition and long-term planning to relationships, grounding Libra's idealism with a focus on responsibility and tradition. You may be drawn to partners who exude maturity, stability, or status, valuing tangible demonstrations of commitment. While this placement can create enduring, meaningful partnerships, it's important to ensure that duty doesn't overshadow affection, allowing space for romance and spontaneity.

If you have Taurus on the cusp, Venus in Capricorn adds structure and determination to your already steady approach to relationships. You're likely to value partners who share your long-term goals and practical mindset, creating a partnership rooted in shared ambition and mutual respect. However, the pragmatic nature of Capricorn may occasionally feel at odds with Taurus's sensuality, so it's essential to keep the emotional and romantic connection alive while building something enduring and meaningful.

Mars in Earth Signs

When Aries or Scorpio rules one of your relationship houses, Mars is the planetary ruler, bringing themes of passion, drive, and ambition to that area of your life. When Mars finds itself in an earth sign—Taurus, Virgo, or Capricorn—it channels its fiery energy into grounded, practical action. Let's look at how earth influences these Mars-ruled houses, highlighting both the strengths and the challenges of these combinations.

Mars in Taurus combines Aries's boldness and Scorpio's intensity with Taurus's steadiness and persistence. This placement slows down the impulsive energy of Mars, creating a more deliberate and methodical approach to relationships. You're determined to achieve what you want in love and intimacy, and once you set your sights on someone, you're unlikely to give up. For houses with Scorpio on the cusp, Mars in Taurus adds a layer of sensuality and reliability, ensuring that deep connections are not only emotional but also practical and secure.

Mars in Taurus can sometimes struggle with taking action because it never wants to start something it can't finish. For houses with Aries on the cusp, this placement dampens the spontaneity and excitement that Aries craves and can lead to frustration or inaction. In houses with Scorpio on the cusp, while your persistence is a gift, it can turn into possessiveness, especially when it comes to shared resources or intimacy.

Mars in Virgo brings precision and a sense of purpose to a house with Aries or Scorpio on the cusp. In relationships, you're driven by a desire to improve and perfect the connection, ensuring everything runs smoothly. This placement excels at problem-solving, making you a reliable partner who works tirelessly to meet shared goals. For houses with Aries on the cusp, Virgo's practicality tempers impulsiveness, while houses with Scorpio on the cusp benefit from Virgo's analytical approach to deeply held emotions.

While Mars in Virgo's attention to detail is an asset, it can also become overly critical or perfectionistic, especially in relationships. For houses with Aries on the cusp, this placement leads to overthinking and hesitation, which can feel at odds with Aries's instinct for bold, immediate action. In houses with Scorpio on the cusp, the tendency to focus on flaws or "fix" emotional dynamics is likely to hinder vulnerability and intimacy.

Mars in Capricorn is exalted, meaning it expresses its energy powerfully and effectively. For houses with Aries or Scorpio on the cusp, this placement adds ambition, discipline, and a focus on long-term goals. In relationships, you approach love and intimacy with a strong sense of responsibility, ensuring your partnerships are built to last. Capricorn's controlled energy brings stability to the passionate, sometimes volatile nature of Aries and Scorpio.

While Mars in Capricorn is highly effective, its focus on achievement and control can overshadow emotional expression in relationships. For houses with Aries on the cusp, this placement may temper spontaneity and excitement, leading to a more calculated approach to romance. In houses with Scorpio on the cusp, the drive for control and power might create challenges in sharing vulnerability or relinquishing dominance within the relationship. With either sign, it's very important not to turn relationships into projects or conquests.

Jupiter in Earth Signs

When Sagittarius or Pisces rules one of your relationship houses, Jupiter is the planetary ruler, bringing themes of expansion, optimism, and growth to what you want from that area of your life. In earth signs—Taurus, Virgo, or Capricorn—Jupiter's expansive energy is tempered by a practical, stable, and focused feeling. Here's how earth influences Sagittarius's adventurous nature and Pisces's empathic approach in these houses.

With Jupiter in Taurus, Sagittarius's natural curiosity and love for exploration take a more practical and steady approach. Relationships in these houses may center around shared values and building lasting security together. You're likely drawn to partners who appreciate the beauty of life's simple pleasures, and your optimism is rooted in creating physical things, like a cozy home or financial stability. While Sagittarius usually craves freedom, Jupiter in Taurus adds a desire for predictability and consistency.

Jupiter in Taurus brings a practical, sensual dimension to Pisces's deep, intuitive nature. In relationships, you want to focus on creating a grounded, supportive connection that feels emotionally secure. While Pisces can sometimes get lost in idealism, Taurus's influence helps you stay grounded, channeling your emotional needs into building a stable and nurturing, more physical bond. While Taurus's material nature helps mitigate the Pisces tendency to sacrifice too much for relationships, be mindful of becoming overly attached to comfort or routine, which can dull the magical quality that Pisces brings to intimacy.

Jupiter in Virgo channels Sagittarius's expansive energy into practical goals and detailed plans. Relationships in these houses might focus on shared projects or personal growth, with an emphasis on improving and refining your connection over time. You're likely drawn to partners who inspire you to grow through discipline and hard work. However, Virgo's critical nature might clash with Sagittarius's more free-spirited vibe, so finding a balance between adventure and practicality is the key.

With Jupiter in Virgo, Pisces's idealistic and intuitive approach to relationships becomes more focused on service and devotion. You may find yourself drawn to partners who can handle the details while still being focused on the big picture. While Virgo's influence helps bring structure to Pisces's sometimes chaotic inner world, it might also bring up insecurities or induce overthinking. Learning to trust your intuition without second-guessing can help you create connections that feel both stable and spiritually fulfilling.

Jupiter in Capricorn grounds Sagittarius's adventurous spirit, with a focus on achievements and ambition. Relationships in these houses are likely built on shared goals, mutual respect, and a commitment to building something together. You may be drawn to partners who share your drive for achievement or inspire you to grow through hard work and discipline. However, Capricorn's serious nature will tone down Sagittarius's playfulness, so remember to allow time for adventure.

For houses with Pisces on the cusp, Jupiter in Capricorn shifts the focus from emotional and spiritual connection to building a stable and likely traditional relationship. While Pisces often seeks emotional merging, Capricorn's influence helps you establish healthy boundaries and ensure that relationships are rooted firmly in reality. This placement encourages you to turn your ideals into concrete plans, creating a connection that balances emotional vulnerability with practical strength.

Saturn in Earth Signs

When Capricorn or Aquarius rules one of your relationship houses, Saturn is charge, bringing a need for structure and discipline and lessons about responsibility to that area of your life. In earth signs—Taurus, Virgo, and Capricorn—Saturn's energy is especially strong, emphasizing practicality, stability, and a focus on tangible outcomes. Here is how earth signs influence Saturn's expression in these houses.

Saturn in Taurus reinforces Capricorn's emphasis on building a solid foundation in relationships. The focus here is on finding stability, with a strong preference for practical, reliable partnerships. This placement encourages you to invest time and energy into creating a life of comfort and security with your partner, but it may also bring challenges around material attachment or possessiveness (or a fear of them). While Capricorn already values perseverance, Taurus ensures that relationships develop slowly and deliberately, avoiding impulsive decisions.

With Saturn in Taurus, Aquarius's need for an intellectual and forward-thinking approach to relationships becomes a grounding influence. You may find yourself drawn to partners who share your desire for meaningful progress but also value the material things in life. Saturn in Taurus can help bring grounding to Aquarius's detached, intellectual energy by encouraging you to build emotional and material security in your relationships. However, be careful not to become too fixated on material goals, which could stifle the innovative spirit of Aquarius.

Saturn in Virgo is aligned with Capricorn's natural attraction to discipline and hard work. This placement adds a detail-oriented and analytical approach to relationships, encouraging you to carefully evaluate your partnerships and set high standards for commitment. While Capricorn focuses on long-term goals, Virgo ensures that every step is planned and executed with precision. Avoid being overly critical, as this could place unnecessary strain on relationships.

With Saturn in Virgo, Aquarius's broad, visionary outlook is tempered by a focus on practicality and problem-solving. You may seek partners who share your passion for improvement and growth but are also grounded and realistic. Saturn in Virgo helps balance Aquarius's tendency to overanalyze by channeling that mental energy into productive relationship-building activities. However, the combined analytical nature of Aquarius and Virgo might make it harder to relax and simply enjoy your connections, so cultivating trust and acceptance is important. Aquarius and Virgo are both big thinkers, so you may need to bring your relationships into the real world and not just live them out in your mind.

Saturn in Capricorn is in its rulership, making this placement a powerhouse of stability and ambition. Relationships in these houses are focused on working together, mutual respect, and long-term commitment. Saturn in Capricorn amplifies the natural strengths of a house with Capricorn on the cusp, ensuring that your partnerships are built to last. However, this placement may also bring challenges around emotional vulnerability or an overemphasis on tradition and status, so it's important to balance work with emotional connection, since Saturn in Capricorn can turn almost anything Capricorn into something that feels like work.

For a house with Aquarius on the cusp, Saturn in Capricorn brings structure and discipline to Aquarius's intellectual and forward-thinking energy. You may be drawn to partners who share your vision for the future but also have the practicality and determination to turn those dreams into reality. Saturn in Capricorn encourages you to approach relationships with patience and a sense of responsibility, but it's important to avoid becoming too rigid or focused on management. Leave some room for movement and emotional connection to let love thrive.

The Planets in Air Signs

Air brings a light and curious energy to whatever it touches. It's the element that thrives on communication, ideas, and friendships. Air energy is all about staying open and connected, keeping ideas in motion, and seeking understanding. Some planets love the freedom that air provides, while others might struggle to focus or feel grounded. When the ruler of your relationship houses lands in an air sign, expect a strong emphasis on intellectual connection, social interaction, and the need to keep things fresh and interesting. Let's explore how breezy, mental energy shapes the way you approach love, partnerships, and deeper connections and how it affects what you're looking for.

The Sun in Air Signs (Gemini, Libra, or Aquarius on the House Cusp)

When Leo is on the cusp of one of your relationship houses, the Sun brings its bold, radiant energy to the forefront of what you're looking for and adds themes of creativity, self-expression, and passion to your connections. But when the Sun itself is in an air sign—Gemini, Libra, or Aquarius—the dynamic shifts, blending Leo's warmth with air's social, intellectual, and communicative qualities. Here is how each air sign adds its unique flair to the Sun's expression.

Gemini's curious, talkative nature lightens Leo's more dramatic and fixed energy. With the Sun in Gemini, you're drawn to partners who stimulate your mind and keep the conversation flowing. Relationships ruled by Leo take on a playful, spontaneous quality, as you seek variety and adventure in your connections. However, the Gemini influence may make it harder to commit fully, as your curiosity keeps you moving from one interest to another. Balancing Leo's need for admiration with Gemini's curious nature and love of exploration is key.

Libra's charm and focus on harmony soften Leo's intensity, creating a dynamic that values partnership and diplomacy in relationships. With the Sun in Libra, relationships ruled by Leo become a space for mutual admiration and shared creativity. You're likely to attract partners who value aesthetics and romance, and your approach to connection is more cooperative than commanding. However, the Libra influence may make you overly reliant on external validation, so it's important to ensure your confidence comes from within.

Aquarius's innovative and independent energy challenges Leo's need for expression, bringing a unique push-pull dynamic to what you're looking for in relationships. With the Sun in Aquarius, the house with Leo on the cusp becomes a space where individuality and connection must coexist. You're drawn to unconventional relationships or partners who inspire you to think outside the box. While Leo thrives on recognition, Aquarius shifts the focus toward shared ideals and community and encourages you to see love as a partnership of equals. This combination can be both inspiring and challenging, as balancing independence with the desire for admiration requires careful navigation.

The Moon in Air Signs

When Cancer is on the cusp of one of your relationship houses, the Moon becomes the guiding force, bringing emotional depth, nurturing energy, and a focus on security to your connections. But when the Moon is in an air sign—Gemini, Libra, or Aquarius—it shifts how this emotional, intuitive energy expresses itself, adding intellect, communication, and objectivity to the mix. Let's explore how the Moon in air signs influences the houses with Cancer on the cusp in your chart.

With the Moon in Gemini, Cancer's emotional and protective nature takes on a lighter, more curious tone. While Cancer traditionally craves deep emotional bonding, Gemini's influence adds a need for mental stimulation and variety in relationships. You're drawn to partners who can engage in meaningful conversations, and you bring a playful, adaptable energy to your connections. However, this placement can make you prone to overthinking your emotions rather than fully feeling them, and you may need to work on balancing logic with vulnerability.

Libra's harmonious and relationship-oriented energy complements Cancer's nurturing side, making you deeply invested in creating balance and mutual care in your partnerships. Relationships ruled by Cancer with the Moon in Libra are marked by a strong desire for emotional reciprocity and fairness. You bring charm, warmth, and a natural ability to mediate conflicts, but you may struggle with confronting deeper emotional issues if they disrupt the peace. Learning to embrace the messier side of connection can help you create more authentic bonds.

Aquarius's independent and forward-thinking energy brings a unique twist to Cancer's traditional focus on home and emotional security. With the Moon in Aquarius, you're drawn to relationships that allow for individuality and intellectual growth. While Cancer seeks closeness and comfort, Aquarius adds a need for freedom and space, which can create a push-pull dynamic in partnerships. You bring an open-minded, innovative approach to relationships, but you may need to work on letting your guard down and connecting on a deeper emotional level. Balancing Cancer's need for intimacy with Aquarius's detachment can lead to meaningful connections that honor both your emotional and your intellectual needs.

Mercury in Air Signs

When Gemini or Virgo rules one of your relationship houses, Mercury takes center stage, bringing a mental, communicative, and curious energy to how you connect. With Mercury in an air sign—Gemini, Libra, or Aquarius—the already cerebral nature of these houses becomes even more dynamic, emphasizing intellectual stimulation, adaptability, and open dialogue. Let's dive into how Mercury in air signs influences the energy of Gemini and Virgo in your chart.

With Mercury in its home sign, Gemini's natural curiosity and versatility shine even brighter. Relationships ruled by Gemini gain a lively, quick-witted, and engaging tone, making communication a cornerstone of connection. You bring an insatiable appetite for conversation and ideas, and you're drawn to partners who can keep up with your mental energy.

However, this placement can make it challenging to stay grounded, as you might flit from one interest to the next. In houses with Virgo on the cusp, Mercury in Gemini lightens Virgo's meticulous focus, encouraging more spontaneity and creativity in relationships. Just be mindful of overthinking or spreading yourself too thin.

Libra's diplomatic and relationship-oriented energy adds a graceful, balanced touch to a house with Gemini or Virgo on the cusp. In Gemini houses, Mercury in Libra encourages meaningful conversations that foster harmony and understanding. You're likely to approach relationships with charm and tact, striving for fairness and mutual respect. In Virgo houses, Mercury in Libra softens Virgo's critical edge, replacing it with a desire for connection and compromise. However, you may struggle with decision-making or a tendency to avoid conflict, so finding your voice in relationships is key.

Aquarius's innovative and forward-thinking energy brings a unique twist to houses with Mercury on the cusp. In Gemini houses, Mercury in Aquarius emphasizes intellectual growth and unconventional ideas, drawing you toward partners who inspire you to think outside the box. You're likely to connect through shared visions and deep, thought-provoking discussions. In Virgo houses, Mercury in Aquarius broadens Virgo's practical focus, encouraging you to explore new perspectives and push boundaries in your relationships. While this placement adds excitement and originality, it can sometimes lead to emotional detachment or difficulty connecting on a deeper level. Balancing your need for intellectual stimulation with emotional presence will help create more meaningful connections.

Venus in Air Signs

When Taurus or Libra rules one of your relationship houses, Venus takes the lead, emphasizing themes of beauty, harmony, and connection. With Venus in an air sign—Gemini, Libra, or Aquarius—the Venusian energy becomes more social, intellectual, and adaptable, influencing what you seek and bring to your partnerships. Here's how Venus in air signs shapes your houses with Taurus or Libra on the cusp.

With Venus in Gemini, relationships ruled by Taurus gain a lively and curious edge. While Taurus typically prefers stability and predictability,

Venus in Gemini introduces a love for variety and intellectual connection. You bring lightheartedness and playfulness to your relationships, and you're drawn to partners who stimulate your mind as much as your heart. For Libra houses, Venus in Gemini enhances your natural charm and social grace, making you a magnet for witty and engaging conversations. However, this placement can make it hard to settle down, as you may crave constant excitement or find it difficult to commit deeply.

When Venus is in its rulership in Libra, the energy of both Taurus and the house with Libra on the cusp is elevated to its fullest Venusian expression. In Taurus houses, Venus in Libra brings a sense of refinement and balance, encouraging you to create relationships rooted in mutual respect and shared values. You're likely to approach love with tact and diplomacy, avoiding conflict whenever possible. In Libra houses, Venus in Libra amplifies your natural ease in social settings and ability to create harmony in partnerships. While this placement enhances beauty and connection, it's important to avoid prioritizing appearances over deeper emotional truths.

Venus in Aquarius adds a sense of individuality and innovation to a house with Taurus or Libra on the cusp. In Taurus houses, Venus in Aquarius challenges your usual desire for stability, encouraging you to embrace unconventional relationships and explore connections that inspire personal growth. You're drawn to partners who value freedom and intellectual engagement, and you bring a fresh perspective to love and partnership. For Libra houses, Venus in Aquarius emphasizes intellectual compatibility and shared ideals, fostering relationships based on mutual respect for independence. However, this placement may make it harder to navigate emotional intimacy, as you may prioritize mental connection over vulnerability. Balancing your need for freedom with your desire for meaningful relationships will help you thrive.

Mars in Air Signs

When Aries or Scorpio is on the cusp of one of your relationship houses, Mars takes the lead, bringing action, drive, and passion into focus. With Mars in an air sign—Gemini, Libra, or Aquarius—the bold, intense energy of this planet becomes more cerebral, social, and adaptable. Here's how

Mars in air signs shapes the dynamic of houses with Aries or Scorpio on the cusp.

With Mars in Gemini, houses with Aries on the cusp gain a quick-witted and versatile edge. While Aries naturally thrives on directness and action, Mars in Gemini adds an intellectual spin, making communication and mental stimulation central to your relationships. You bring energy and enthusiasm, but your attention span can waver, as you may jump from one idea or connection to another. For Scorpio houses, Mars in Gemini introduces a lighter, more playful energy to what is typically a deep and intense space. While this placement can ease the emotional weight of Scorpio, it may also bring inconsistency or a tendency to intellectualize emotions rather than feeling them fully.

Mars in Libra softens Aries's bold independence, channeling that energy into connection, cooperation, and shared decision-making. In Aries houses, Mars in Libra makes you more inclined to seek balance and fairness in relationships, though this can sometimes lead to indecision or a tendency to avoid conflict. You're motivated by harmony and bring charm and diplomacy to your connections, though you might struggle to assert yourself when needed. For Scorpio houses, Mars in Libra adds a sense of grace to the intensity of this house. While this placement can help you navigate shared resources and deep emotional bonds with fairness, there's a risk of being passive-aggressive if you avoid addressing deeper issues directly.

Mars in Aquarius brings a unique and innovative energy to houses with Aries on the cusp. Whereas Aries typically values direct action, Mars in Aquarius encourages a more thoughtful, unconventional approach. You're motivated by ideals and driven to connect with partners who share your vision for the future. While this placement brings originality and independence to relationships, it can also make you resistant to traditional commitments. In Scorpio houses, Mars in Aquarius shakes up the emotional depth and intensity with a more detached, analytical energy. This placement can make you crave intimacy on your own terms, emphasizing intellectual and emotional freedom. However, the challenge lies in balancing your need for independence with the vulnerability required for true connection.

Jupiter in Air Signs

When Sagittarius or Pisces is on the cusp of one of your relationship houses, Jupiter takes the lead, bringing expansion, optimism, and growth to your connections. With Jupiter in an air sign—Gemini, Libra, or Aquarius—the expansive energy of Jupiter blends with the intellectual, communicative, and social qualities of air. Here's how Jupiter in air signs influences the themes of these houses.

With Jupiter in Gemini, houses with Sagittarius on the cusp take on an extra dose of curiosity and versatility. Relationships become an exciting exchange of ideas and knowledge, and you're drawn to partners who challenge your intellect and broaden your perspective. However, Jupiter's natural love for expansion paired with Gemini's tendency to scatter energy can lead to restlessness or inconsistency in commitments. In Pisces houses, Jupiter in Gemini shifts the dreamy, emotional energy of Pisces into a more cerebral and conversational space. While this can bring lightness and adaptability to your connections, it's important to balance intellectual stimulation with emotional depth to avoid feeling disconnected.

Jupiter in Libra enhances the relationship-focused energy of Sagittarius houses, emphasizing harmony, balance, and mutual growth. You're drawn to partners who reflect your values and help you create a sense of shared purpose. With this placement, you bring charm and fairness to your connections, though there's a risk of overcompromising to keep the peace. In Pisces houses, Jupiter in Libra adds grace and diplomacy to the emotional depth of Pisces energy. This combination fosters spiritual and romantic connections that feel harmonious and balanced. However, you may need to watch for a tendency to idealize relationships or avoid confronting deeper emotional issues.

Jupiter in Aquarius brings an innovative, forward-thinking energy to Sagittarius houses, encouraging you to seek partners who align with your ideals and share your vision for the future. Relationships are seen as opportunities for growth and collaboration, with a strong emphasis on individuality and freedom. However, this placement can make traditional commitment feel restrictive, as you value partnerships that allow for independence. In Pisces houses, Jupiter in Aquarius introduces a sense of innovation and intellectual exploration to Pisces's natural emotional depth. This combination supports unique, unconventional connections that feel both inspiring and spiritually fulfilling. Just be mindful of staying grounded, as the airy nature of Aquarius might make it harder to fully engage with the emotional and intuitive side of relationships.

Saturn in Air Signs

When Capricorn or Aquarius rules one of your relationship houses, Saturn sets the tone, bringing structure, responsibility, and life lessons to your connections. With Saturn in an air sign—Gemini, Libra, or Aquarius—the grounded energy of Saturn merges with the intellectual, communicative, and social qualities of air. Here's how Saturn in air signs influences what you're looking for and what you bring to houses with Capricorn or Aquarius on the cusp.

With Saturn in Gemini, houses with Capricorn on the cusp take on a more analytical and conversational tone. You seek relationships where communication is key, and you value partners who are thoughtful and open to intellectual exchange. However, Saturn's influence may make you cautious about speaking your mind, fearing rejection or misunderstanding. Learning to trust your voice and communicate your needs clearly will strengthen your partnerships. In Aquarius houses, Saturn in Gemini brings an emphasis on flexibility and learning through connection. You may feel drawn to partners who challenge your thinking or introduce you to new ideas, but the airy, dual nature of Gemini could make it hard to fully commit unless you find a partner who values growth as much as you do.

Saturn in Libra enhances Capricorn houses with a focus on fairness, balance, and long-term partnership. You're drawn to partners who are responsible and share your sense of commitment. This placement may make you cautious about entering relationships, as you want to ensure that the connection is stable and equitable before investing fully. While this can protect your heart, it can also delay the deep intimacy you crave. In Aquarius houses, Saturn in Libra emphasizes collaboration and harmony in unique or unconventional partnerships. You value fairness and equality in your connections and are willing to work through differences to create a balanced relationship. However, you may need to be mindful of overcompromising or avoiding confrontation in order to maintain peace.

Saturn in Aquarius reinforces the structured energy of Capricorn houses with an innovative and forward-thinking approach. You seek relationships that offer stability while allowing for independence and individuality. This placement can make you cautious about traditional relationships, as you prioritize connections that align with your values and long-term vision. In Aquarius houses, Saturn in Aquarius doubles down on themes of authenticity and self-reliance. You bring a serious, disciplined approach to partnerships and may be drawn to unconventional dynamics that challenge societal norms. While this placement can make it hard to fully open up, it also fosters deep, meaningful connections when both partners respect each other's autonomy.

The Planets in Water Signs

Water brings emotional depth and a sense of flow to whatever it touches. In astrology, it's the element that goes beneath the surface, connecting with feelings, memories, and the unseen currents of life. Water energy is sensitive, nurturing, and deeply attuned to connection, but it can also feel overwhelming or elusive at times. When the ruler of your relationship houses lands in a water sign, it can shift what you're looking for in love and partnership. It can add or increase a need for emotional intimacy, vulnerability, and a bond that feels deeply meaningful. Trust, safety, and the ability to share your true self become themes in your search. Let's see how this soulful, reflective energy shapes not only the way you connect but also what you seek in your relationships.

The Sun in Water Signs (Cancer, Scorpio, and Pisces)

When Leo is on the cusp of one of your relationship houses, the Sun's placement can bring energy, vitality, and self-expression to that area of life. The Sun wants to shine, drawing attention and admiration. But when the Sun finds itself in a water sign—Cancer, Scorpio, or Pisces—it takes on a more emotionally attuned, sensitive, and intuitive quality. Let's explore how the Sun's typically confident energy is affected by the fluidity and emotional nature of the water signs.

With the Sun in Cancer, Leo's usual boldness is softened by Cancer's nurturing and protective qualities. While Leo thrives on external recognition, Cancer's energy turns the focus inward, emphasizing emotional security. In relationships, this combination suggests a need for partners who appreciate your sensitivity and ability to create a sense of home and comfort. You bring warmth and loyalty to your connections, but your pride may sometimes mask a vulnerable core. Trust and emotional safety are nonnegotiable, and once those are established, you'll shine as a devoted and caring partner. Leo is a fixed sign, and this energy becomes changeable when the Sun is in Cancer. Be mindful not to let your nurturing instincts overshadow your own needs for attention and admiration.

The Sun in Scorpio adds a layer of emotional depth and magnetic intensity to the Sun's energy. This placement can bring a focus on power dynamics, loyalty, and trust in relationships. You're drawn to connections that challenge and urge you to dig deep, seeking partners who can match your passion and emotional resilience. While Leo on the house cusp craves recognition, Scorpio energy shifts the focus toward shared experiences and emotional vulnerability. Your pride may occasionally clash with Scorpio's need for privacy, so finding a balance between self-expression and maintaining the depth of connection is key.

With the Sun in Pisces, Leo's vibrant energy is blended with Pisces's dreaminess and empathy. This creates a natural romantic who thrives on connection and shared inspiration. Relationships for you are about creating and sharing a vision, whether it's a creative project or an emotional bond. However, the Sun in Pisces may struggle with boundaries, and Leo's pride could be vulnerable to feeling unappreciated or unseen. You bring warmth, creativity, and compassion to your partnerships, but it's essential to stay grounded and ensure your needs are met, even as you prioritize others.

Moon in Water Signs

When Cancer is on the cusp of one of your relationship houses, the Moon's placement is important in understanding how your emotional needs and habits affect your connections. The Moon's energy already resonates deeply with Cancer, emphasizing themes of emotional expression, intuition, and caregiving. But when the Moon itself is in a water sign—Cancer, Scorpio, or Pisces—it takes these themes to a deeper level, adding layers of sensitivity, intensity, and empathy.

With the Moon in its own sign, Cancer's natural traits of nurturing, emotional depth, and protective instincts are amplified. You bring an incredible ability to care for and understand your partner on an intuitive level, often anticipating their needs before they've voiced them. However, this placement can also make you highly sensitive, and you may find yourself retreating into your shell when you feel hurt or unappreciated. In relationships, you seek emotional safety and a deep sense of belonging. You'll thrive with a partner who values family, home, and emotional connection as much as you do. The challenge is to avoid overgiving and to ensure your needs are met too.

The Moon in Scorpio adds intensity and emotional complexity to the house with Cancer on the cusp. While Cancer seeks to nurture and protect, Scorpio's influence brings a focus on vulnerability, trust, and transformation. You're drawn to relationships that challenge you emotionally, craving deep, all-encompassing connections. You bring a fierce loyalty and protective instinct to your partnerships, but your emotions can be overwhelming at times, for both you and your partner. It's essential to navigate feelings of jealousy or control, as Scorpio energy can heighten these tendencies. The key to harmony lies in balancing your emotional intensity with Cancer's innate need for security and stability.

The Moon in Pisces brings a dreamy, compassionate energy to the house with Cancer on the cusp. You approach relationships with a sense of romantic idealism, seeking partners who share your emotional depth and creative spirit. This placement amplifies your intuitive connection to others, making you highly empathetic and attuned to your partner's feelings. However, boundaries can be a challenge, as you may struggle to distinguish your emotions from those of others. While Cancer's energy provides a grounding influence, the Moon in Pisces encourages you to open your heart and explore the spiritual dimensions of love. The challenge is to balance your giving nature with self-care, ensuring your emotional needs aren't overlooked.

Mercury in Water Signs

When Gemini or Virgo rules one of your relationship houses, Mercury's placement gives insight into how you communicate and connect with others and analyze your relationships. Mercury thrives in the intellectual realms of these signs, focusing on logic and conversation. But when Mercury lands in a water sign—Cancer, Scorpio, or Pisces—it brings an emotional, intuitive, and sometimes mysterious edge to the way Gemini and Virgo operate. Let's explore how Mercury in water signs influences what you're looking for and what you bring to relationships in these houses.

Mercury in Cancer softens Gemini's quick-witted and curious nature with a dose of emotional awareness. Conversations take on a nurturing tone, and you're more interested in understanding feelings than just exchanging ideas. In relationships ruled by Gemini, this placement makes you an excellent listener and someone who can communicate with heartfelt empathy. However, your sensitivity may make you prone to overanalyzing emotional cues or taking things personally. For Virgo, Mercury in Cancer adds an intuitive dimension to your typically methodical and detail-oriented approach. You're likely to consider how your words impact others on a deeper level, making you a thoughtful and considerate communicator. The challenge here is to avoid retreating into your shell when conversations get tough.

With Mercury in Scorpio, Gemini's natural curiosity becomes more focused and intense. You want to dig beneath the surface, uncovering secrets and exploring topics that others might shy away from. This adds depth and passion to relationships governed by Gemini, but it can also lead to a tendency to overthink or fixate on certain dynamics. For Virgo, Mercury in Scorpio transforms your analytical nature into something more probing and investigative. You're drawn to uncovering the emotional motivations behind your partner's actions, which can lead to profound connections—or potential power struggles if trust becomes an issue. This placement pushes you to balance your investigative instincts with openness and trust.

Mercury in Pisces blends Gemini's mental agility with Pisces's dreamy, intuitive energy, creating a poetic and imaginative approach to relationships. You're likely to communicate in a way that's emotionally resonant, even if it lacks some of Gemini's usual precision. In relationships ruled by Gemini, this placement encourages you to connect on a spiritual or emotional level, but you may need to work on clarity and boundaries in your communication. For Virgo, Mercury in Pisces softens your practical, detail-focused tendencies, encouraging you to think more holistically about your connections. This placement helps you see the bigger picture in relationships, but it may also make it harder to stick to the facts or address practical concerns.

Venus in Water Signs

When Venus is in a water sign—Cancer, Scorpio, or Pisces—it infuses relationship houses with Taurus or Libra on the cusp with a more emotional vibe. These placements prioritize emotional connection, vulnerability, and a sense of soulful unity in connecting. However, this depth of feeling can bring challenges, such as heightened sensitivity or an idealized view of love.

When Venus is in Cancer, Taurus's love of comfort and stability gains a nurturing, protective edge. Your relationships are likely to center around creating a safe, emotionally fulfilling home. You bring a tender and caring energy to connections, but you may also feel vulnerable to rejection or betrayal, making it essential to build trust slowly. For Libra, Venus in Cancer deepens your need for harmony, shifting it from a social level to a more personal, heartfelt one. Partnerships become about emotional safety and shared nurturing, though you may find yourself struggling to set boundaries when the emotional tides get overwhelming.

With Venus in Scorpio, Taurus's love of the tangible and sensual dives into the world of emotional intensity and transformation. You crave depth in relationships, seeking a bond that transcends the physical and ventures into the realm of shared secrets and vulnerability. However, this intensity can sometimes clash with Taurus's steady nature, creating a dynamic where you must learn to balance passion with patience. For Libra, Venus in Scorpio brings a layer of magnetism and intrigue to your desire for partnership. You seek meaningful, transformative connections, but the darker side of Venus in Scorpio can lead to power struggles or a tendency to test your partner's loyalty.

When Venus is in Pisces, Taurus's grounded approach to love gains a dreamy, romantic quality. You're drawn to relationships that feel spiritual or otherworldly, though this can sometimes lead to idealizing partners or overlooking practical compatibility. Your natural appreciation for beauty is enhanced by Pisces's artistic and intuitive energy, making shared creative or emotional pursuits especially meaningful. For Libra, Venus in Pisces amplifies your romantic side, infusing your partnerships with compassion, empathy, and an almost magical sense of connection. While this can lead to beautiful, soul-level bonds, it's important to watch for a tendency to sacrifice too much of yourself or get lost in unrealistic expectations.

Mars in Water Signs

When Aries or Scorpio is on the cusp of one of your relationship houses, Mars takes center stage, bringing energy, drive, and a sense of determination to those connections. But when Mars is in a water sign—Cancer, Scorpio, or Pisces—there are layers of emotion, intuition, and depth that shape what you're looking for and what you bring to relationships. Here's how water influences these houses with Mars on the cusp.

Mars in Cancer softens the typical fiery and intense nature of Mars, as it operates in a deeply emotional and nurturing space. For Aries on a house cusp, this placement transforms its usual bold, action-oriented energy into something more protective and family-focused. You're driven by emotional connections, and your need to protect those you care about often fuels your actions. In relationships, you may struggle with direct confrontation, as Mars in Cancer prefers passive resistance or emotional withdrawal when things get tough.

For Scorpio on the cusp, Mars in Cancer deepens the emotional intensity. While Scorpio already seeks deep, transformative connections, this placement emphasizes vulnerability and emotional bonding. Trust becomes the cornerstone of your relationships, and you may find yourself fiercely protective of your partner or shared resources. However, watch out for emotional defensiveness or manipulative tendencies when feeling insecure.

Mars in Scorpio is in its rulership, expressing its full intensity and power here. For Aries on the cusp, this placement adds a layer of emotional depth and strategy to your usual boldness. Relationships become about more than surface-level attraction—they're a battleground for deep emotional transformation. You're drawn to partners who challenge you, help you grow, and push you to explore your limits. However, Mars in Scorpio can also bring possessiveness and a need for control, so it's important to balance independence with connection.

For Scorpio on the cusp, Mars in Scorpio doubles down on themes of power, intimacy, and emotional depth. You approach relationships with a no-holds-barred intensity, seeking complete vulnerability and trust. This placement demands emotional honesty and may drive you to explore the darker sides of love and connection. While this intensity can be magnetic, it's essential to guard against destructive tendencies such as jealousy or an all-or-nothing mindset in relationships.

Mars in Pisces maneuvers using intuition and emotional resonance, making it the most subtle and least direct expression of Mars. For Aries on the cusp, this placement shifts a usually headstrong and straightforward nature into a more empathic and intuitive way of operating. You're motivated by idealism and spiritual connection, and you may find yourself drawn to partners who share your creative or compassionate outlook on life. However, this placement can make it harder to set boundaries or assert your needs, so you'll need to practice clarity in communication.

For Scorpio on the cusp, Mars in Pisces softens the sign's intensity, introducing a more spiritual and inspired approach to relationships. Emotional and physical intimacy becomes intertwined with creativity and a sense of higher purpose. While you're deeply intuitive in relationships, this placement can also lead to blurred boundaries or romanticized ideals that don't align with reality. Learning to ground your dreams in measurable action will help you navigate love and connection.

Jupiter in Water Signs

When Sagittarius or Pisces rules one of your relationship houses, Jupiter takes the lead, bringing expansion, optimism, and a quest for meaning. But when Jupiter finds itself in a water sign—Cancer, Scorpio, or Pisces—it infuses this energy with emotional depth, intuition, and a desire for profound connection. Let's explore how Jupiter's placement in water signs influences the qualities of these houses.

Jupiter is exalted in Cancer, meaning it operates with emotional wisdom and a nurturing touch. For Sagittarius on the cusp, this placement softens the fiery, adventurous nature of Sagittarius, creating a desire to build relationships rooted in emotional security and care. You're likely drawn to partners who feel like "home" and share your values of family and emotional safety. While this placement emphasizes warmth and connection, it may also lead to a tendency to play it safe, avoiding risks that could bring greater growth.

For Pisces on the cusp, Jupiter in Cancer amplifies the emotional and intuitive qualities of Pisces, adding an extra layer of nurturing energy. Relationships take on a deeply supportive and protective tone, as you're motivated to create a sanctuary where both you and your partner feel emotionally safe. However, this placement may heighten sensitivity, making you prone to absorbing your partner's emotions and losing sight of your own needs.

Jupiter in Scorpio blends Jupiter's expansive energy with Scorpio's depth and intensity, creating a drive to explore the transformative aspects of relationships. For Sagittarius on the cusp, this placement shifts your usual openness into something more guarded and strategic. While you're still drawn to big ideas and grand adventures, relationships must also offer emotional depth and shared growth. You're likely to attract partners who challenge you to dig deep and confront your fears, helping you grow on a soul level.

For Pisces on the cusp, Jupiter in Scorpio brings a profound emotional intensity to your relationships. You crave spiritual and emotional merging, seeking partners who inspire transformation and shared vulnerability. This placement may also heighten themes of power dynamics, trust, and control in your connections. While the depth of this placement can create profound bonds, it's essential to balance emotional investment with healthy boundaries.

Jupiter is at home in Pisces, expressing its full capacity for compassion, creativity, and spiritual growth. For Sagittarius on the cusp, this placement softens the fiery, outgoing nature of Sagittarius with a dreamy, introspective quality. You're likely drawn to partners who share your ideals and inspire your imagination, creating connections that feel almost otherworldly. However, this placement may also lead to a tendency to idealize relationships, leaving you disillusioned when reality doesn't match your dreams.

For Pisces on the cusp, Jupiter in Pisces is a double dose of Piscean energy, emphasizing themes of emotional connection, empathy, and spiritual growth. Relationships take on an almost magical quality, as you're deeply attuned to your partner's emotions and needs. While this placement encourages profound compassion and understanding, it may also blur boundaries, making it essential to ground your relationships in reality and maintain a clear sense of self.

Saturn in Water Signs

When Capricorn or Aquarius rules one of your relationship houses, Saturn steps in as the planetary ruler, adding structure, responsibility, and a need for long-term stability. But when Saturn finds itself in a water sign—Cancer, Scorpio, or Pisces—it can take on a more emotional and intuitive tone. Let's look at how Saturn in water signs influences these houses.

Saturn in Cancer brings a focus on emotional security and family-oriented commitments. For Capricorn on the cusp, this placement softens the typically practical and achievement-driven energy of this sign. While you still value structure and reliability in relationships, there's a stronger emphasis on creating emotional safety and nurturing connections. This placement may draw you to partners who feel like "home" or help you build a strong emotional foundation. However, Saturn in Cancer can also create a fear of vulnerability, making it difficult to open up fully until trust is deeply established.

For Aquarius on the cusp, Saturn in Cancer adds an emotional depth to your typically intellectual and forward-thinking approach to relationships. While you're still drawn to unconventional or innovative connections, this placement encourages you to ground your ideals in emotional reality. You may find yourself more focused on creating a supportive and nurturing environment in your partnerships, but you'll need to guard against withdrawing emotionally when things feel uncertain.

Saturn in Scorpio intensifies Saturn's natural discipline with Scorpio's emotional depth and transformative energy. For Capricorn on the cusp, this placement brings a focus on power dynamics, trust, and control within relationships. You're likely drawn to partnerships that challenge you to confront your fears and grow on a deep emotional level. While Capricorn's practical energy values stability, Saturn in Scorpio pushes you to explore the deeper, more vulnerable aspects of connection. This can lead to incredibly strong bonds, but it may also create struggles around trust and letting go of control.

For Aquarius on the cusp, Saturn in Scorpio adds emotional intensity to your typically detached approach to relationships. While Aquarius energy thrives on innovation and independence, Saturn in Scorpio demands emotional honesty and a willingness to navigate the complexities of intimacy. This placement can make you more cautious about forming deep connections, but it also gives you the ability to create transformative and lasting partnerships when you're ready to fully commit.

Saturn in Pisces blends Saturn's need for structure with Pisces's idealistic and empathetic qualities. For Capricorn on the cusp, this placement brings a spiritual and compassionate dimension to your relationships. While you still value practicality and long-term planning, Saturn in Pisces encourages you to connect on a more intuitive and emotional level. You may be drawn to partners who inspire your imagination and help you explore the softer side of life. However, balancing the dreamy nature of Pisces with Saturn's need for boundaries is crucial to avoid overcommitting or taking on too much responsibility in your relationships.

For Aquarius on the cusp, Saturn in Pisces shifts your focus from intellectual ideals to emotional and spiritual connections. This placement encourages you to ground your visionary ideas in empathy and compassion, creating partnerships that are both innovative and deeply meaningful. While you may initially struggle with the lack of clear boundaries that Pisces energy brings, Saturn's influence helps you develop the tools to navigate these complexities and build lasting relationships that align with your higher ideals.

The Wrap-Up: Ruling Planets and What They Add to the Story

Here's the thing: The sign your house ruler is in can change the dynamic of your relationship houses. Sometimes it turns the volume up, making certain traits or themes really obvious. Other times it tones things down, making the energy more subtle—or even feel a little "off." Either way, it adds an important layer to your story about love, connection, and commitment.

If the planet's energy works well in its sign, then everything flows a bit more easily. You may find that it feels easier to navigate certain types or phases of relationships. But if the planet struggles in a sign, there's probably some learning to do before you can get the kind of connection you're after. These lessons show up in all kinds of ways: conflicts, patterns you can't seem to break, or even attracting partners who embody the planet's energy in ways that teach you more about yourself and what you want and don't want.

The beauty is that every placement, even the tricky ones, has something to teach you. Whether it's bringing passion, stability, curiosity, or emotional depth—or working through impatience, overthinking, or insecurity—it all adds to your understanding of what you bring to relationships and what you need in return. The more you lean into the lessons, the closer you get to the connections that truly fulfill you.

The Plot Twists in Your Love Story

Grab your journal or the notebook you've been working with, and let's pull all the pieces together with this exercise.

> The sign on my 5th house is __________,
>
> the planetary ruler of my 5th house is __________,
>
> and the sign this ruler is in is __________.

Does the energy of the sign on the 5th house match the sign the ruling planet is in? If yes, how is it enhanced or supported? If your answer is no, how does the sign the ruling planet is in change the tone of the sign on the house cusp? What does the sign the ruler is in add to your 5th house story? For example, if Aries is on the 5th house cusp and its ruling planet, Mars, is in Pisces, does Pisces enhance Mars's fire or does it tone it down?

The sign on my 7th house is _________,

the planetary ruler of my 7th house is _________,

and the sign this ruler is in is _________.

Does the energy of the sign on the 7th house match the sign the ruling planet is in? If yes, how is it enhanced or supported? If your answer is no, how does the sign the ruling planet is in change the tone of the sign on the house cusp? What does the sign the ruler is in add to your 7th house story?

The sign on my 8th house is _________,

the planetary ruler of my 8th house is _________,

and the sign this ruler is in is _________.

Does the energy of the sign on the 8th house match the sign the ruling planet is in? If yes, how is it enhanced or supported? If your answer is no, how does the sign the ruling planet is in change the tone of the sign on the house cusp? What does the sign the ruler is in add to your 8th house story?

Do you see relationship patterns with any of these signs and houses?

Do any of the associated traits hold lessons you've learned, are working on, or need to embrace? If so, which planet or sign in your chart seems most connected to that theme?

Planet: _________

Sign: _________

Examples of Patterns to Notice

Now let's look for patterns. These questions can help you spot recurring themes in who you're drawn to—and how that might link back to planets or houses in your chart.

- Do you tend to have many friends with the same Sun sign? If so, is that sign connected to one of your relationship houses (5th, 7th, or 8th)? Which one? If not, which house cusp in your chart is that sign on, and what might that reveal about the kinds of people you're drawn to?
- Do you tend to date or connect with people who share your mother's or father's Sun sign?
- Is there a particular Sun sign you're attracted to? If so, which planet and house are associated with that sign in your chart?

6

The Relationship House Rulers in the Houses

Where Love Shows Up in Your Life

As you've seen in the previous chapter, the planetary ruler of a house adds another layer to your relationship story. In this chapter we'll look at how the ruler of each house carries its energy to the house it's in, linking those two areas of your life. This connection not only shows how different parts of your life influence your relationships but also offers clues about *where* to find the kinds of connections you're looking for.

For example, if the ruler of your 7th house of partnership is in your 10th house of career, it might mean you're more likely to meet a partner through work or public life. If the ruler of your 5th house of romance is in your 12th house, your love life might involve private or spiritual connections or be tied to themes of healing and introspection—or it might even mean that you have secret love affairs.

This chapter of the book is where it all comes together to point to where you are more likely to make connections. By exploring where the planetary rulers of your relationship houses are in your birth chart, you'll uncover a practical map for navigating love, intimacy, and partnerships. These placements don't just tell you *what* you're drawn to; they also show you *where* to look for it—and can keep you from wasting time looking in the wrong places.

Before we explore where the planetary rulers of your relationship houses are—and how they shape your experiences of love, partnership, and intimacy—it's important to review the twelve houses. Understanding the energetic differences between them will help you interpret where those rulers land in *your* chart.

Your Chart's Foundation: Understanding the Houses

Each house in a birth chart has its own level of activity, which can influence how easily its themes show up in your life. The angular houses—1st, 4th, 7th, and 10th—are the most energetic and visible. The events and themes tied to these houses tend to feel more obvious and easier to activate. Then there are the succedent houses—2nd, 5th, 8th, and 11th—which are a bit quieter. They take time to fully develop and unfold, but they hold steady, enduring energy. Finally, there are the cadent houses—3rd, 6th, 9th, and 12th. These are the reflective and lesson-oriented spaces of the chart, and planets here may require more effort to express themselves or be noticed, even by you.

As you explore the chart further, keep in mind which quadrant a relationship planet falls in: whether it's in the first quadrant, where self-reliance and personal growth are emphasized; the second quadrant, focused on close-to-home relationships and private life; the third quadrant, rich with the chart's coupling energy; or the fourth quadrant, where partnerships may take on public, collective, or spiritual significance.

1st House: You, Your Identity, and What You Project into the World

The 1st house represents your *self*, your physical body, and how you present yourself to the world. It's about your approach to life and the energy you put out into the world, which shapes the way others perceive you. While the Ascendant is the specific degree marking the start (cusp) of the 1st house and describes your outward demeanor or "mask," the 1st house itself is about your individuality, your personal style, and how you interact with your environment in general.

In relationships, the 1st house can influence how you draw people in through your presence and how your sense of self impacts partnerships.

2nd House: Values, Self-Worth, and Your Stuff

The 2nd house is all about values: what you value, how you value yourself, and even the material things you accumulate as a reflection of those values. Often called the house of possessions, the 2nd doesn't just cover money and belongings, but also your personal sense of worth and security. This house reveals how you approach stability, what you're drawn to in terms of comfort, and how you build a foundation for your life.

In relationships, the 2nd house speaks to the importance of shared values and the tangible aspects of a connection. It's where you figure out what you truly need to feel secure, both emotionally and financially. Whether it's about creating a comfortable home, aligning priorities with a partner, or knowing your own worth, the 2nd house helps set the stage for what you bring to and expect from your connections. It's grounded, practical, and deeply tied to your sense of what makes life meaningful and comfortable.

3rd House: Connection, Communication, and Siblings

The 3rd house is all about how you communicate, think, and connect with the world around you. It's the domain of your neighborhood, siblings, and day-to-day interactions. This house rules the exchange of ideas, curiosity, and how you absorb and share information. It's where we explore the power of words, storytelling, and even casual conversations.

In relationships, the 3rd house reflects how you express yourself and engage with others on a mental level. It's about the give-and-take of communication, whether it's deep discussions or lighthearted banter. Think of the 3rd as the house that lays the groundwork for understanding and being understood.

4th House: Home, Family, and Your Roots

The 4th house is your personal sanctuary—the heart of your chart. It's all about home, family, roots, and security. This is where you go to feel safe and connected, whether that's through your literal home or the people who feel like "home" to you. It also represents your foundations, the things you carry forward from childhood, and the traditions or values that ground you. The 4th house is deeply personal—it's the space where your private life lives, away from the world's spotlight. This house is about what grounds you on an internal level, whether that's through your family, your ancestry, or the refuge you create for yourself. It's all about finding your anchor in this life.

5th House: Creativity, Joy, and Children

The 5th house is where joy, creativity, and self-expression come to life. It's the part of your chart that reflects your ability to play, take risks, and explore life through personal expression and the connections you make along the way. This house is often associated with fun, hobbies, romance, and even the concept of children—not just in a literal sense, but also as symbols of what we "birth" creatively, like art or passion projects.

Unlike the deeper commitments of the 7th house or the emotional vulnerability of the 8th house, the 5th house focuses on connection for the sake of enjoyment and exploration. It's the spark of romance, the thrill of creative pursuits, and the excitement of discovering new passions. It governs the activities that bring pleasure and allow for carefree moments of self-discovery.

The 5th house invites you to embrace spontaneity, take risks in love or creative projects, and let go of expectations. It's not about permanence or obligation, but about finding what lights you up and brings joy to your life. Whether it's through romance, artistic expression, or playful activities, the 5th house is where you explore what makes life feel vibrant and fulfilling.

6th House: Health, Routines, and Work

The 6th house in astrology is all about your daily routines and responsibilities and the work you do to maintain your life. It's the house of effort, health, and the systems that keep things running smoothly. This is where we focus on practical matters such as jobs, well-being, and habits, but also how we approach our duties and commitments.

The 6th house isn't about the grand career aspirations of the 10th house; it's more about the day-to-day jobs—what you do consistently, how you manage your time, and how you care for your wellness. It's where you'll find themes around work environments, coworkers, and the tasks that make up your daily life. It connects to health and wellness through focusing on the routines or regimens that support your physical and mental vitality.

The 6th house carries a tone of responsibility and asks how you contribute to the larger system, whether it's through your work, your care for others, or the way you support yourself. It's a space where discipline meets practicality, encouraging a focus on the small, consistent actions that lead to lasting results. I've always found it fascinating how small animals are associated with this house. After all, what better way to establish a routine based on basic needs than by getting a pet? They thrive on having their daily needs met on a predictable schedule, and they might just help you find structure in your own life too.

7th House: Partnership and Commitment

The 7th house is where we move beyond the self and start thinking about the "other." It's the house of one-on-one relationships, covering all kinds of partnerships—from romantic and business collaborations to legal agreements and even open conflicts with others. This house reflects how we engage in committed relationships, where there's a sense of mutual dependency, for better or worse.

Unlike the exploratory nature of earlier houses, the 7th house is about creating balance and finding ways to connect and collaborate. This is where we learn to navigate the give-and-take dynamics of relationships, discovering what we need from others and what we're willing to give in return. It's the house of agreements, where we make commitments and define the roles we play in each other's lives.

Interestingly, the 7th house also governs open enemies, highlighting that not all one-on-one dynamics are positive. These relationships, whether personal or professional, can challenge us to see things from another perspective or test our ability to maintain our boundaries.

Ultimately, the 7th house isn't just about the people we attract—it's also a reflection of how we approach relationships. It shows the qualities we look for in others, what we value in partnership, and how we negotiate the complexities of connection.

8th House: Sex, Death, and Taxes

The 8th house delves into the realms of life's deeper mysteries—sex, death, and transformation are central here. This is the house where we face the inevitable cycles of endings and beginnings, learning to navigate the emotional and spiritual shifts they bring. It's also a place of fascination with the unknown, tied to themes of the occult, metaphysics, and anything hidden beneath the surface.

The 8th house governs intimacy, not just in the physical sense but also in the emotional and energetic merging with others. It's where vulnerability and trust come into play, offering the potential for profound connection or, conversely, the fear of betrayal or loss. The 8th house challenges you to explore what it means to truly share yourself with another and what you're willing to risk in doing so.

The 8th house is also tied to shared resources and other people's stuff, whether that's finances, inheritances, debts, or energetic exchanges. There's a magnetism here, a draw toward what others possess, whether that's material, emotional, or spiritual. The allure of power and control can be a part of the story of this house.

Ultimately, the 8th house teaches us about surrender and renewal. Whether you're navigating shared finances, confronting fears of mortality, or embracing the power of real intimacy, this house asks you to face life's darker corners to uncover deeper truths about yourself and your connections. It's a space of profound growth—but only if you're willing to embrace the discomfort that comes with it.

9th House: Higher Learning, Travel, and Philosophy

The 9th house is all about expanding your worldview, whether that's through higher learning, spiritual growth, or literal journeys to far-off places. This house speaks to the quest for meaning, where we explore big ideas and connect to something larger than ourselves. It's where we seek out experiences that challenge our perspectives and help us grow.

The 9th house is tied to education and wisdom, not just in the formal sense but in how we learn through life. It encourages us to explore philosophies, cultures, and beliefs that give us a sense of purpose. Whether it's through travel, studying different traditions, or asking the big existential questions, the 9th house will have us craving a deeper understanding of the world.

There's a social aspect to the 9th house—one that connects us to others through shared values, ideals, or causes. It's about finding common ground across differences and building bridges through shared experiences or mutual curiosity. This house also touches on the role of mentorship or teaching, whether you're the one learning or the one guiding others.

10th House: Public Role and Achievements

The 10th house represents your public life, your aspirations, and the roles you step into in the broader world. It's where we see how you show up in society, the mark you want to leave, and the reputation you build. This house speaks to your ambitions and the external recognition you strive for, whether through career, achievements, or how you contribute to the collective.

Unlike the deeply personal houses, the 10th is outward-facing, focusing on how you're perceived and the legacy you create. It's tied to positions of authority or responsibility and can describe the impact you aim to make on others. This house also points to long-term goals and the highest of your achievements.

The 10th house is not solely about work—it's also connected to our purpose. Whether it's a career, a personal mission, or a broader calling, this house helps define the area of life where you're most likely to seek recognition and fulfillment. It's the house of visibility, where your efforts and ambitions shine for others to see.

11th House: Groups, Organizations, and the Larger Community

The 11th house is where community, connection, and shared goals take the stage. It's often called the house of friendships, but it's about more than casual acquaintances—it's where we align with groups, causes, and networks that reflect our ideals. Whether it's your closest circle of friends, a professional network, or a community organization, the 11th house represents the collective energy that helps you work toward common goals.

The 11th house is also tied to hopes and dreams, specifically the ones that feel bigger than yourself. It's the space in the chart where you envision the future and find the support to help make it a reality. Here, individuality blends with shared purpose, as you balance your personal identity with the larger groups or movements you're a part of.

In relationships, the 11th house emphasizes the social aspects of connection: partners who share your ideals, friends who feel like family, or a shared cause that brings you closer to others. It's where you see how collaboration and community can enrich your life.

12th House: Solitude, Introspection, and Institutions

The 12th house represents the hidden and often intangible aspects of life, encompassing themes like solitude, introspection, and the parts of ourselves we may not immediately recognize. It's the house of what's unseen—unconscious patterns, repressed emotions, and private experiences that shape us in subtle ways.

A significant theme of the 12th house is institutions, places like hospitals, prisons, and retreat centers that remove us from everyday life. These spaces can provide healing, rehabilitation, or reflection, but they can also feel isolating, depending on the context. The 12th house speaks to how we handle being "on the inside," whether that's within ourselves or within a larger system.

The 12th house also invites us to step away from the noise of the external world, offering opportunities for quiet moments of self-awareness and rest. It's where we might find a calling to help others or to work behind the scenes, supporting the greater good without needing recognition. The 12th house encourages a deep connection to yourself and the ability to navigate life's more subtle, unseen layers.

The 5th House Ruler of Romantic Connections in the Houses

The ruler of the 5th house is the planet that governs the sign on the cusp of that house. For instance, if your 5th house cusp falls in Leo, then the Sun is the ruler of your 5th house. The position of your 5th house ruler in your natal chart provides key insights into your romantic experiences and where you might find love.

Why the Ruler of Your 5th House Matters

The ruler of your 5th house is your compass to help you discover the areas of life where you'll find romance, creativity, and joy. Where your 5th house ruler is by sign, house, and aspect can show how you express affection, where you find pleasure, and the kinds of romantic experiences you're likely to attract and want to attract.

Understanding this layering adds depth to how you approach and reflect on your dating history. Sometimes the place where romance or creativity is waiting for you isn't where you'd expect to find it. These subtle cues can help you connect the dots between your chart and the patterns you've experienced. Let's look at what the ruler of the 5th house reveals when it is placed in each of the twelve houses.

When the Ruler of the 5th Is in the 1st House

If the ruler of the 5th house is in the 1st house, your sense of self is very connected to love, joy, and creativity. Romantic connections and personal expression are closely tied to how you see yourself and how others see you. You've got a natural charm and energy that draws people in, and your relationships and creative outlets tend to reflect who you really are at your core.

With this placement, you probably bring a playful, warm, and even dramatic vibe to the table. You want romantic connections that let you be yourself, and you're likely drawn to partners who really get—and appreciate—your individuality. There's a spark of excitement in how you approach relationships, making things lively and fun.

That said, because the 1st house is about identity, there's a chance you might seek a little too much validation from your romantic life or creative achievements. It's important to make sure your sense of self isn't dependent on matters of the 5th house. If it is, you'll learn a lot about who you are through romantic relationships. At its best, this placement helps you shine authentically, using love and creativity as ways to express your unique personality.

When the Ruler of the 5th Is in the 2nd House

When the ruler of your 5th house lands in the 2nd house, your romantic life and creative expression are tied to themes of value, stability, and security. You're likely drawn to relationships that feel grounded, where you can build something tangible together—whether that's a financial foundation, a cozy home, or just a shared sense of security. Romance might also spark in practical places, like work settings or financial discussions, or even while shopping or indulging in life's comforts.

Creativity for you isn't just about self-expression; it's something you take seriously. You might focus on creating things that last—projects or hobbies that have a practical or financial benefit. You're not just playing around; you're building something meaningful.

In dating, you're probably looking for someone who shares your values and sees the worth in what you bring to the table. Affection could be shown through acts of generosity or giving and receiving gifts, and you're likely to appreciate a partner who helps you feel secure in every sense of the word. With this placement, the quality of your romantic relationships often reflects the strength of your own self-worth. If you find yourself attracting duds, taking time to work on yourself first can help break the cycle and lead to more fulfilling connections.

When the Ruler of the 5th Is in the 3rd House

When the ruler of your 5th house lands in the 3rd house, romance and creativity become all about connection through communication. You're drawn to partners who stimulate your mind and keep the conversation flowing. Whether it's engaging in witty banter, long discussions about everything under the sun, or flirty texts, the mental spark is just as important as the emotional or physical one.

You might find romantic opportunities through your neighborhood, your local community, or even casual interactions such as running errands or chatting with someone at a café. Siblings or mutual acquaintances could also play a role in setting you up with potential partners. Creative expression for you often involves words, writing, or storytelling—anything that lets you share your ideas and thoughts with the world.

This placement suggests that communication is at the heart of your romantic connections. Whether through heartfelt conversations, shared stories, love letters, or creative projects that involve writing or speaking, you'll find joy in exchanging ideas and building intellectual rapport. The key is to stay open and engaged with the world around you, as your next connection might be just a conversation away.

When the Ruler of the 5th Is in the 4th House

When the ruler of your 5th house lands in the 4th house, your approach to romance, creativity, and joy is closely tied to your home, family, and personal foundations. Love and self-expression often come with a deep need for emotional security, and you may find that the relationships you pursue reflect or challenge the core values and patterns you've inherited from your family. There's an instinct to bring the energy of joy and romance to your private life, whether that's by creating a loving home environment with your romantic partner or turning to creativity as a way to process your emotions or difficult family stuff.

Romantic connections might start in intimate or familiar settings, like through family friends or at home-based gatherings, or they might take on a nurturing, protective quality. You could be drawn to people who make you feel safe and grounded or who share a desire to build something lasting and meaningful together. Your creative side likely thrives when you feel emotionally stable and supported, so cultivating a strong sense of inner security can help you express yourself more fully.

On the flip side, if your early experiences at home were challenging, this placement might show patterns you're working to heal in your love life. Learning to separate your personal story from your romantic connections can be key to creating relationships that feel truly nourishing and aligned with who you are. Whether it's through finding joy in traditions, creating a sanctuary for yourself, or exploring the layers of your emotional world, the 5th house ruler in the 4th reminds you that love and creativity flourish when they're rooted in authenticity and trust.

When the Ruler of the 5th Is in the 5th House

When the ruler of the 5th house is in the 5th house, romance, creativity, and self-expression become a major focus in your life. This placement amplifies the themes of the 5th house, suggesting that you're deeply connected to exploring creativity, play, and personal expression. Romantic relationships for you are less about practicalities or emotional entanglements and more about shared experiences that light up your world.

In your romantic story, you're likely drawn to partners who inspire your sense of play and imagination. Relationships for you might feel like a stage for expressing yourself and discovering new facets of who you are. You might find yourself caught up in the excitement of love and the rush of new connections, enjoying the thrill of romance and the unfolding possibilities it brings.

This placement also highlights a strong desire for creative fulfillment. Whether through art, hobbies, or passion projects, your love life often intersects with your creative pursuits. Partners might even be drawn into these activities, becoming part of the joy you create or helping you bring your ideas to life.

However, the amplification of the 5th house can also lead to challenges. There's a tendency to idealize romance or treat relationships as sources of entertainment or competition, which could make it harder to build deeper, more committed connections. It's essential to balance the fun and play of the 5th house with the realities of building lasting bonds.

Ultimately, this placement shows a life filled with opportunities to explore love, creativity, and joy. By learning to integrate your love of play with a willingness to deepen connections, you can create relationships that are exciting and centered on commitment.

When the Ruler of the 5th Is in the 6th House

When the ruler of your 5th house is in the 6th house, romance, creativity, and joy take on a practical feeling. This placement suggests you might find love in the everyday rhythms of life—work, errands, or health-related activities. You're drawn to partners who share your dedication to daily responsibilities or complement your routines. There's a sense of connection through shared tasks, whether it's meal prepping, walking the dog, or hitting the gym together.

Creativity here might focus on refining processes, improving systems, or creating beauty through organization. You likely find joy in hobbies that have a functional or productive element, like gardening, cooking, or even DIY projects. Play becomes about finding fulfillment in the small, meaningful acts of service that make life flow more smoothly.

Romance can feel more grounded with this placement, but it's important to make space for spontaneity. When love feels like just another item on the to-do list, it can lose some of its spark. Learning to balance responsibilities with leisure and play keeps relationships thriving.

This placement also highlights the importance of self-care in relationships. If you're constantly giving or prioritizing others' needs, it's easy to lose sight of your own joy. Taking time to indulge in what makes you happy—even if it feels frivolous—ensures you don't burn out on love or life.

When the Ruler of the 5th Is in the 7th House

When the ruler of the 5th house lands in the 7th house, romance and creativity weave directly into your partnerships. Relationships might feel like a natural playground for self-expression and joy. This placement suggests you're someone who thrives in committed connections where there's room for playfulness and shared passions. Romantic partnerships may even start casually, evolving into deeper commitments as you realize how much joy and creativity the other person brings into your life.

You may seek partners who embody the spirit of the 5th house—someone who sparks inspiration, encourages your creative pursuits, or brings an element of fun and excitement to your life. This placement can also mean your romantic relationships have a unique way of blending the lightheartedness of the 5th house with the more serious commitment of the 7th.

On the flip side, the line between casual and committed could blur, and you may find it hard to separate romance from partnership. It's important to stay mindful of whether you're pursuing relationships for the joy they bring or because you feel a need to merge your identity with someone else's.

Ultimately, with the ruler of the 5th in the 7th, your relationships can become a stage for exploring your passions, expressing your creativity, and finding true joy in connection. When balanced, this placement can create partnerships that are not just functional but also deeply fulfilling and inspiring.

When the Ruler of the 5th Is in the 8th House

When the ruler of your 5th house is in the 8th house, romance and creativity take on a deeper, more intense meaning. This placement connects your playful, creative energy with the themes of intimacy, vulnerability, and transformation. It's not just about fun dates or casual flirtation; it's about connections that push boundaries, peel back layers, and leave a lasting impact.

In romance, you're drawn to relationships that feel significant and transformative. Surface-level connections just won't do—you crave the depth of physical and emotional merging. There's a magnetic quality to the way you approach love, and you might find yourself attracting (or being attracted to) people who hold some kind of power or mystery. Relationships here are not for the faint of heart. They'll teach you about trust, shared vulnerability, and what it means to truly let someone in.

This placement can also bring a fascination with exploring the more private, taboo, or unspoken aspects of relationships, including sexuality and power dynamics. It's no surprise that Mata Hari, the world-famous exotic dancer, courtesan, and spy, had the rulers of her 5th and 8th houses tightly conjunct in her chart.

Creatively, this placement asks you to dig deep. Your best work often comes from a place of emotional truth or through processing life's darker or more transformative moments while pushing beyond social boundaries. Whether it's through writing, art, or other forms of self-expression, your creativity likely carries an intensity that resonates deeply with others.

Ultimately, with the 5th house ruler in the 8th, your journey in romance and creativity is one of transformation. The more you're willing to face fears of vulnerability or loss, the more fulfilling and meaningful your connections can become. It's a placement that asks for courage—but the rewards are likely profound.

When the Ruler of the 5th Is in the 9th House

When the ruler of your 5th house of romance, creativity, and joy lands in the 9th house, your love story might be tied to bigger ideas, adventures, and a search for meaning. This placement can mean you find joy in connections that broaden your understanding of the world, whether that's through travel, higher education, or exploring philosophical ideals. Relationships are more than just fun for you; they're an opportunity to grow and learn.

You might be drawn to partners who inspire you to think beyond your immediate environment or who come from different backgrounds. A shared sense of adventure and a curiosity about life's big questions could play a significant role in your romantic experiences. You're not just looking for a partner; you're looking for a fellow explorer, someone who can take you on intellectual or spiritual journeys.

Creativity for you may be tied to the pursuit of knowledge and expressing your big ideas. Writing, teaching, or even creative storytelling might be outlets where your passion shines—the 9th *is* the house of publishing. You likely feel most alive when you're sharing discoveries or creating something that reflects your distinctive worldview.

In romance and creative expression, you might be fueled by a desire to connect on a higher level. This placement can also make you prone to romanticizing ideals or seeing relationships as part of a grand quest. Balancing this with practical expectations can help you build connections that are both inspiring and grounded.

When the Ruler of the 5th Is in the 10th House

When the ruler of your 5th house of romance and creativity is in the 10th house, your dating life and creative self-expression often intersect with your public or professional life. This placement suggests you might meet romantic partners through your career or public engagements or while pursuing long-term goals. It also indicates that creativity or personal passions could play a role in shaping your reputation or aspirations.

You may be drawn to partners who share your ambition or appreciate the public-facing side of your personality. For you, relationships aren't just personal; they're tied to your broader sense of purpose and how you're perceived by others. Whether it's a romantic connection or a creative endeavor, there's a drive to make it meaningful in a way that leaves a lasting impression on the world.

This placement can also suggest that your romantic life and professional life are tightly connected—one may influence the other. However, there's a potential for overlap that requires balance, as the pressures of public recognition or ambition could spill into personal relationships, leading to challenges if boundaries aren't clearly defined.

Ultimately, with this placement, love, creativity, and ambition intertwine. You're likely to find fulfillment in partnerships and projects that align with your goals and support the legacy you're building.

When the Ruler of the 5th Is in the 11th House

When the ruler of your 5th house lands in the 11th house, romance and creativity are intertwined with community and shared goals. You may find romantic connections within your social circles or through group activities. Your relationships often begin with a foundation of friendship or shared interests, and these connections can feel most fulfilling when they align with your bigger dreams or collective endeavors.

This placement suggests that your creative energy flourishes when it's shared or connected to others in meaningful ways. You may be drawn to partners who encourage your aspirations or inspire you to think about how your relationship contributes to your overall sense of fulfillment. Relationships formed through shared activities, group settings, or mutual interests and causes can feel particularly rewarding and supportive.

At its best, this placement brings a sense of camaraderie and shared vision to romance, but you might also face challenges in balancing personal intimacy with the broader social or collective focus of the 11th house. Finding ways to nurture one-on-one connections while staying true to your ideals and group commitments will help you create relationships that feel meaningful and are aligned with the bigger picture.

When the Ruler of the 5th Is in the 12th House

When the ruler of the 5th house finds itself in the 12th house, your romantic and creative life can feel like it's happening behind a veil. There's a natural pull toward private or even secretive relationships. You may find yourself drawn to connections that feel deeply personal but aren't always visible to the outside world. This could mean quiet, soulful romances or relationships that thrive away from public scrutiny.

Creativity, too, might feel like a private sanctuary for you—a spiritual experience you don't want to share. You could be someone who pours your heart into art, writing, or other creative outlets but prefers to keep these expressions hidden or shared only with a trusted few. This placement suggests that your inspiration may stem from deep introspection, your dreams, or even subconscious influences.

The 12th house also connects to institutions, which might influence how and where you encounter love or creativity. For example, you might find romantic or creative fulfillment in spaces like retreats, hospitals, or other environments where solitude and reflection are encouraged.

One potential challenge with this placement is learning to balance your private world with the need for authentic connection. While it's perfectly fine to keep certain parts of your life under wraps, it's important to ensure you're not using secrecy as a shield to avoid vulnerability. When you allow your creative talents and romantic desires to emerge from the shadows, you'll find they can enrich not only your own life but also your connections with others.

The 5th House Ruler in Action

Let's revisit David Bowie's chart (page 68) and explore his 5th house ruler and its placement. Bowie has Gemini on the 5th house cusp, with its ruler, Mercury, positioned in the 11th house (but very close to the 12th house cusp). This suggests a strong connection between romance and friendships, groups, or organizations. In his romantic life, he likely valued and even expected friendship as a foundation for deeper connections. Creatively, this placement points to a relationship between his art and social causes or political commentary.

With the ruler of his 5th house in the 11th, we'd expect Bowie to have a large social circle and an active social life as well as many collaborations throughout his creative career. The influence of the collective would play a significant role in his art, and Mercury's chameleon-like nature reflects his ability to adapt to and shape cultural trends. Bowie's fashion and artistic transformations were influenced by the collective style of the time, and in turn, he influenced the collective.

This 5th-11th house combination can also indicate meeting romantic partners through friends, which is how he met Iman, his second wife. They were set up on a blind date for a party—a perfect blend of 11th house themes (friends and parties) and the 12th house influence (the unseen, like a blind date).

Mapping Your Joy and Romance

Now it's your turn.

- Which house is the ruler of your 5th house in?
- What themes does this house bring to your 5th house story?
- Are there any of these themes you'd like to explore further in order to go deeper into how they may connect to creativity, joy, romance, or children in your life?

When you look back, are there any patterns you can see when you consider these house themes?

The 7th House Ruler of Committed Relationships in the Houses

The 7th house is all about relationships that help define us—the partnerships we commit to, the people who mirror us, and the connections that help us grow. While the sign on the cusp of the 7th house, or the Descendant, sets the tone for what we're drawn to in others, the ruler of this sign can give us even more clues to the who, what, and where of our partnership stories. This ruling planet of the 7th not only gives us the tone and energy of our partnerships but also shows where those relationships are likely to show up in our lives, based on the house the planet occupies. This placement can show you where you're likely to find meaningful connections and how those relationships might play out.

Why the 7th House Ruler Matters

The Descendant is a reflection of your Ascendant—it can be the shadow side of your outward identity. It reveals what you may not easily see in yourself but often look for in others. If the Ascendant is "me," then the Descendant is "we." I believe this is where the idea "what we dislike in others is something we don't like in ourselves" comes from. This dynamic makes the 7th house ruler incredibly important. It tells a story not just about the people you're drawn to but also about what you might need to learn about yourself through those connections.

The ruler of the 7th house isn't just about the "fun" parts of relationships, though there's plenty of that too. It can also highlight where you might need to do some personal growth—where you're projecting, resisting, or learning from others. It's like a cosmic breadcrumb trail leading you toward the partnerships you're meant to have and the lessons they bring.

When the Ruler of the 7th Is in the 1st House

When the ruler of your 7th house lands in your 1st house, relationships play a defining role in how you see yourself. Partners and one-on-one connections aren't just people in your life—they reflect parts of your identity. It's likely that you attract strong, dynamic individuals who actively shape your sense of self, pushing you to grow and evolve through your partnerships. You feel more confident when you have opportunities to demonstrate what you know and guide others.

This placement can also make you very relationship-focused. You may feel incomplete without a partner or find that your personal identity is heavily influenced by the people you're close to. This can also be the placement of a professional who deals in one-on-one relationships. Clients, patients, and collaborators all fall in the 7th house, so building identity can also come from these therapeutic or work relationships. The energy of the 7th house ruling planet in the 1st suggests that lessons about compromise, collaboration, and asserting your own individuality will be central themes in your life.

In relationships, you might find that you're quick to adapt to the needs and desires of your partners, sometimes to the detriment of your own goals or identity. Finding a balance between "me" and "we" is vital. When you integrate the lessons of this placement, your relationships not only strengthen your self-image but also give you a deeper sense of purpose and authenticity.

When the Ruler of the 7th Is in the 2nd House

When the ruler of your 7th house lands in your 2nd house, partnerships and security are deeply intertwined. Relationships aren't just about connection for you—they're about shared values, stability, and wanting to build something tangible with a partner. Whether it's pooling resources, creating financial stability, or simply feeling emotionally secure, this placement ties your partnerships to themes of value and worth.

You might attract partners who emphasize material or emotional security or share your vision for building a stable foundation. Conversely, a lack of partnership or recurring relationship challenges may highlight areas where your own sense of self-worth needs attention. If you don't value yourself fully, you may find that you attract partners who reflect those insecurities back to you or challenge your ideas around what you deserve.

Money can also play a significant role in your partnerships. You may find yourselves navigating how to share resources, divide responsibilities, or align financial goals. This placement can lead to great success when you and your partner are on the same page, but it may also bring lessons about boundaries and ensuring fairness in financial matters.

Ultimately, this placement is about learning to recognize your own value—independent of any partnership. If you feel like you lack value without a partner, it would be a good idea for you to work on this *before* entering into a committed relationship. When you understand your worth and align with people who share your values, you can create partnerships that are not only secure but also deeply fulfilling.

When the Ruler of the 7th Is in the 3rd House

When the ruler of your 7th house is in the 3rd house, communication becomes a cornerstone of your relationships. Partnerships thrive on conversation, shared ideas, and intellectual connection. You're likely drawn to people who stimulate your mind, whether that's through witty banter, deep discussions, or shared interests.

This placement often points to relationships forming in environments connected to learning, teaching, or exchanging information. School friends, writing groups, language classes, or even a shared love of books or podcasts could set the stage for a meaningful partnership. The 3rd house is still in the *self* quadrant of the birth chart, so partnerships can reflect how we feel about ourselves within our sibling group, how we communicate, and our intellect.

To nurture lasting relationships, focus on building shared interests and fostering curiosity together. Whether it's taking a road trip, attending workshops, or collaborating on creative projects, this placement encourages partnerships that grow through intellectual engagement and mutual learning. When you lean into the energy of the 3rd house, your relationships become a space for discovery and connection.

When the Ruler of the 7th Is in the 4th House

When the ruler of your 7th house is in the 4th house, partnerships are tied to your personal sense of foundation and security. Having the 7th house ruler here can bring a focus on creating a shared life that feels grounded, where mutual support and connection are key. Partners may play a pivotal role in helping you establish or redefine what "home" means to you.

You might find that significant relationships develop in private or familiar settings, like at home, in your community, or through family introductions. There's likely a desire for your partnerships to reflect shared values about home, family, and long-term commitment—and there's the potential to attract partners who resemble the parent associated with this house.

This placement can illuminate inherited relationship patterns. The 7th house ruler in your 4th house points to understanding how early life experiences shaped your expectations of committed relationships, and getting a handle on any issues you have is an important step in forming healthy bonds—although it's quite likely you'll learn a lot about your family dynamics through your 7th house connections. Breaking unhelpful patterns or honoring traditions can lead to much more fulfilling connections.

In your partnerships, you likely thrive when you can build something lasting and tangible together, whether that's a home, a legacy, or shared goals that provide a strong foundation. This placement asks you to balance personal needs with partnership goals, ensuring that your relationships enhance—not diminish—your sense of stability and security.

When the Ruler of the 7th Is in the 5th House

When the ruler of your 7th house is in your 5th house, partnerships and creativity are deeply intertwined. Romantic relationships may feel like a form of self-expression, and you're likely to be drawn to partners who bring a sense of joy, playfulness, and spontaneity to your life. This placement suggests a natural ability to find connection through shared sports, artistic pursuits, or children.

Your approach to relationships often centers on experiencing life's pleasures together, whether that's through creative projects, shared passions, or even casual dating before settling into a more serious commitment. Relationships for you need to be romantic and offer opportunities to have fun and celebrate life's lighter side.

With this placement, you might find that love and romance inspire you to tap into your own creativity. Whether it's through art, music, or some other form of creative expression, your connections with others can spark your most imaginative ideas. Sometimes, though, there's a risk of putting excitement and the thrill of romance ahead of the deeper aspects of a committed partnership.

If the planets and signs related to the 5th and 7th houses aren't particularly creative or romantic, partnerships might be seen as simply a way to procreate—where one might feel like a marriage isn't complete without children. To make the most of this placement, it's important to balance the need for fun and joy with an awareness of what you need for lasting connection. By weaving the fun and creative energy of the 5th house with the commitment-oriented nature of the 7th, you can create relationships that are both vibrant and meaningful.

When the Ruler of the 7th Is in the 6th House

When the ruler of your 7th lands in your 6th house, relationships can take on a practical vibe. You're likely drawn to partnerships where working together, sharing responsibilities, or building a life grounded in routines feels natural. Partners might come into your life through work settings, daily habits, or shared commitments that bring a sense of purpose and structure to your connection.

This placement can indicate a strong focus on mutual support in relationships. You might find satisfaction in helping your partner thrive, or vice versa, and teamwork is often a defining feature of your bonds. There's an emphasis on "showing up" for one another, whether that means navigating daily responsibilities together or supporting each other through life's challenges.

Sometimes this placement can bring an imbalance if one partner assumes more of the supportive or caregiving role. It's important to ensure that both of you feel valued and appreciated for the ways you contribute to the partnership. Clear communication about expectations and boundaries will go a long way in creating harmony.

Romantic connections with this placement thrive when you share a sense of purpose or a goal-oriented mindset. Whether it's building a healthy lifestyle, working on shared projects, or simply supporting each other's day-to-day efforts, relationships become stronger when they're grounded in shared goals and a commitment to growth.

When the Ruler of the 7th Is in the 7th House

When the ruler of your 7th house is in the 7th house, partnerships take center stage in your life. Relationships aren't just important to you; they're a defining aspect of how you navigate the world. You likely place a strong emphasis on connection and commitment, seeing partnerships as essential for your personal growth and fulfillment.

This placement can suggest a natural ability to build one-on-one connections. You might be someone who thrives in close relationships, whether they're romantic, professional, or platonic. Because partnerships are so central to your life, there's a chance you could lose sight of your own needs or identity within them. Learning to balance "me" and "we" is crucial. This placement encourages you to assert your own desires while still maintaining the harmony you crave in relationships.

The danger of this placement can be the tendency to have relationships just to have a relationship. Knowing who you are as an individual is going to be important for you in order to have a partnership that fosters growth and honors your personal goals. Without a strong sense of self, you could find yourself too focused on what the relationship provides instead of the quality of it—this can happen no matter what type of 7th house relationship it is. Taking time to develop your own identity and desires will help ensure that your connections are mutually enriching.

If challenges come up, they often point to lessons about boundaries, compromise, and mutual respect. When the energy of this placement is integrated, you have the potential to form deeply fulfilling, balanced connections that elevate both you and the other.

When the Ruler of the 7th Is in the 8th House

When the ruler of your 7th house lands in the 8th house, relationships are tied to themes of trust, vulnerability, and shared commitments. This placement suggests that partnerships can bring opportunities for profound connection, often requiring you to navigate the complex issues of emotional intimacy and the blending of resources. The 8th house is a place of "all in" energy—there's no halfway, and the partnerships you form will reflect this.

You may attract partners who are drawn to shared goals or resources, and relationships can involve financial entanglements. This placement can highlight the importance of transparency in how shared responsibilities are handled, whether that's managing joint finances or dividing emotional labor.

Relationships with this placement act as catalysts for personal growth and might challenge you to confront fears around letting others in or relying on another. There's a vulnerability required here, but it's one that can lead to deeper, more fulfilling partnerships.

This placement can also indicate a need to understand boundaries within partnerships. There are three dangers with this placement. There can be a tendency to turn every relationship into a therapeutic one, marry only for financial reasons, or commit to someone based simply on good sexual chemistry. Developing boundaries and self-awareness/self-reliance will help you avoid these pitfalls in your relationships.

With the 7th house ruler in the 8th, partnerships are a space for profound connection and mutual trust. By finding a balance between shared resources and vulnerability, you can create partnerships that are deeply meaningful and transformative in the best ways.

When the Ruler of the 7th Is in the 9th House

When the ruler of your 7th house is placed in the 9th house, your partnerships are often tied to exploration, growth, and expanding your worldview. Relationships might form with people from different backgrounds, cultures, or belief systems, or you might find that meaningful connections develop through shared interests in travel, education, or religious beliefs.

You could be drawn to partners who inspire you to think bigger, challenge your perspectives, or encourage you to embrace new experiences. Partnerships for you often come with a sense of adventure, whether that's literal travel or the excitement of learning and growing together. These connections may open doors to new philosophies, higher education, or opportunities to broaden your understanding of the world.

This placement can also suggest that you find partners in settings tied to teaching, publishing, or cultural exploration. A chance meeting in a classroom, at a seminar, or even during an international trip could lead to significant relationships. Your connections are often enriched by a shared curiosity and a desire to learn from each other.

In partnerships, you may prioritize intellectual stimulation and shared aspirations. However, there's a need to balance the lofty ideals of this placement with the practical realities of building a life together. Beware of falling for guru types. Relationships here thrive when both partners respect each other's independence and foster a mutual drive for intellectual and experiential growth.

When the Ruler of the 7th Is in the 10th House

When the ruler of your 7th house is in the 10th house, relationships can become part of your public or professional life. This placement suggests that partnerships—whether romantic, business, or otherwise—can influence your career path, your public image, or the aspirations you pursue. You might be drawn to partners who are prominent in their field or play a role in helping you achieve recognition in some way.

You're likely to attract people who are outwardly focused. This might mean meeting partners through work settings, professional networks, or public events. It can also suggest that your partnerships might be more visible to others, whether you intend them to be or not.

This placement highlights the importance of having your partnerships and personal ambitions aligned. You may find that your partner's influence or support helps you reach greater heights or that your relationships open doors to new opportunities. However, it's important to make sure your connections are grounded in genuine affection and understanding rather than only shared goals or external expectations.

Having the 7th house ruler in the 10th asks you to think about how your partnerships impact your broader life direction. Do they support your ambitions or do they take you off course? This is a key question when navigating relationships with this placement. For you, partnerships can intertwine with your public life and long-term pursuits. Building relationships that complement your ambitions and maintain authenticity and personal connection can lead to meaningful, supporting partnerships.

When the Ruler of the 7th Is in the 11th House

When the ruler of your 7th house is in the 11th house, your partnerships are likely to be influenced by group dynamics, shared goals, or social causes. This placement connects partnership with friendships, social networks, or involvement in collective causes. You're drawn to people who share your social concerns and inspire you to work toward a shared vision.

This placement brings an emphasis on camaraderie. You may find that your closest relationships begin as friendships or that you thrive in partnerships where there's a sense of equality and teamwork. Partners who encourage your dreams and share your ideals are especially appealing to you. The focus here isn't just on the one-on-one connection but also on how the partnership fits into your broader social or aspirational world.

One potential challenge with this placement is learning to balance your personal connections with your social goals. While friendships and shared causes are key to your sense of purpose and fulfillment, it's important to make sure your partnerships don't become secondary to your larger ambitions. Finding ways to mix your personal and social worlds will help you build fulfilling and harmonious relationships.

Sometimes a person with this placement isn't interested in a committed partnership, and that's perfectly fine. With the 7th house ruler in the 11th, partnerships thrive on shared goals, friendships, and community involvement. Aligning your relationships with your larger aspirations creates connections that are both meaningful and supportive.

When the Ruler of the 7th Is in the 12th House

When the ruler of your 7th house is in the 12th house, partnerships can be complex and even have an air of mystery to them. This placement suggests that relationships may be connected to themes of solitude, retreat, or institutions such as hospitals, retreats, or organizations where service to others plays a role. You might attract partners who are deeply private or help you uncover hidden parts of yourself through the relationship.

The 12th house has a way of veiling things, so connections could feel karmic, fated, or unusually intense. You may be drawn to people who challenge you to confront fears or explore the parts of yourself that you might usually keep hidden. There's a deep emotional bond that can develop with this placement, one that needs vulnerability and trust to grow.

The hidden nature of the 12th house can also mean that relationships might involve secrecy, whether it's private feelings you keep to yourself or even connections that are secret by design. Alternatively, this placement can indicate a partner who is a support from behind the scenes. No matter the nature of the relationship, with this placement you'll always need sufficient time on your own.

With the ruler of the 7th house in the 12th, relationships enable you to explore deeper, even hidden parts of yourself. While the connections may feel private or otherworldly, they hold the potential for profound spiritual growth if you embrace the lessons of trust and self-awareness they provide.

The 7th House Ruler in Action

Yoko Ono is an interesting character. Although a prolific artist in her own right, in most circles she's more famously known for her relationship with John Lennon and her role in breaking up what many believe was the greatest band ever. I don't remember what even led me to check her chart, but I'm glad I did. When I saw the placement of the ruler of her 7th house, I laughed out loud.

Ono has Mars ruling her 7th house and it's in her 12th house, very close to the 11th house cusp. If you don't know the story of Yoko and John and you google them, a picture of them protesting in bed is always among the top images that'll pop up. This reflects the rest and solitude of the 12th house but also the activism of the 11th house. Lennon was still married when he and Ono met, so they had an affair, which is a good example of the 12th house and secrets. They even married in secret!

Tracing Your Path to Partnership

Use the following prompts to reflect on how the placement of your 7th house ruler shapes your approach to relationships and what it reveals about your personal journey toward lasting partnership.

- Which house is the ruler of your 7th house in?
- What themes does this house bring to your 7th house story?
- Are there any of these themes you'd like to explore further in order to go deeper into how they may connect to partnerships and commitments in your life?

When looking back, are there any patterns you can see when you consider these house themes?

The 8th House Ruler of Intimate Connections in the Houses

The 8th house is about deep, authentic connections. It's where trust, vulnerability, and shared resources and intimacy live, and the ruler of this house points to where these themes might show up in your life. Whether we're talking about emotional intimacy, shared finances, or deep emotional healing, the 8th house ruler offers clues to where and how you will experience or can find inner communion.

Why the Ruler of the 8th House Matters

The ruler of the 8th house can guide you to understanding how you navigate the most vulnerable and deeply psychological parts of life. This placement doesn't just highlight where you might experience trust, shared intimacy, or emotional growth—it shows where you're being asked to open up, let go, and connect on a deeply authentic level.

Unlike the sometimes surface or practical connections of other houses, the 8th house ruler points to the places where relationships challenge you to grow, whether through shared experiences, emotional healing, or navigating power dynamics. It also reveals where themes of merging—financially, emotionally, physically, or even spiritually—can bring both reward and risk.

By exploring the ruler of the sign on your 8th house cusp, you can gain insights into how you approach trust, intimacy, and the deeper bonds connecting you to others. It's not just about where you might find connection but also about how you transform through those connections.

When the Ruler of the 8th Is in the 1st House

When the ruler of your 8th house is in the 1st house, the themes of trust, intimacy, and transformation become deeply personal. Your approach to life and the way you present yourself to the world are influenced by your ability to navigate vulnerability and create authentic connections. There's a sense that your identity is shaped by the deep emotional bonds you form, as well as the challenges and growth they bring.

This placement suggests that you carry a natural intensity in your interactions with others. You may find that people are drawn to your presence, sensing your ability to hold space for profound emotional experiences. At the same time, relationships often mirror back aspects of your identity that you're still learning to understand or embrace. This dynamic can create a cycle of self-discovery through connection.

With this placement, you may be asked to confront themes of personal empowerment and how much of yourself you're willing to share in relationships. Trust and transparency become key components of your journey as you learn to integrate the deeper, more complex parts of yourself into your outward identity. At its best, this placement helps you cultivate a sense of self that is not only authentic but also rooted in emotional resilience.

Boundaries may be an ongoing lesson for you, as the blending of 8th house intimacy with 1st house selfhood can blur the line between what's yours and what's shared. Learning to assert your individuality while still embracing meaningful connections is crucial. When you embrace the lessons of this placement, your personal growth is catalyzed by the depth and richness of your relationships, allowing you to step into a version of yourself that is both vulnerable and empowered.

When the Ruler of the 8th Is in the 2nd House

When the ruler of your 8th house lands in the 2nd house, deep connections intersect with themes of personal value, stability, and resources. This placement highlights how relationships and shared experiences influence what you prioritize and what you're willing to invest in, both emotionally and materially.

You might find that partnerships challenge you to reflect on your sense of security and whether it's tied to external factors or comes from within. Intimate connections often bring lessons about ownership, of both physical possessions and your personal sense of worth. There's an emphasis on understanding what you truly value and how those values shape the way you engage with others.

With this placement, you're likely to be drawn into situations where trust and sharing play a role in building something lasting. However, the 2nd house ruler here also asks you to establish clear boundaries around what's yours and what you're willing to share. This placement encourages self-reflection about the balance between giving and receiving and whether your contributions—whether emotional or financial—are reciprocated.

At its heart, this placement emphasizes building confidence in your ability to stand on your own while navigating close connections. Relationships aren't just about merging with others but also about strengthening your own sense of stability and independence. When you lean into the 2nd house energy, you create partnerships that honor your values and help you cultivate a lasting sense of self-assurance.

When the Ruler of the 8th Is in the 3rd House

When the ruler of your 8th house is in the 3rd house, deep connections are expressed through communication, curiosity, and shared ideas. This placement suggests that your relationships thrive on honest dialogue and intellectual exchange, making open conversations a cornerstone of intimacy for you. Words, whether spoken or written, carry weight—they become a bridge for emotional depth and connection.

You might find that trust and vulnerability grow through the act of sharing thoughts, secrets, and stories. Partnerships could form in environments where communication flows naturally, such as in learning settings, online communities, or even casual conversations with neighbors or siblings. This placement brings an ease to uncovering what lies beneath the surface, as long as both parties are willing to talk about it.

Sexual intimacy can also take on a mental or verbal component with this placement. You're likely drawn to partners who stimulate your mind as much as your emotions, and conversations might play a big role in creating closeness. However, the 8th house ruler here also asks you to be mindful of trust within communication—learning when to speak and when to listen and being discerning about who you open up to.

With this placement, you're learning that intimacy isn't just about big emotional breakthroughs; it's also found in the everyday exchanges of thoughts, ideas, and shared moments. When you embrace the energy of the 3rd house, your connections become a space for exploring both the depth of your emotions and the breadth of your curiosity. By grounding your relationships in meaningful dialogue, you build partnerships that are both mentally stimulating and emotionally fulfilling.

When the Ruler of the 8th Is in the 4th House

When the ruler of your 8th house is in the 4th house, deep emotional bonds and trust are tied to your personal foundation. This placement suggests that the core of your sense of intimacy and connection comes from feeling secure and rooted in your sense of home—whether that's your physical environment, your family dynamics, or your inner emotional world.

Partnerships often highlight themes connected to family or inherited patterns, pushing you to explore how early experiences have shaped your understanding of closeness and trust. You may find that the relationships you form mirror or challenge the emotional landscape of your upbringing, creating opportunities to redefine what home and belonging mean to you.

The blending of the 8th and 4th houses often brings a focus on privacy and shared emotional space. Your most meaningful connections might develop in intimate or familiar settings, like within your home, or through shared experiences that feel grounding and secure. There's an emphasis on creating a safe space for both yourself and your partner to express vulnerability and build trust.

This placement can also highlight the importance of generational healing. Exploring the emotional legacy of your family can bring clarity and help you form healthier relationships. The 4th house ruler here encourages you to acknowledge the ways that your sense of inner stability influences the depth of your partnerships.

At its best, this placement allows you to cultivate intimate relationships that feel deeply anchored. By integrating the lessons of the 4th house, you can create connections that feel like a true safe haven, offering both emotional security and opportunities for growth.

When the Ruler of the 8th Is in the 5th House

When the ruler of your 8th house is in the 5th house, intimacy intertwines with creativity, passion, and personal expression. This placement suggests that your deepest connections are sparked through shared joy, playfulness, and the pursuit of life's pleasures. Sexual intimacy, in particular, can feel like an art form—something that brings depth and beauty to your relationships.

Your romantic life is likely a significant area where trust and vulnerability come into play. You may be drawn to partners who inspire your creativity or awaken your sense of adventure. These connections can feel deeply exciting and transformative, but they may also challenge you to explore the balance between emotional depth and the thrill of romance.

With this placement, you might find that intimacy is tied to your sense of self-expression. Being seen, appreciated, and celebrated for who you truly are becomes a key part of feeling close to someone. Relationships have the potential to inspire your creative side, whether that's through artistic endeavors, shared hobbies, or simply living life more boldly together.

There's also an emphasis on pleasure and enjoyment, but this placement asks you to explore the difference between fleeting attraction and meaningful connection. Physical and emotional intimacy blend here, and you'll likely learn that satisfying relationships require both passion and trust.

When the ruler of the 8th house is in the 5th, your partnerships thrive when they honor your need for both fun and emotional depth. By embracing this energy, you can create connections that are not only exhilarating but also deeply fulfilling, where intimacy is celebrated as a joyful and transformative part of life.

When the Ruler of the 8th Is in the 6th House

When the ruler of your 8th house is in the 6th house, themes of intimacy, trust, and shared vulnerability merge with your daily life, routines, and sense of purpose. This placement suggests that close relationships often revolve around the practical aspects of life: working together, supporting one another, and navigating the responsibilities of everyday life.

Sexual intimacy can take on a grounded, consistent quality here, tied to acts of care and mutual effort. There's a focus on the connection that grows through shared habits and routines and even the work you do side by side. Building trust in your relationships may come from the small, seemingly ordinary moments where you show up for one another in tangible, reliable ways.

This placement can also highlight the importance of mutual support. You may find that intimacy deepens when you and your partner share goals, whether it's maintaining a healthy lifestyle, managing responsibilities, or tackling challenges as a team. The bonds you form often require effort and dedication, but the rewards come through the sense of stability and mutual care you create together.

Boundaries around roles and expectations can be an important lesson with this placement. It's crucial to ensure that the emotional depth of your connections doesn't get lost in the practicalities of daily life. When balanced, this placement encourages relationships where intimacy feels integrated into the rhythm of life, rather than existing as something separate or occasional.

By embracing the 6th house energy, you can build connections that feel deeply meaningful and sustaining, where trust and closeness are rooted in the shared effort of creating a life together. This placement reminds you that intimacy doesn't always need grand gestures—it can thrive in the quiet consistency of mutual care and support.

When the Ruler of the 8th Is in the 7th House

When the ruler of your 8th house is in the 7th house, the themes of trust, vulnerability, and emotional depth flow directly into your one-on-one relationships. This placement suggests that close partnerships are a space where you explore the deeper layers of connection, with trust and intimacy acting as foundational pillars in your unions.

Partnerships for you often carry an intensity that goes beyond surface-level compatibility. You're likely drawn to relationships where shared experiences, emotional bonding, and mutual growth are prioritized. The blending of these houses can bring profound partnerships, but it also means these connections may challenge you to confront fears, open up fully, and navigate the complexities of shared lives.

With this placement, commitment becomes a gateway to exploring emotional closeness and merging resources, whether that's time, energy, or finances. Sexual intimacy often takes on a meaningful role in your partnerships, becoming a way to deepen your connection and solidify trust. However, the 8th house ruler here also highlights the importance of honesty and transparency in building these close bonds.

There's an emphasis on partnerships as a transformative force in your life. Relationships may teach you about the balance between reliance and independence, as well as the courage it takes to be truly vulnerable with another person. The key is learning to navigate these waters without losing your own sense of self or becoming overly dependent on the relationship itself for emotional stability.

When the ruler of the 8th house is in the 7th, your relationships thrive when trust, shared goals, and emotional depth are at the core. These partnerships are a space for mutual healing and growth, offering the opportunity to build connections that are both deeply intimate and genuinely supportive.

When the Ruler of the 8th Is in the 8th House

When the ruler of your 8th house is in the 8th house, themes of trust, shared resources, and intimacy are amplified, making these areas of life central to your experiences. This placement suggests a natural pull toward exploring the deeper layers of connection, whether through emotional closeness, financial partnerships, or uncovering the hidden dynamics that shape relationships.

You may have an innate ability to navigate the complexities of shared responsibilities and trust. Whether it's blending resources with others or building profound emotional bonds, there's a focus on creating connections that are meaningful and authentic. Sexual intimacy can also take on a significant role in your relationships, serving as a space where trust and vulnerability come together in powerful ways.

This placement can highlight the importance of understanding boundaries, both your own and those of others. The ruler of the 8th house here often draws you into situations that ask for a deep level of honesty and emotional investment. Relationships may require you to work through fears of loss, betrayal, or dependency, helping you to build resilience and confidence in navigating the complexities of trust.

There's also the potential for a strong interest in the mysteries of life, whether that's through studying psychology, finances, or anything that dives below the surface. Partnerships might serve as a mirror, reflecting back hidden truths about yourself and encouraging emotional growth.

When the ruler of the 8th house is in the 8th, your life is enriched by the meaningful connections you form with others. By embracing the lessons of trust and openness, you can build relationships that not only support but also deepen your understanding of what it means to truly connect. This placement invites you to lean into the transformative potential of authentic intimacy.

When the Ruler of the 8th Is in the 9th House

When the ruler of your 8th house is in the 9th house, the themes of trust, intimacy, and shared experiences intersect with the pursuit of knowledge, exploration, and expanded perspectives. This placement suggests that deep emotional connections and shared resources may be tied to your beliefs, your quest for meaning, or your willingness to explore beyond the familiar.

You're likely to find that trust and vulnerability grow through shared intellectual or philosophical pursuits. Intimacy for you often involves conversations and experiences that open up new ways of thinking, whether that's through study, travel, or engaging with ideas that challenge your worldview. Relationships may flourish in environments where learning and exploration are central.

With this placement, there's often a connection between emotional closeness and shared aspirations. You may be drawn to partners who inspire you to reach for broader horizons or who share your passion for uncovering life's deeper truths. Sexual intimacy might also carry a sense of discovery, with partners who encourage you to explore both physical and emotional dimensions in meaningful ways.

This placement encourages you to bridge emotional depth with intellectual curiosity. Partnerships often become a space where trust is built not only through emotional connection but also through shared values and goals. At its best, this placement helps you create relationships that are both deeply personal and enriched by a shared vision for the future.

When the ruler of the 8th house is in the 9th, your partnerships thrive when they combine emotional depth with mutual growth. Whether through shared knowledge, goals, or experiences, your relationships have the potential to expand both your inner and outer worlds, offering a profound sense of connection and purpose.

When the Ruler of the 8th Is in the 10th House

When the ruler of your 8th house is in the 10th house, themes of trust, intimacy, and shared resources become intertwined with your public life, career, and reputation. This placement suggests that deep connections and transformative experiences often play a role in shaping your professional path or how you're seen by others.

You might find that relationships, whether personal or professional, are pivotal in helping you achieve your goals or gain recognition. Partnerships can have a significant impact on your public standing, and trust plays a crucial role in these connections. Shared responsibilities, joint ventures, or collaborations may become stepping stones to building something substantial, and how you navigate these shared experiences can shape your broader trajectory.

Sexual intimacy and emotional trust may also find an unexpected link to your sense of purpose or ambition. Relationships that thrive on mutual effort and respect might inspire you to pursue goals or create a sense of stability that allows you to reach new heights. Conversely, challenges in trust or resource-sharing could highlight areas that need attention to prevent potential disruptions in your public life.

This placement asks you to consider how much influence intimate relationships should have on your external life. Learning to balance the depth of 8th house themes with the visibility and responsibilities of the 10th house is key. Boundaries around trust and shared effort become even more essential when navigating relationships in a public or professional context.

When the ruler of the 8th house is in the 10th, you're called to integrate emotional depth with a clear sense of purpose. By cultivating meaningful connections that support your broader ambitions, you can create partnerships that enrich both your personal and your public life, helping you build a legacy of trust and accomplishment.

When the Ruler of the 8th Is in the 11th House

When the ruler of your 8th house is in the 11th house, themes of trust, intimacy, and shared experiences are tied to friendships, social networks, and collective goals. This placement suggests that your closest connections often emerge within group settings or shared aspirations or through collaboration on larger visions. Relationships in your life have the potential to be both deeply personal and socially impactful.

You may find that trust and vulnerability develop most naturally in friendships or in spaces where mutual ideals are pursued. These connections often inspire you to open up and share on a deeper level, especially when there's a shared goal or cause. Sexual intimacy can take on a unique dynamic here, often blending with the need for emotional closeness and camaraderie, creating bonds that feel both deeply personal and connected to a broader purpose.

This placement often asks you to explore how intimacy and shared responsibilities can coexist within larger networks or communal environments. You may be drawn to partnerships that begin in group settings or through shared social efforts, and the strength of those connections lies in their ability to honor both individual and collective needs.

Boundaries can be an important lesson with this placement. It's essential to ensure that the depth of your personal connections doesn't get overshadowed by group dynamics or collective responsibilities. Finding a balance between intimate relationships and your involvement in wider networks will help you navigate this placement with greater ease.

When the ruler of the 8th house is in the 11th, your relationships thrive when they blend emotional depth with shared aspirations. By creating connections that honor both your personal needs and your desire to contribute to something larger, you can form bonds that are both meaningful and fulfilling.

When the Ruler of the 8th Is in the 12th House

When the ruler of your 8th house is in the 12th house, the deep themes of trust, intimacy, and shared experiences connect to private, hidden, or secluded areas of life. This placement suggests that much of your growth through relationships happens behind the scenes, in spaces where you can explore vulnerability away from the public eye.

Intimate connections may carry a sense of mystery or require you to confront aspects of yourself that are usually kept hidden. Trust and emotional closeness can feel deeply personal and tied to your inner world, with relationships becoming a space for profound self-discovery and healing. Sexual intimacy might also hold a sacred or reflective quality, serving as a way to bridge the gap between your inner and outer realities.

This placement encourages you to explore how privacy and emotional depth intersect. You may be drawn to relationships that feel deeply private or transformative, where both you and your partner support each other in navigating life's complexities. These connections often challenge you to let go of old fears or patterns that no longer serve you.

With the 8th house ruler here, it's important to build trust both with others and within yourself. This placement often asks you to navigate boundaries, ensuring that the emotional depth of your relationships doesn't become overwhelming or lead to feelings of isolation. Time spent in reflection can help you process the lessons these connections bring.

When the ruler of the 8th house is in the 12th, your relationships thrive when they honor both the depth of your emotions and your need for introspection. These connections have the potential to guide you toward a deeper understanding of yourself, offering a space for healing and meaningful growth.

The 8th House Ruler in Action

This area of the chart can be trickier to find examples for because of its intimate nature. Information about the 8th house tends to stay private, with discussions often limited to shared finances or surface-level mysticism. The 8th house also comes up frequently in career discussions when it's tied to the overall story, but for our purposes, finding examples proved a bit more challenging.

Marilyn Monroe, however, stood out in the search for examples of famous sex scandals—and her chart doesn't disappoint. Monroe has the same ruler for her 5th and 8th houses: Jupiter, which is placed in her 7th house of marriage and partnerships. Adding to the picture, the ruler of her 7th house, Saturn, is located in her 4th house of family. This connection is significant because her first marriage, at age sixteen, was arranged as an alternative to returning to an orphanage (the choice had to do with her home). The arrangement was made by her legal guardian (Saturn), a family friend of her mother. Saturn often appears in the astrology of those in arranged marriages, and having the ruler of the 7th house in the 4th ties partnerships to the family and home.

When the 5th, 7th, and 8th houses are interconnected like this, it often points to a pattern of serial monogamy or a series of love affairs that lead to partnerships. Monroe was married three times in her short life (she died at the age of thirty-six).

With the ruler of both sex houses (5th and 8th) in the house of partnerships (7th), Monroe may have viewed sexual relationships as naturally leading to commitment. This astrological pattern offers insight into her deep heartbreak over her affair with John F. Kennedy never progressing beyond the affair stage.

Finally, adding Aquarius energy (the sign of the ruler of the 5th and 8th houses and the sign on the Descendant) to the story highlights the importance of friendship as well. With the relationship houses so intertwined in her chart, Monroe's connections blurred the lines between friends, lovers, and partners, making these roles interchangeable in her life.

If we boil it down and simply look at the ruler of the 8th in her 7th house, we could say that deep intimacy is tied to partnership and commitment. Through partnership there's the potential to dive deep into the psyche, which can be both scary and transformative. There's the potential for deep healing from both partnerships and an appropriate therapeutic practitioner.

Following the Thread of Intimacy

Use the following questions to reflect on how the placement of your 8th house ruler influences your experiences of intimacy, trust, and emotional depth and where those lessons tend to unfold in your life.

- Which house is the ruler of your 8th house in?
- What themes does this house bring to your 8th house story?
- Are there any of these themes you'd like to explore further in order to go deeper into how they may connect to intimacy, vulnerability, sex, or shared resources in your life?

When you look back, are there any patterns you can see when you consider these house themes?

To Sum It Up

In this chapter we've explored what the rulers of the relationship houses—or key houses for understanding romance, partnership, and intimacy—can show us when placed in each of the twelve houses of the chart. Each placement weaves together the themes of the relationship houses with the distinct focus of the house they land in, showing how and where these themes manifest in your life.

- **The 5th house ruler** emphasizes romance, creativity, children, and the spark of connection that brings joy and excitement to relationships. It highlights where we seek pleasure, self-expression, and the thrill of infatuation and romance.
- **The 7th house ruler** focuses on partnerships and legal unions, showing where and how we relate to others in meaningful one-on-one relationships. This placement is about building connection and fostering mutual support.
- **The 8th house ruler** delves into the deeper layers of intimacy, trust, and shared experiences, revealing where we merge with others on emotional, financial, and physical levels. It's where vulnerability and authentic connection play a transformative role.

By looking at the house placements of these rulers, we can learn where and how the themes of these houses come to life. These placements act like a beacon, helping us find and understand the dynamics we encounter in relationships and the environments that foster each kind of connection.

7

Aspects to the Relationship House Rulers

The Potential Twists and Turns in Your Love Story

In astrology, aspects are the mathematical connections between the planets and points in your chart. Think of them as conversations—some flow easily, while others can feel more like debates or conflicts. Each aspect carries its own energy, shaping how the planets involved interact with each other.

Here's a quick breakdown of the aspects we'll be focusing on in this chapter, along with their psychological energy:

Sextile (60°): Opportunity-filled energy. Sextiles create a sense of ease, encouraging you to explore possibilities without *overwhelming* effort (they do take effort to activate). Psychologically, they're like a door left slightly open—inviting you to step through if you're ready.

Square (90°): A challenging energy that pushes you to take action. Squares can feel like friction or inner tension, creating a sense of urgency to resolve the issues they bring up. Psychologically, they often reflect conflict, frustration, or pressure, but they also pave the way for amazing growth when tackled head-on.

Trine (120°): A very easy connection between planets. Psychologically, trines foster confidence and a feeling of alignment, making it easy to lean into the areas they influence. However, they can make you complacent if you don't actively engage with their positive potential, as trines can tend to be the *default setting* in a natal chart—something we easily go back to, even when it's not in our best interest.

Quincunx (150°): A slightly more subtle but persistent energy that brings a need to make adjustments or shifts. It's energy that can't relax. Psychologically, quincunxes generate unease or insecurity, making you question your instincts or feel like circumstances are out of sync. This aspect asks for patience, introspection, and acceptance to find clarity. With any quincunx, success will almost certainly come from an unanticipated direction.

Opposition (180°): A reflective aspect, where two planets sit across from each other, asking you to find compromise. Psychologically, oppositions can create feelings of being pulled in opposite directions or attracting external challenges as mirrors of internal struggles. Oppositions offer powerful opportunities for self-awareness, objectivity, and integration when you acknowledge that both sides exist inside you.

Aspects show us the dynamics at play in our chart: where things feel easy, where challenges come up, and where shifts are necessary. When we apply this to the Descendant and the rulers of the 5th, 7th, and 8th houses, we can see how these dynamics influence love, partnerships, and intimacy.

Planetary Connections to the Relationship House Rulers and the Descendant

Aspects to the rulers of the 5th, 7th, and 8th houses or to the Descendant reveal how each planet's energy shapes your relationship astrology. Each house ruler and the Descendant represent key facets of your love story:

- Aspects to the 5th house ruler highlight conflict or ease in romance, play, children, and casual connections.

- Aspects to the 7th house ruler show us difficulty or ease in finding and having committed partnerships (including marriage), emphasizing one-on-one interactions.
- Aspects to the 8th house ruler helps us see where we'll find ease and flow or difficult obstacles when we explore intimacy, trust, and the deeper bonds that shape our connections.
- Aspects to the Descendant reflect how we engage with others in relationships. Aspects to the Descendant can influence our sense of self versus others, mirroring internal dynamics that can show up in our partnerships. Knowing which planets are aspecting this point in your chart can help you understand parts of yourself or others that might help or sabotage committed relationships.

These aspects are external, showing conflicts you might have between people or other areas of your life when it comes to the relationship houses—but they also describe internal experiences, revealing how you might feel tension, flow, or the need to adjust your attitude or expectations in your approach to relationships. By recognizing these connections, you can gain insight not only into how you relate to others but also into the patterns shaping your love life.

We're going to look at how each planet making aspects to the house rulers or the Descendant might play out in your experiences and personality. In some charts there are several aspects being made to one planet, and sometimes there aren't many. None if this is good or bad. When there are many challenging aspects, it usually means there is some learning to do and self-awareness is needed to have a healthy interaction. This might mean relationships come a little later in life, after you've had the chance to grow, gain clarity, and come to understand what genuinely supports your well-being.

Sun Themes

The Sun in the natal chart represents your core identity, life force, and sense of purpose. It's the part of you that seeks to shine and express itself authentically. The Sun reflects how you approach individuality, creativity, and personal growth—it's your vitality. It also represents the ego, the father, and men.

Sun Aspects

When the Sun is in a house or forms an aspect to a relationship house ruler or to the Descendant itself, there's a direct connection between who we are and the themes of the house. The Sun can bring attention and vitality to the themes of the house, often making the matters of that house feel central to your identity. Depending on the nature of the aspect, the interaction can inspire confidence and creativity in that area or create tension and obstacles that challenge you to integrate your personal goals with the house's themes. When the Sun interacts with a house, the areas ruled by that house are central in you becoming who you're meant to be.

The Sun Conjunct a House Ruler

A conjunction between the Sun and a house ruler creates a powerful link between your core identity and the themes of the house, making these areas feel vital to who you are. This aspect brings creativity, warmth, and potential generosity to your connections, fostering opportunities for personal growth through 5th, 7th, and 8th house interactions. Relationships, intimacy, and joy become key pathways for developing self-awareness, as these experiences mirror your strengths and vulnerabilities.

However, the ego can get in the way. With this aspect, rejection or perceived failure in these areas can feel deeply personal, leading to difficulty taking risks or putting yourself out there. There's also a tendency to seek identity through relationships or become overly self-centered in how you approach the house's themes. Balancing the confidence and creativity of the Sun with the need for collaboration and connection is key to making the most of this aspect.

The Sun Conjunct the Descendant

When the Sun is conjunct the Descendant, your identity is shaped largely through your partnerships. You may see yourself most clearly when you're in one-on-one relationships or through how others reflect your strengths and weaknesses back to you. This can bring warmth and charisma to your connections but also a tendency to define yourself through others. Learning to balance self-expression with collaboration is key. Your path to selfhood often runs right through your relationships.

The Sun Sextile to a House Ruler

A sextile from the Sun to a house ruler creates an opportunity-rich connection between who you are and the themes of the house. This aspect can bring a sense of ease and curiosity, encouraging growth and exploration in areas tied to romance, partnerships, or intimacy. The sextile supports your creativity and generosity, making it easier to express your vitality and individuality in relationships. The sextile can foster confidence without pressure, allowing you to take risks and engage with others with more ease. This aspect can help you navigate challenges in these areas without feeling a threat to your identity. While the sextile doesn't push intensely like a harder aspect might, it opens doors for personal growth and connection if you choose to step through them.

The Sun Sextile the Descendant

When the Sun is sextile the Descendant, you naturally bring warmth, charm, and a sense of ease to one-on-one relationships. Others tend to respond well to your presence, and you may find that opportunities for partnership or connection come more easily. While this isn't a high-pressure aspect, it supports mutual growth if you're willing to show up authentically. The key is not to take that ease for granted, as nurturing what comes naturally can lead to deeply rewarding bonds.

The Sun Square to a House Ruler

A square from the Sun to a house ruler creates tension and challenges between your core identity and the themes of the house. This aspect often brings an intense drive to prove yourself in areas tied to romance, partnerships, or intimacy, but it can also highlight insecurities or conflicts in these relationships. The square pushes you to confront obstacles and navigate power struggles, which can feel frustrating but ultimately lead to growth.

Psychologically, the square can make you feel like the house's themes demand more than you're ready to give or that your ego is at odds with your desires in these areas. There's a risk of reacting defensively, avoiding vulnerability, or letting rejection threaten your sense of self. However, the square's pressure can also spark creativity, self-awareness, and a deeper understanding of what you need to feel fulfilled. Success here comes from understanding and integrating the lessons brought by your solar conflicts. Once you're secure in who you are, these squares can lead to extremely productive and fulfilling relationships described by the house involved in its ruler square your Sun.

Because the Sun can represent the father, a square from the Sun can indicate conflict with the father when it comes to partnerships. For example, perhaps your father wasn't a positive role model or actively blocked your love life. Getting over these father issues may be part of your relationship journey.

The Sun Square the Descendant

When the Sun is square the Descendant, your identity development is often shaped by conflict or contrast in relationships. You may wrestle with asserting yourself while staying connected to others or feel like being seen requires you to shrink or compromise who you are. These dynamics can create friction in partnerships but also push you toward deep personal growth. The key is learning to stay rooted in your sense of self without needing to dominate or disappear.

The Sun Trine to a House Ruler

A trine from the Sun to a house ruler creates a harmonious and supportive connection between your core identity and the themes of the house. This aspect often brings ease and natural confidence in areas tied to romance, partnerships, or intimacy. It enhances creativity, generosity, and self-expression, making it easier to connect with others and find joy in the house's themes. There's a natural flow to these relationships, providing positive reinforcement from early experiences or comfort in navigating these areas.

But the ease of the trine can also lead to complacency. It's very easy to fall into old patterns, going from one person to the next and having the same relationship over and over again. The father archetype can be very supportive, both directly and by modeling something you end up attracting. The trine can create blind spots to behaviors or patterns that don't serve you in the long term, trapping you in loops that are hard to discontinue. While the trine offers easy flow, its lack of challenge can prevent you from pushing beyond what feels familiar, which can result in missed opportunities for deeper, more fulfilling connections.

When we approach it consciously, the trine's supportive energy can help us build strong, fulfilling relationships. Success lies in recognizing and breaking free from any unhelpful patterns while still leaning into the confidence this aspect offers.

The Sun Trine the Descendant

When the Sun is trine the Descendant, you naturally shine in one-on-one connections. There's often a warm, magnetic quality that draws others in, and relationships can feel like an easy extension of who you are. You're likely to attract people who affirm your sense of self, but that ease can also keep you stuck in familiar patterns. It's important to stay conscious of how you show up in relationships so you don't lose yourself in the comfort of connection.

The Sun Quincunx (Inconjunct) to a House Ruler

A quincunx between the Sun and a house ruler creates a feeling of misalignment between your core identity and the themes of the house. This aspect generates a deep sense of insecurity, making it hard to trust yourself or feel at ease in areas tied to romance, partnerships, or intimacy. You might experience a sense of bad timing in relationships or feel as though you have to hide parts of yourself to make things work. This can lead to avoidance, self-doubt, or a lingering feeling of failure when it comes to these connections.

Quincunxes with the Sun can make you question who you are in relationships, sometimes highlighting gaps between your desires and reality. Learning to embrace and accept your true self is a key part of this journey, and so is recognizing that relationships may look different from what you were expecting but still hold incredible value. This aspect can teach flexibility, asking you to appreciate what you have and find beauty in the unexpected.

While the quincunx may never feel as smooth as other aspects, it offers profound opportunities for self-discovery and growth. Success comes from going with the flow, letting go of rigid expectations, and learning to trust that your unique path can lead to fulfilling relationships.

The Sun Quincunx (Inconjunct) the Descendant

When the Sun is quincunx the Descendant, there can be a persistent discomfort—sometimes subtle, sometimes not—in how you relate to others. It might feel like you're never quite seen clearly or like your efforts to connect somehow miss the mark. Relationships may trigger questions about your identity, or you may feel the need to shift who you are to make things work. But as long as you stay true to yourself and let curiosity and flexibility guide your interactions, partnerships can become a powerful space for growth. The key is not letting your expectations of how a relationship *should* look get in the way of showing up fully as your whole self.

The Sun in Opposition to a House Ruler

An opposition from the Sun to a house ruler creates a dynamic tension between your core identity and the themes of the house. This aspect acts like a cosmic mirror, shining an objective light on the house ruler, often through interactions with others. There's a constant pull between focusing on your own needs and identity and addressing the needs represented by the house, creating a push-pull dynamic that requires compromise.

This tension can lead to projection, where you attribute qualities of the house ruler onto others rather than acknowledging them within yourself. For example, you may attract romantic situations that reflect a part of yourself you deny or that are in conflict with your personal goals. Realizing that both sides reflect parts of your own psyche will lead to a fuller experience and help put an end to difficult relationship patterns.

Learning to integrate these opposing forces is key. It takes time and experience to figure out how to honor both sides, allowing your identity to coexist with the qualities of the ruling planet and the themes of the house. When approached with awareness, this opposition leads to a richer understanding of yourself and your relationships. Success lies in giving both sides time, attention, and space to thrive, instead of swinging too far in either direction.

The Sun in Opposition to the Descendant

When the Sun is in opposition to the Descendant, there's often a tug-of-war between self-definition and relationship. You might find yourself pulled toward people who embody qualities that you've disowned or that are underdeveloped in yourself. This can create powerful attraction—and equally powerful conflict. The challenge is to stop seeing these "separate parts" as detached from you and instead recognize how your relationships reflect aspects of your own identity.

This opposition can show up differently depending on where your Sun sits. If it's in the 12th house (just above the Ascendant), then part of your personal development involves working through unconscious patterns that can quietly sabotage relationships and learning not to get in your own way. If it's firmly in the 1st house (below the horizon), then there may be a strong, even overdeveloped, sense of self. In this case, relationships—and the people who challenge you—become essential mirrors for growth.

Over time, this aspect can help you integrate the parts of yourself that you've projected outward, leading to more balanced, mutual connections where your sense of self doesn't interrupt relationships forming or get lost in the *other person*.

Moon Themes

The Moon in the natal chart represents your emotional world, intuition, and deepest sense of security. It reflects how you nurture yourself and others, process feelings, and react and respond to the ebb and flow of life. The Moon reveals your inner needs, habits, and subconscious patterns, acting as a guide to what makes you feel safe.

The Moon also symbolizes the mother, caregivers, and nurturing energy in your life. It speaks to your instinctual reactions and the way you seek comfort, belonging, and emotional fulfillment. In relationships, the Moon's position can show how you express vulnerability and connect on a deeper emotional level.

Moon Aspects

When the Moon is in a house or forms an aspect to a house ruler, a house cusp, or the Descendant, there's a deep emotional connection between your emotional security and the themes of the house. The Moon brings sensitivity, receptivity, and emotional instinct to the area it touches, often making the related themes central to your well-being. Depending on the aspect, the interaction can feel emotionally aligned and comforting or stir up reactive/instinctive patterns that need awareness and healing. The Moon's aspects, whether to a house or the Descendant, reveal where emotional needs, intuition, and vulnerability shape your experience of connection to others.

The Moon Conjunct a House Ruler

A conjunction between the Moon and a house ruler creates a strong emotional link between your inner world and the themes of the house. This aspect makes the matters of the house feel deeply personal, tied to your sense of comfort, security, and emotional well-being. You may find yourself instinctively drawn to the house's themes, nurturing them as a way to feel comfortable.

Psychologically, the Moon is instinctual, and this conjunction can heighten your sensitivity, making you highly attuned to the experiences and dynamics related to the house. However, it can also lead to overidentifying with the themes of the house, so your moods and sense of self become tied to what's happening in these areas of your life. This aspect offers opportunities for self-awareness and emotional growth, but it also challenges you to manage the fluctuating, instinctual nature of the Moon.

The Moon Conjunct the Descendant

When the Moon is conjunct the Descendant, emotional fulfillment is often found in one-on-one relationships. You may crave closeness and security through partnerships and feel most at ease when you're emotionally attuned with someone else. There's often a strong instinct to care for partners or to be cared for, and your mood can fluctuate depending on how your relationships are going. This aspect can bring deep empathy and sometimes a tendency to overidentify with others' feelings. Creating emotional boundaries and cultivating self-soothing strategies is essential for building sustainable partnerships where you don't lose yourself in the emotional current of "we."

The Moon Sextile to a House Ruler

A sextile from the Moon to a house ruler creates an easy and supportive connection between your emotions and the themes of the house. This aspect helps you feel emotionally secure and comfortable in these areas, encouraging you to explore and grow without a lot of pressure. There's a natural flow here that makes it easier to trust your instincts and engage with the house's themes in a caring, intuitive way.

The sextile opens doors for meaningful experiences in relationships, creativity, or intimacy, but it doesn't push you. It's up to you to take advantage of the opportunities it brings. When you do, this aspect helps you build emotional confidence and create connections that feel genuinely fulfilling.

The Moon Sextile the Descendant

When the Moon forms a sextile to the Descendant, your emotional nature supports the formation of balanced, caring relationships. You tend to approach one-on-one connections with warmth, understanding, and an openness that puts others at ease. This aspect can bring opportunities to form emotionally supportive bonds, but they may show up subtly, requiring you to be receptive and take the initiative. If you lean in, this aspect can help you build partnerships where mutual care, trust, and emotional flow come naturally.

The Moon Square to a House Ruler

A square from the Moon to a house ruler creates tension between your emotions and the themes of the house. This aspect can feel like an emotional tug-of-war, where the needs of the house conflict with your sense of comfort and security. It pushes you to confront unresolved feelings, develop emotional resilience, and work through patterns that might feel frustrating or overwhelming.

Conflicts with the mother or maternal figures can show up here, especially if early experiences shaped how you view the relationships associated with the house. You might find yourself repeating emotional patterns or struggling to meet both your needs and the expectations tied to the house's themes. The tension of the square can highlight where you're out of sync with your own emotional needs, leading to growth when you address it head-on.

While challenging, the square has the potential to bring powerful emotional breakthroughs. By navigating the discomfort and learning to balance your feelings with the house's demands, you can create stronger, more fulfilling connections that align with what you truly need to fulfill your emotional needs and not just the habits you've previously relied on.

The Moon Square the Descendant

When the Moon is square the Descendant, your emotions, unconscious behaviors, and instinctive need for safety can come into conflict with the people represented by the 7th house, especially emotional connections like partners. This aspect can make relationships feel emotionally charged or unpredictable, as your instinctive reactions get triggered easily. You may crave closeness yet pull back the moment vulnerability feels risky, or you might overrespond to a partner's moods without realizing you're doing it. Early attachment patterns often surface here, creating moments where your emotional responses don't align with what the relationship needs. The square pushes you to slow down, name what you're feeling, and develop emotional boundaries that keep you grounded. With awareness, this aspect becomes a path to deeper maturity, helping you build partnerships where your sensitivity and someone else's needs can coexist without constant friction.

The Moon Trine to a House Ruler

A trine from the Moon to a house ruler creates an effortless connection between your emotions and the themes of the house. Therefore, you'll likely be drawn to the themes of the house to find emotional comfort. And conversely, if the affairs of the house aren't fulfilled, you may feel unsafe or unsettled. You may find it easy to nurture these areas and feel supported by them in return, creating a sense of comfort and stability.

While the trine's ease is a gift, it can also lead to falling into familiar patterns without questioning them. Emotional habits, especially those modeled by your mother or maternal figures, may seem "right" simply because they're comfortable, even if they don't truly serve you. This can create blind spots, where you unconsciously repeat behaviors that limit growth or prevent deeper emotional fulfillment.

When approached with awareness, the trine is an opportunity to easily access your emotional strengths while staying open to new ways of relating. By balancing the natural flow with conscious effort, you can create satisfying relationships and experiences in the areas tied to the house.

The Moon Trine the Descendant

When the Moon is trine the Descendant, it's often easy for you to form emotionally attuned relationships. You're naturally receptive to others' needs and tend to offer a sense of emotional safety in close connections. This aspect supports emotional closeness and comfort in one-on-one dynamics, especially when there's mutual trust and a willingness to care for each other. While the flow is smooth, it's important not to rely solely on emotional familiarity. Sometimes you may gravitate toward what feels emotionally "safe," even if it doesn't foster emotional growth. Awareness helps you make the most of this natural gift for connection without falling into patterns that no longer support you.

The Moon Quincunx (Inconjunct) to a House Ruler

A quincunx between the Moon and a house ruler creates an uneasy and often confusing relationship between your emotions and the themes of the house. This aspect can leave you feeling deeply insecure about these areas, sometimes even afraid to engage with them fully. The emotional disconnect of the quincunx can make it hard to trust yourself, leading to a sense of discomfort or failure when navigating the relationships or experiences tied to the house.

Psychologically, this aspect can manifest as an underlying fear or avoidance of the house's themes, as they can feel unpredictable or out of sync with your inner world. You might find yourself second-guessing your instincts or intuition or questioning whether you belong in certain situations. This insecurity can create emotional blocks, making it difficult to feel safe or grounded in the areas governed by the house.

The key to working with the quincunx is learning to accept your emotional responses, even when they don't make immediate sense. By embracing the discomfort and the lessons it offers, you can develop a deeper understanding of yourself and find ways to create balance and growth. Success comes from recognizing that it's okay for these areas to be different or challenging and allowing yourself to grow through the process of adapting and adjusting. More often than not, this aspect suggests that your most fulfilling relationships might not fit neatly into traditional relationship norms or societal expectations.

The Moon Quincunx (Inconjunct) the Descendant

When the Moon is quincunx the Descendant, your emotional needs and relationship instincts may feel mismatched. You may long for closeness but find yourself pulling back, or you may give more than you get, unsure why certain dynamics leave you unfulfilled. There's likely a subtle dissonance in one-on-one partnerships, as if your emotional rhythms and others' expectations just don't sync up. This aspect invites you to explore how your caregiving behaviors or emotional reactions may need reevaluating. With time, self-reflection, and flexibility, you can learn to adjust without abandoning yourself, creating partnerships that honor your sensitivity without you having to twist yourself into someone you're not.

The Moon in Opposition to a House Ruler

An opposition between the Moon and a house ruler lights up a tension between your emotional needs and the themes of the planet and the house. This aspect often plays out in relationships or experiences that feel like they're pulling you in two directions, making it hard to satisfy both sides at once. Compromise becomes the key. Figuring out how to acknowledge these parts of yourself and meet your emotional needs while still addressing the demands of the house's themes can take self-acceptance, time, and effort.

This opposition can create projection, where you see the house's qualities in others rather than acknowledging them in yourself. Learning to honor both sides of the opposition is an ongoing process. While you might never fully "balance" the two, finding ways to give each side time to operate without sacrificing your emotional well-being is the healthiest approach.

Over time, this aspect can teach you a lot about your emotional patterns and help you form relationships that feel more authentic and supportive.

The Moon in Opposition to the Descendant

When the Moon opposes the Descendant, emotional reactions and relationship patterns often feel entangled. You may find yourself overidentifying with your own emotional landscape while struggling to read or respond to others' cues, or you might flip the script, being overly attuned to others while ignoring your own needs. This dynamic often points to early experiences where emotional safety felt conditional or inconsistent. In adult partnerships, that can play out as an emotional push-pull, projection, or the sense that you're either too much or not enough. The work here is learning to hold space for both—your emotional sensitivity and someone else's perspective—without swinging too far toward self-abandonment or emotional defensiveness.

Mercury Themes

Mercury is all about how you think, communicate, and process information. It's the part of you that's curious, adaptable, and always looking to connect the dots. Mercury shows how you learn, express ideas, and share your thoughts with others. It's your mental style—whether you're quick-witted or methodical or somewhere in between.

Mercury also governs movement and connection, like how you navigate your environment and engage with others. In relationships, it reflects how you communicate, listen, and handle the back-and-forth flow of ideas and conversations. Whether through words, writing, or gestures, Mercury helps you connect with the world around you.

Mercury Aspects

When Mercury is in a house or forms an aspect to a house ruler or the Descendant, it creates a direct link between how you think, communicate, and process information and the themes of the house or the dynamics of one-on-one relationships. Mercury's energy brings curiosity and a need to understand, giving the house's themes a mental focus. Whether through conversations, learning, or planning, these areas become places where your mind stays active and engaged.

Depending on the nature of the aspect, Mercury's influence can help you express yourself clearly, develop a sharper perspective, or, in some cases, create overthinking or miscommunication around the house's themes. When Mercury interacts with a house, it invites you to explore and articulate how those areas of life shape your worldview and connections with others.

Mercury Conjunct a House Ruler

A conjunction between Mercury and a house ruler creates a direct connection between your mental world and the themes of the house. This aspect makes the house's matters a focal point for your mental exploration and communication, encouraging you to think, talk, and learn about them constantly. These areas might even define how you express yourself, as your thoughts are often tied to the house's themes. This makes it easy or necessary for you to express yourself when it comes to the themes of the house. Conjunctions can entangle the planets involved, including their themes and the themes of the houses, so talking, writing, or creating with your hands can help you untangle the ideas if they become confused.

The conjunction can make you incredibly sharp and quick-witted in the areas governed by the house, but it can also lead to overthinking or getting stuck in analysis mode. You might feel a constant need to talk things through or seek external input to process what's happening in these areas. The other trip wire can be living out the house themes in your mind only, not through experience.

With this conjunction, there's a huge potential for mental growth and adaptability, but you'll need to watch for times when overanalyzing or second-guessing gets in the way of trusting your instincts. Finding ways to quiet the mind and focus your energy can help you utilize this aspect's full potential.

Mercury Conjunct the Descendant

When Mercury is conjunct the Descendant, relationships are mental terrain; you process, analyze, and often talk your way through connections. One-on-one partnerships are likely where you do some of your best thinking (or overthinking), and conversation and a mental connection are essential to feeling close. You may be drawn to witty, articulate people or feel most seen when someone really listens. But there's a risk of overanalyzing your feelings or trying to fix relationship issues with logic rather than allowing yourself to feel the emotions and work through them. Creating space for quiet, reflective connection, where presence matters more than words, can bring balance and depth to your partnerships.

Mercury Sextile to a House Ruler

A sextile between Mercury and a house ruler creates a supportive and opportunity-rich connection between your mental energy and the themes of the house. This aspect brings curiosity, adaptability, and a natural ease in communicating or exploring these areas. It can feel like these themes just make sense to you, allowing you to connect with them in a way that feels both effortless and rewarding.

The sextile can also point to an unexplored talent or gift in the house's themes. You may have a knack for understanding or expressing these areas, but you need to actively engage with them to unlock their potential. Whether it's through learning, writing, speaking, or collaborating, this aspect offers plenty of room for growth if you step into the opportunities it presents.

While the sextile doesn't demand action, it opens doors for creative and intellectual development. By exploring this energy, you can discover new ways to express yourself and build confidence in the areas governed by the house.

Mercury Sextile the Descendant

When Mercury forms a sextile to the Descendant, communication is a natural bridge in your relationships. You're likely to connect with others through conversation, humor, or shared curiosity and may find that talking things out brings people closer to you. This aspect supports playful banter, thoughtful exchanges, and an easy mental rapport in one-on-one dynamics. Just be sure not to take this ease for granted, as nurturing real interaction (and not just clever talk) can help you build deeper and more authentic bonds.

Mercury Square to a House Ruler

A square between Mercury and a house ruler creates tension between your mental energy and the themes of the house. This aspect can feel like a mental battle to make sense of these areas, which leads to overthinking and mental restlessness. Your mind may feel overstimulated when dealing with the house's themes, as if there's always something to solve, fix, or figure out.

This square can highlight an overactive nervous system. You might find it hard to let go of thoughts related to the house's matters, replaying conversations or planning endlessly in an attempt to gain control. This can create cycles of anxiety or frustration and also conflict—especially if you feel stuck or unable to find clarity in these areas.

At its best, the square can push you to develop mental clarity and resilience. By learning to slow down, quiet your mind, and trust the process, you can turn the square's tension into an opportunity for growth. When you have this aspect, learning to listen to your intuition and not just your thoughts can take pressure off your analytical skills. It's about finding ways to work through the mental noise without letting it take over, allowing you to engage with the house's themes in a more beneficial and balanced way.

Mercury Square the Descendant

When Mercury squares the Descendant, communication in close relationships can feel like a minefield. You may second-guess what you say or what others say, leading to misunderstandings, overanalysis, or mental tension in partnerships. There's often a strong desire to be understood, but the delivery or timing can miss the mark. This aspect invites you to become aware of how your words (or silence) shape your connections. With time, you can learn to soften your stance, listen more openly, and communicate with trust so the other person hears and understands you.

Mercury Trine to a House Ruler

A trine between Mercury and a house ruler makes it easy for you to mentally connect to and express the themes of the house. This aspect brings clarity, adaptability, and a knack for understanding and communicating in these areas. You may find it easy to express your thoughts and ideas in ways that align seamlessly with the house's themes, giving you a sense of confidence.

While the trine's ease is a gift, it can also lead to autopilot behavior. You might rely too much on what comes naturally, sticking to familiar ways of thinking or communicating without challenging yourself to grow. This can create blind spots or keep you from developing new perspectives that could enrich your connection to the house's themes. The trine helps you harness your natural mental strengths while encouraging curiosity, self-reflection, and a willingness to stretch beyond what feels easy. By pushing yourself to explore beyond the familiar, you can make the most of this aspect's potential.

Mercury Trine the Descendant

When Mercury is trine the Descendant, conversations feel like the natural bridge to connection. You're likely skilled at expressing yourself in one-on-one relationships and may instinctively know how to put others at ease with your words. This aspect brings openness and verbal rapport, quick understanding, and mental harmony with partners. Just be mindful not to lean too hard on charm or familiarity, as relationships thrive when you're also willing to challenge your thinking and stay open to perspectives that stretch you beyond what's comfortable.

Mercury Quincunx (Inconjunct) to a House Ruler

A quincunx between Mercury and a house ruler creates an uneasy connection between your thoughts and the themes of the house. This aspect can make these areas feel awkward or out of sync, leaving you second-guessing yourself or struggling to communicate effectively. You might feel insecure about your ideas or find it hard to express your needs or figure out how to approach the house's topics.

This discomfort can lead to overthinking, avoidance, or feeling like you're never saying or doing the "right" thing in these areas. It may take time and effort to build confidence and trust your instincts, but the quincunx offers valuable lessons in flexibility and self-acceptance. By learning to adapt and go with the flow, you can turn the quincunx into an opportunity to develop clarity and find creative ways to navigate the house's themes.

Mercury Quincunx (Inconjunct) the Descendant

When Mercury is quincunx the Descendant, communication in relationships can feel slightly off, like you're not quite speaking the same language. You might overexplain, hold back, or find that your words don't land the way you intended. There's often a mismatch between your thinking style and how others process or respond to your words, which can lead to second-guessing or frustration. This aspect encourages you to be patient—with yourself and with others—and to stay curious instead of critical. Over time, honing your listening skills and letting go of the need to get it "just right" can lead to more genuine, responsive connections.

Mercury in Opposition to a House Ruler

An opposition between Mercury and a house ruler highlights a mental tug-of-war between your perspective and the issues represented by the other planet, especially as they relate to the themes of the house. This aspect often shows up as external conflicts or situations that force you to see both sides, creating tension in how you communicate or approach these areas.

You might find it easier to project the house's themes onto others, focusing on their actions rather than recognizing your own role. The key to working with this opposition is compromise—learning to give both sides attention and understanding. By doing so, you can bridge the gap and use this tension to gain greater self-awareness and improve communication in the house's matters.

Mercury in Opposition to the Descendant

When Mercury opposes the Descendant, your mind can be deeply engaged with how others think, speak, or interpret your words. You may attract partnerships that challenge your perspective or push you to articulate your ideas more clearly. Sometimes this aspect shows up as a tendency to debate, defend yourself, or assume you're being misunderstood, which can complicate communication. The invitation here is to listen as much as you speak and to recognize that not every disagreement is a threat. Objectivity is the secret to partnership success. Over time, this aspect can help you develop more thoughtful, reciprocal dialogue and deepen your relational intelligence.

Venus Themes

Venus is fundamentally about what you want. It represents your desires, your values, and what you're naturally drawn to. Venus is at the root of everything you attract, whether it's people, experiences, or material things. It reflects your sense of beauty, your taste, and what brings you joy and satisfaction.

Venus also speaks to your self-worth and how you prioritize what matters most to you. It's the planet that reveals how you align your desires with your values, shaping the way you seek pleasure and fulfillment in life.

Venus Aspects

When Venus is in a house or aspecting a house ruler or the Descendant, it highlights the connection between your desires and the themes of those houses. Venus's influence brings an emphasis on attraction, values, and what you want in these areas of life, shaping how you experience romance, partnerships, and intimacy.

These aspects reveal how you align your wants with your relationship dynamics. They can show ease or tension in how you attract and express love or even challenges in understanding what truly fulfills you. Venus's influence here isn't just about external relationships—it also speaks to your self-worth and how it shapes the connections you build.

Depending on the aspect, Venus can make the house ruler's themes feel easy and magnetic, or it might point to struggles with finding balance between your desires and the realities of relationships. In either case, Venus's involvement offers a chance to deepen your understanding of what you truly value and how to create more meaningful connections.

Venus Conjunct a House Ruler

A conjunction between Venus and a house ruler creates a strong link between what you want and the themes of the house. This aspect makes what you want and attract in these areas feel central to your sense of value and fulfillment. It enhances your ability to draw in relationships, experiences, or resources tied to the house, often with a sense of ease or magnetism.

While the conjunction amplifies your charm and appeal in these areas, it can also lead to overindulgence or relying too much on external validation. Fulfillment comes from aligning your values with the house's themes and making sure your desires fit with your long-term happiness rather than quick gratification.

Venus Conjunct the Descendant

When Venus is conjunct the Descendant, attraction and connection become central to how you relate to others. You're drawn to relationships that feel easy, affectionate, and in line with your personal ideals of love and beauty. You likely have a magnetic quality that draws people to you. Relationships can reflect your level of self-worth, which makes them both deeply fulfilling and occasionally fraught with pressure to maintain peace or be desirable. The key is to build connections where you don't compromise your values just to be loved.

Venus Sextile to a House Ruler

A sextile between Venus and a house ruler creates an easy and supportive connection between what you want and the themes of the house. This aspect highlights opportunities for attracting relationships, experiences, or resources tied to the house's topics, often with natural harmony and flow.

The sextile can also point to an unexplored talent or gift in these areas. You may have a knack for understanding or expressing the house's themes but need to actively engage with them to fully realize their potential. While this aspect doesn't demand effort, stepping into its opportunities can lead to personal growth and fulfillment. By aligning your desires with the house themes, you can create meaningful connections that feel both enjoyable and rewarding.

Venus Sextile the Descendant

When Venus is sextile the Descendant, forming or deepening one-on-one relationships tends to feel easy and inviting. There's often a natural sense of cooperation or mutual appreciation in your partnerships. This aspect can reflect social charm, grace in navigating the dynamics of relationships, or an instinct for knowing how to make others feel seen and valued. While the sextile might not force growth, embracing connection when it feels good and letting others in can open up pathways for emotional fulfillment and self-discovery.

Venus Square to a House Ruler

A square between Venus and a house ruler creates tension between what you want and the themes of the house. This aspect can bring challenges in aligning your desires with the realities of relationships, experiences, or resources tied to the house. You may find yourself attracted to people or situations that clash with your long-term goals or values, creating frustration or inner conflict in these areas.

The square can highlight struggles with self-worth or values, making it easy to fall into patterns of overcompensation or avoidance. It can push you to question whether your desires are truly fulfilling or if they're rooted in external pressures or short-term gratification. Sometimes this aspect can produce a feeling of not knowing what you want, which leads to false starts and unsatisfying connections.

Even though it's challenging, the square brings an opportunity for personal growth. By facing the conflict head-on, you begin to develop an understanding of what you want and learn to navigate the house's themes with awareness and honesty.

Venus Square the Descendant

When Venus squares the Descendant, relationships can stir up internal friction about worth, value, and reciprocity. You might feel pulled between wanting connection and resisting vulnerability or struggle to believe you're truly wanted for who you are. This aspect can reveal patterns where you give too much, expect too little, or mistake intensity for love. It asks you to get honest about what you want from others…and what you're offering in return. With time, clarity comes from learning to value yourself enough and hold out for relationships that are both meaningful and mutual.

Venus Trine to a House Ruler

A trine between Venus and a house ruler creates an easy connection between what you want and the themes of the house. This aspect makes it easy and feel natural to attract relationships, experiences, or resources tied to the house. You're likely to approach these areas with confidence, often finding support or positive outcomes without much effort.

While the trine's ease is beneficial, it can also lead to complacency. You might stick to familiar patterns without questioning if they actually fulfill you or depend too much on what feels comfortable instead of exploring new possibilities. This can create blind spots and limit personal growth. By using both the trine's natural flow and conscious effort, you can make the most of this aspect, creating connections that are aligned with your values and provide much greater gratification.

Venus Trine the Descendant

When Venus is trine the Descendant, there's often a natural ease and magnetism in one-on-one relationships. You may instinctively know how to make others feel appreciated, and you often attract partners who reflect your values or boost your sense of well-being. This aspect supports harmony and mutual affection and often makes it easier to form connections that feel aligned and mutually enjoyable from the beginning. But that same ease can lead to settling into patterns that feel pleasant but lack depth. Knowing what truly satisfies you—beyond comfort and ease—helps ensure that your relationships remain both fun and enriching.

Venus Quincunx (Inconjunct) to a House Ruler

A quincunx between Venus and a house ruler creates a disconnect between your desires and the house's themes. You can feel out of sync or uncertain about how to approach relationships, experiences, or resources tied to the house. There may be a sense of awkwardness or frustration, as if the pieces don't quite fit together. This discomfort can produce insecurity about your desires or a tendency to question whether what you're drawn to is "right." You might struggle to trust your instincts, overcompensating in some areas or avoiding the house's themes altogether. Timing can feel off, and it might seem like what you want is just out of reach.

The key to working with this aspect is adaptability and self-acceptance. By allowing the discomfort and learning to adjust your expectations, you can find creative ways to engage with the house's themes. Over time, the quincunx offers important lessons in appreciating what you have and aligning your desires with your reality.

Venus Quincunx (Inconjunct) the Descendant

When Venus is quincunx the Descendant, your desires in relationships may feel slightly misaligned with how partnerships tend to show up in your life. You might long for connection but find that your style of relating doesn't quite match what others expect, or vice versa. This aspect can create tension or insecurity around how love and affection are exchanged, leading you to second-guess what you want or how you are in one-on-one situations. With time and self-awareness, you learn to adjust without abandoning your values, creating space for authentic relationships that allow for difference without disconnection.

Venus in Opposition to a House Ruler

An opposition between Venus and a house ruler creates tension between what you want and the themes of the house. It can feel like a tug-of-war, where focusing on one side leaves the other neglected. You may attract relationships or situations that highlight imbalances, pushing you to face issues around your desires, values, and self-worth.

This aspect can lead to projecting the Venus or house themes onto others instead of recognizing your role in the dynamic or pattern or how you already embody those qualities yourself. Learning to compromise and honor both sides of the opposition helps create more satisfying connections. While the perfect balance isn't attainable, this aspect encourages deeper self-awareness and alignment with your true needs.

Venus in Opposition to the Descendant

When Venus is in opposition to the Descendant, relationships often act as a mirror, reflecting your desires and values back to you, sometimes in ways that feel provoking. You might attract partners who embody traits and attributes you long for but struggle to claim for yourself, or you find that your wants clash with what others expect from you. This aspect can bring both magnetic attraction and tension, especially if you tend to seek validation through others. Over time, learning to recognize your projections and take ownership of your needs allows for more mutual, grounded connection—where love is shared, not chased.

Mars Themes

Mars is about how you take action, your drive, and how you go after what you want. It represents your energy and ambition and the way you assert yourself in the world. Mars is the planet of initiative and courage—it shows where and how you're willing to take risks and fight for your goals.

Mars also reflects your passions, from what motivates you to what fuels your physical and emotional energy. It's tied to desire and determination, as well as how you handle conflict, frustration, and competition. Mars helps you understand how you take charge, respond to challenges, and channel your drive toward achieving what matters most.

Mars Aspects

When Mars is in a house or forms an aspect to a house ruler or the Descendant, it brings energy, motivation, and a sense of urgency to the themes of that house or to your one-on-one relationships. Mars's influence highlights where you feel compelled to take action, assert your will, or push through limitations.

These aspects reveal how you approach challenges and pursue what you desire. They can show confidence and determination—or highlight struggles with impatience, anger, impulsiveness, or frustration. Mars's involvement often pushes you to take bold action, but it can also bring heat or conflict to the house's themes.

Mars Conjunct a House Ruler

A conjunction between Mars and a house ruler creates an intense connection between your passion and the themes of the house. This aspect makes the house's matters a focal point for what you're driven to go after, encouraging bold steps and brave moves in these areas. You're likely to approach the house's themes enthusiastically or with a sense of urgency, feeling motivated to swing into action and make things happen.

While the conjunction amplifies courage and ambition, it can also bring impulsiveness, impatience, or conflict. You may find yourself pushing too hard or struggling to balance assertiveness with sensitivity in these areas. This aspect can intensify passions, including sexual energy, tying the house themes to deeper desires and motivations. To make the most of this conjunction, focus on channeling Mars's energy productively.

Mars Conjunct the Descendant

When Mars is conjunct the Descendant, relationships spark your drive. You may be drawn to bold, assertive partners or find that close connections activate your own assertiveness and desire to take charge. This aspect often brings passion, chemistry, and directness to one-on-one dynamics, but it can also lead to power struggles or a tendency to provoke (or be provoked). Learning how to assert yourself without overpowering others—and how to handle conflict without escalating it—is key to building strong, passionate, and respectful partnerships.

Mars Sextile to a House Ruler

A sextile between Mars and a house ruler is a supportive and energizing connection between what you'll go for and the themes of the house. This aspect supports confident action and opens doors to opportunities in these areas. You're likely to be motivated to pursue the house themes with enthusiasm, even like it's your mission, depending on other Mars factors.

The sextile offers a natural ease, but it also points to untapped Mars potential. There may be talents or strengths related to Mars and the house themes you haven't fully explored. By taking action in these areas, you can unlock new ways to channel your energy and zeal. This aspect can help you assert yourself without the potential conflict of the hard aspects, making it easier to align your passions with meaningful goals. It's a chance to act decisively and build momentum in the house's areas of focus.

Mars Sextile the Descendant

When Mars is sextile the Descendant, you're likely to bring energy, initiative, and a collaborative spirit to your relationships. This aspect supports healthy assertiveness. You can stand your ground without sparking conflict and you may attract partners who motivate you or mirror your drive. While this dynamic brings some ease to the Mars energy, it still invites growth. Noticing where you hold back or where you could pursue connection more directly will help you make the most of this easy flow between desire and action in relationships.

Mars Square to a House Ruler

A square between Mars and a house ruler creates tension and conflict between your drive and the themes of the house. This aspect can feel like constant tension, where your desires and actions clash with the challenges or expectations tied to the house. It can bring frustration, impatience, or a sense of being blocked in these areas.

This strain can lead to reactive behavior, where you might push too hard, act impulsively, or struggle to assert yourself effectively. The square can highlight where you need to learn self-control and patience, develop resilience, and refine how you go after what you want.

Even though it's challenging, the square with Mars has the potential to fuel important growth. By facing the obstacles head-on and working through the frustration, you can build strength and clarity. Success comes from channeling Mars's energy in a focused way, turning dissatisfaction into determination and progress in the house's topics.

Mars Square the Descendant

When Mars squares the Descendant, relationships can become battlegrounds or you could avoid confrontation altogether. You may feel on edge in partnerships, as if you're fighting to be heard or struggling to compromise without losing ground. This aspect can provoke power struggles, misdirected anger, or a pattern of attracting combative dynamics. But it also offers a powerful invitation: to understand how you express frustration, desire, and assertiveness in close connection. Learning to differentiate between real conflict and reactive habits can help you build relationships where passion doesn't turn into polarization.

Mars Trine to a House Ruler

A trine between Mars and a house ruler creates a natural connection between your passions and the themes of the house. This aspect makes it easy to take action and pursue goals related to these areas with confidence. You're likely to feel motivated and empowered, often achieving success with less effort than expected.

The trine's ease can also lead to falling into familiar patterns. You might rely on what comes naturally without pushing yourself to grow or explore new possibilities. This can result in missed opportunities to fully develop your potential in the house's themes.

With self-awareness, the trine can allow you to harness Mars's energy effectively while staying open to growth. By combining the trine's flow with conscious effort, you can maximize the potential and make meaningful progress in the house's areas of focus. Remember, just because something comes easily doesn't mean it can then be ignored.

Mars Trine the Descendant

When Mars is trine the Descendant, there's often an effortless ability to assert yourself in relationships. You likely know how to take the initiative without overwhelming others and may attract partners who are confident, direct, or inspiring in some way. This aspect encourages healthy expressions of sexuality and desire in partnerships, but ease can lead to operating on autopilot. It's worth asking whether you're doing what's easy or actively choosing the kind of connection you want. Staying engaged and intentional helps turn natural compatibility into something truly dynamic, lasting, and fulfilling.

Mars Quincunx (Inconjunct) to a House Ruler

A quincunx between Mars and a house ruler creates an uneasy connection between your drive and the themes of the house. This aspect often feels awkward or out of sync, making it challenging to know how to take action or approach the house's topics. You feel unsure of yourself, hesitant to act, or frustrated by a sense of misalignment.

This discomfort can lead to impulsive or misguided efforts, as if you're trying to force things to fit that don't naturally align. Alternatively, you might avoid engaging with the house's themes altogether, feeling they're too hard to navigate. Timing can also feel off, which adds to the sense that your efforts aren't producing the results you were expecting.

The quincunx pushes you to adapt and find new ways to go after what you want. By accepting the discomfort and experimenting with different approaches, you can learn to work with the house's themes. Over time, this aspect offers important lessons in persistence, flexibility, and finding satisfaction in unexpected places. It's the quincunx aspect that produces innovation and unexpected solutions in any realm, so don't be afraid to buck convention.

Mars Quincunx (Inconjunct) the Descendant

When Mars is quincunx the Descendant, your approach to relationships may feel mismatched or misdirected at times. You might struggle to assert yourself appropriately in partnerships, either holding back too much or coming on stronger than intended. Feeling unsafe sexually in partnerships can be a product of this aspect, and there's often dissonance between your intentions and how they land with others. This aspect requires experimentation: trying new ways of expressing desire, handling conflict, or initiating connection. With patience and curiosity, you can find your rhythm—one that doesn't rely on conventional roles but feels honest, adaptive, and genuinely you.

Mars in Opposition to a House Ruler

An opposition between Mars and a house ruler creates tension but also objectivity between your drive and the themes of the house. This aspect can feel like a constant tug-of-war, where focusing on one side leads to conflicts with the other. Relationships, experiences, or goals tied to the house can challenge your ability to assert yourself or push you to find compromises.

This friction often plays out in interactions with others, where you might project your frustrations, faults, or ambitions onto another instead of owning those feelings yourself. It can lead to conflicts, highlighting areas where you need to balance your own desires with the needs or expectations of others.

The opposition challenges you to integrate these opposing forces. While it's not about perfect balance, learning to attend to both sides can lead to deeper self-awareness and progress. By working through the tension, you can develop a stronger sense of purpose and learn to navigate the house's themes with confidence and clarity.

Mars in Opposition to the Descendant

When Mars is in opposition to the Descendant, partnerships can stir up powerful reactions, sometimes pulling you into conflict, competition, or struggles with control. You might attract strong-willed or assertive partners or feel like you have to fight for space, respect, or autonomy in relationships. This aspect can provoke you to examine how you express anger, desire, or initiative and how those expressions are received. Over time, the tension teaches you where to stand your ground and where to soften. Integration doesn't mean shrinking; it means choosing connection that honors both your strength and your willingness to grow.

Jupiter Themes

Jupiter represents growth, expansion, and the pursuit of wisdom. It's the planet of optimism, faith, and abundance, showing where you look for opportunities and how you align with your sense of purpose. Jupiter reflects your ability to see the bigger picture, take risks (due to a sense of optimism versus Mars's drive), and believe in your potential.

Jupiter is also tied to your philosophy, ethics, and sense of adventure. It's about what inspires you and how you explore the world, whether through travel, learning, or connecting with ideas that broaden your perspective. At its best, Jupiter is generous and visionary. At its worst, it can be overconfident, excessive, or unrealistic.

Jupiter Aspects

When Jupiter is in a house or aspecting a house ruler or the Descendant, it highlights how growth, opportunity, and belief systems intersect with the house's themes. Jupiter's influence expands the house's topics, encouraging exploration, optimism, and faith in the process. It often brings a layer of meaning tied to your personal philosophy or a sense of purpose, connecting the house's themes to your broader outlook on life.

These aspects reveal how you go after opportunities and align your beliefs with the relationships, resources, or experiences tied to the house. The aspects will show ease or highlight struggles with overconfidence, judgmental attitudes, or unrealistic expectations. Jupiter's involvement asks you to examine whether your approach is aligned with what truly fulfills you or is based on external pressures or overly idealistic visions.

Depending on the aspect, Jupiter can create opportunities for meaningful growth or challenge you to find a balance between optimism and practical effort. By working with Jupiter's energy, you can expand your understanding of the house's themes, turning them into areas of abundance and wisdom.

Jupiter Conjunct a House Ruler

A conjunction between Jupiter and a house ruler creates a powerful connection between your beliefs and drive for growth and the themes of the house. This aspect expands the house's topics, usually bringing optimism, opportunity, and a sense of purpose to these areas. You're likely to approach the house's themes with enthusiasm and a belief that things will work out in your favor.

This conjunction imparts Jupiter's natural gifts, such as generosity, wisdom, and a desire to explore, onto the house and its ruler. It might manifest as optimistic expectations or go deeper, adding a layer of meaning connected to your belief systems and life philosophy to the house's topics. You may find a sense of personal fulfillment or alignment when you engage with these areas, as they can feel tied to *your* bigger picture or mission in life.

However, Jupiter's influence can also lead to an exaggerated ego, feelings of superiority, or inflated idealism. There's a risk of assuming things will always work out without considering practical steps or limits. This aspect asks you to balance faith with effort, ensuring your expansive vision doesn't overlook the details needed to bring it to life.

Jupiter Conjunct the Descendant

When Jupiter is conjunct the Descendant, relationships can feel meaningful, expansive, or guided by a sense of destiny. You may be drawn to partners who broaden your worldview—people who inspire, teach, or encourage you to dream bigger…to be bigger. There's a strong desire for connection that aligns with your personal ideals and sense of purpose. But this aspect can also lead to overidealizing others, making excuses for bad behavior, or expecting more than someone can realistically give. The growth comes not just from being with someone who "elevates" you but also from learning how to bring wisdom, generosity, and perspective into your relationships without losing discernment.

Jupiter Sextile to a House Ruler

A sextile between Jupiter and a house ruler creates an opportunity-rich connection between your beliefs and need to expand and grow and the themes of the house. This aspect supports optimism, learning, and expansion, making it easier to explore the house's topics and align them with your sense of purpose and life philosophy.

The sextile encourages a willingness to take small risks that can lead to big rewards. It also adds a layer of meaning to the house's topics, connecting them to your beliefs or broader outlook on life. While the sextile brings natural ease, these opportunities may require conscious effort to be fully realized. There's often untapped potential—skills or opportunities related to the house's themes may come naturally but need active engagement to flourish. By stepping into these opportunities, you can bring a sense of meaning and abundance to the house's topics.

Jupiter Sextile the Descendant

When Jupiter is sextile the Descendant, there's often a natural openness in partnerships that feel uplifting or growth-oriented. You may have a gift for spotting potential in others, offering encouragement, or being a source of optimism in your close relationships. This aspect supports mutual generosity—emotional, intellectual, or even material—in one-on-one dynamics. But as with all sextiles, the energy needs to be activated. If you consciously cultivate connection through shared values, curiosity, and a spirit of exploration, your relationships can become a steady source of inspiration and expansion.

Jupiter Square to a House Ruler

A square between Jupiter and a house ruler creates tension between your beliefs and desire for growth and the themes of the house. This aspect can bring challenges in aligning your optimism (expectations) with the realities of the house's topics. You may feel pulled in different directions, struggling to reconcile your aspirations with practical limitations or competing priorities.

The square can highlight overconfidence or a tendency to take on more than you can handle in these areas. You might pursue opportunities tied to the house's themes with enthusiasm, only to find your expectations are unrealistic or your efforts lead to frustration. On the other hand, this aspect can lead to self-doubt or have you making unfair judgements of others.

Despite its challenges, the square offers important lessons in moderation, patience, and self-awareness. By addressing the conflict head-on, you can turn Jupiter's expansive energy into focused growth. Success comes from learning how to temper your expectations with practical effort, allowing the house's themes to evolve in a way that's meaningful and sustainable.

Jupiter Square the Descendant

When Jupiter is square the Descendant, your desire for meaningful connection can clash with reality. You might expect too much from others, gloss over red flags in the name of "potential," or find yourself frustrated when relationships don't live up to an ideal. This aspect can point to a pattern of giving too much—or not enough—in pursuit of partnership that feels purposeful. Over time, the tension invites you to adjust your expectations and recognize that growth in relationships doesn't always come through ease or wishful thinking. Sometimes the most expansive connections are forged through honesty, boundaries, and mutual effort.

Jupiter Trine to a House Ruler

A trine between Jupiter and a house ruler creates a natural and supportive connection between your beliefs and growth and the themes of the house. This aspect often makes it feel effortless to pursue opportunities tied to the house's topics. You're likely to approach these areas with optimism and confidence, and they tend to line up well with your personal philosophy or bigger life goals.

While the trine's ease is a gift, it can lead to passivity. You might rely on what comes naturally, sticking to familiar patterns without questioning whether they fulfill you or align with your deeper needs and values. This can create blind spots or missed opportunities for growth.

When approached with intention, the trine allows you to harness Jupiter's optimistic and expansive energy while staying open to new experiences. By combining the trine's natural flow with some effort, you can make the most of this aspect and bring a sense of purpose and fulfillment to the house's themes.

Jupiter Trine the Descendant

When Jupiter is trine the Descendant, there's often a natural ability to bring warmth, wisdom, and perspective to close relationships. You may have a talent for seeing the best in others and creating space for mutual support and growth. This aspect can reflect a kind of relational optimism, an underlying belief that partnership should be meaningful, expansive, and even joyful. Still, that same ease can lead to coasting or avoiding deeper conversations. When you meet this grace with intention, your relationships can become a powerful source of shared purpose and growing understanding.

Jupiter Quincunx (Inconjunct) to a House Ruler

A quincunx between Jupiter and a house ruler creates an uncomfortable connection between your desire to grow, learn, and expand and the themes of the house. This aspect feels like a mismatch, where what you want to achieve doesn't align with how things unfold in these areas. Timing or circumstances can feel off, leaving you to question whether your efforts are worth it or if the house's topics can bring the opportunities you're hoping for.

Jupiter's influence delivers benefits, but usually not in the way you were expecting. The key to working with this aspect is learning to recognize the value in what you have, even if it looks different from what you thought you wanted. Gratitude and adaptability become essential tools for navigating this aspect.

The quincunx can push you to expand your perspective, helping you see unintended benefits or opportunities that might otherwise go unnoticed. Letting go of rigid expectations and embracing the surprises that Jupiter brings can turn this aspect's discomfort into meaningful growth and unexpected rewards.

Jupiter Quincunx (Inconjunct) the Descendant

When Jupiter is quincunx the Descendant, your relational ideals may be out of sync with the reality of one-to-one dynamics. You might envision a partnership that uplifts and inspires but find yourself bumping up against mismatched expectations, awkward timing, or differences in beliefs. This aspect can leave you wondering whether you're asking too much or not dreaming big enough. Over time, it teaches you to appreciate growth that doesn't follow a perfect script. Deep connection can emerge when you stay open to learning, release the need for certainty, and let relationships evolve in their own imperfect but expansive way.

Jupiter in Opposition to a House Ruler

An opposition between Jupiter and a house ruler creates a tug-of-war dynamic between your need to expand and the themes of the house. This aspect often highlights tension between opposing forces, such as personal beliefs versus external expectations or opportunities for expansion versus the need for balance.

The opposition can project Jupiter's energy outward, making it easier to see growth or abundance in others but harder to recognize your own potential in these areas. This might manifest as relying on external validation or feeling that opportunities lie outside your control. There's also a tendency to overextend yourself in the house's topics, taking on too much or expecting more than is reasonable—either from the themes of the house or from others involved in this particular area of your life.

This aspect asks you to compromise and remain objective. Success comes from integrating both sides of the opposition, allowing you to honor Jupiter's expansive energy while staying grounded in reality. By balancing enthusiasm with discernment, you can create meaningful opportunities for growth and fulfillment in the house's themes.

Jupiter in Opposition to the Descendant

When Jupiter is in opposition to the Descendant, relationships can reflect your highest ideals—or challenge them. You may be drawn to people who seem wise, inspiring, or full of potential, expecting them to bring purpose or direction to your life. But this aspect can point to a pattern of placing too much faith in others' visions, goals, or beliefs, losing sight of your own in the process. Growth comes from recognizing that shared inspiration doesn't mean surrendering your autonomy. Healthy connection means walking beside someone toward a meaningful future.

Saturn Themes

Saturn in the natal chart represents structure, discipline, and the lessons that shape personal growth. It's the planet of responsibility, boundaries, and perseverance, highlighting where you are challenged to build something meaningful over time. Saturn is associated with delays, hard work, and the rewards that come from patience and persistence.

Saturn also governs fear, limitations, and self-doubt and can reveal where you might feel restricted or lack confidence. However, its influence is not just about obstacles; it's about learning to overcome them and develop resilience. Saturn represents mastery, showing where you have the potential to turn challenges into enduring success.

At its best, Saturn provides the foundation for stability and maturity, helping you achieve goals that align with your long-term vision. It teaches the value of commitment and the strength that comes from facing life's difficulties with courage, hard work, and determination.

Saturn Aspects

When Saturn is in a house or aspecting a house ruler or the Descendant, responsibility, structure, and *lasting* growth in those areas of life are emphasized. Saturn's influence brings challenges or delays, asking you to approach the house's themes with discipline and a willingness to work through obstacles.

These aspects reveal how you handle limitations and build stability in the relationships, resources, or experiences tied to the house. They can highlight areas where you feel pressure or fear, but also where you have the potential for mastery and long-term success. When Saturn aspects the Descendant, these themes often show up through relationship dynamics requiring patience, boundaries, or a willingness to grow together through challenge. Saturn doesn't offer quick rewards. It requires persistence and effort, but the results are lasting and deeply satisfying.

Depending on the aspect, Saturn can either help you establish solid foundations or point to struggles with insecurity, resistance, or feeling burdened by responsibility. By working with Saturn's energy, you can develop resilience, gain clarity, and create meaningful progress in the house's themes.

Saturn Conjunct a House Ruler

A conjunction between Saturn and a house ruler creates a strong connection between your sense of responsibility and the themes of the house. This aspect puts the house's topics front and center, making them areas where you feel a significant weight of duty, expectation, or challenge. You may approach these areas with caution, seriousness, or a desire for stability and structure.

This conjunction promotes maturity and long-term commitment, but it can also bring feelings of restriction, self-doubt, or fear of failure. You might feel the need to prove yourself or work harder than others to achieve success in the house's themes. This aspect can sometimes lead to delays or obstacles, but these challenges are usually opportunities to develop resilience and authority.

While Saturn's influence can feel heavy, it also offers the potential for lasting success. By embracing the hard work and discipline the conjunction demands, you can create a strong foundation and achieve meaningful progress in the house's areas of focus. Patience, perseverance, and self-trust are key to making the most of this aspect.

Saturn Conjunct the Descendant

When Saturn is conjunct the Descendant, relationships may carry a sense of seriousness, duty, or even karmic weight. You might be drawn to partners who are older or more established or who challenge you to grow up emotionally. This aspect can create a cautious or reserved approach to partnership—connection doesn't come lightly, and trust may need to be earned over time. At its best, this conjunction supports loyalty, endurance, and shared commitment. But it also asks you to examine fears around intimacy, rejection, or vulnerability so you can build something solid without walling yourself off.

Saturn Sextile to a House Ruler

A sextile between Saturn and a house ruler creates a supportive connection between your sense of responsibility and the themes of the house. This aspect encourages steady and practical effort, making it easier to approach the house's topics with discipline and a focus on long-term stability.

The sextile gives opportunities to build a strong foundation in the areas governed by the house involved, but it requires effort to make full use of the potential. It doesn't bring the urgency of harder aspects, but it offers a chance to develop resilience and create meaningful progress when you actively engage with it.

This aspect features untapped strengths or talents related to the house's themes and encourages you to take purposeful and deliberate steps toward achieving your goals. By combining Saturn's practical energy with a willingness to explore opportunities, you can make steady progress that lasts.

Saturn Sextile the Descendant

When Saturn is sextile the Descendant, there's a quiet strength in your approach to relationships. You may naturally seek—or become—a steady, reliable partner, someone who values commitment and shows up with consistency. This aspect supports building partnerships that grow stronger over time, especially when you choose connection intentionally rather than by default. While not dramatic or flashy, this energy helps you cultivate trust and mutual respect through small, consistent actions that build stable foundations.

Saturn Square to a House Ruler

A square between Saturn and a house ruler creates tension between your sense of responsibility and the themes of the house. This aspect often highlights challenges, delays, or feelings of restriction in these areas, pushing you to confront obstacles and develop perseverance. You might feel intense pressure to prove yourself or meet high expectations, either self-imposed or external, in relation to the house's topics.

The square can bring up fears of failure, self-doubt, or a sense of being blocked from achieving your goals. It might feel like you're working harder than others for less reward, which can lead to frustration or a tendency to avoid the house's themes altogether. Alternatively, you may become overly rigid or perfectionistic in your approach, striving for control at the expense of flexibility or growth. This aspect can also manifest as conflict with authority figures when it comes to the house topics involved, requiring either adjustments or a need to set boundaries for yourself.

While the square is challenging, it offers a chance for profound maturation. By facing Saturn's tests head-on, you can develop strength, tenacity, and mastery in the areas tied to the house. Success comes from learning to balance determination with self-compassion and finding ways to work through obstacles without being defined by them.

Saturn Square the Descendant

When Saturn is square the Descendant, relationships can sometimes feel like a relentless source of pressure, especially to prove you're worthy. You might find yourself in relationships where responsibility feels lopsided, either because a partner challenges your limits or because the weight of expectation leaves you feeling overwhelmed. This aspect can stir fears of rejection, abandonment, or failure, making it tempting to withdraw or control relationship dynamics. Over time, Saturn teaches you to set healthy boundaries, take emotional responsibility, and build connections that are strong because they're authentic and grounded in reality. Saturn teaches that intimacy is about showing up, staying steady, and being honest, even when that feels vulnerable.

Saturn Trine to a House Ruler

A trine between Saturn and a house ruler creates a steady and supportive connection between your sense of responsibility and the themes of the house. This aspect brings natural discipline, focus, and a long-term perspective to these areas, which makes it easier to create structure and achieve goals. You're likely to approach the house's topics with determination and a sense of purpose.

Even a trine with Saturn can feel heavy, but there are likely clear rewards for your efforts, which help you build a strong foundation in the house's themes. This allows you to make progress without the resistance or setbacks of harder aspects. It encourages patience and perseverance, giving you the ability to create stability and lasting results.

While the trine is largely positive, you might rely too much on what feels natural or traditional, sticking to familiar methods instead of pushing yourself to innovate or change. To make the most of this aspect, combine its supportive energy with intentional effort, so you don't miss opportunities for deeper mastery and stability.

Saturn Trine the Descendant

When Saturn is trine the Descendant, you're likely to approach relationships with commitment, maturity, and resilience. You may naturally gravitate toward long-term partnerships that offer stability and responsibility, or you may become the steady presence others depend on. This aspect supports trust, loyalty, and slow but steady relationship growth that deepens over time.

A warning about the ease of this aspect: Saturn trine the Descendant can make it difficult to leave when things aren't working. You can stay in relationships out of duty or a belief that longevity equals success, even when the emotional connection has worn out. The lesson here is to balance staying power with self-honesty, so your loyalty serves your growth and happiness. When intentional, this aspect helps you build bonds that are not just lasting but truly supportive.

Saturn Quincunx (Inconjunct) to a House Ruler

A quincunx between Saturn and a house ruler creates an uncomfortable connection between your sense of responsibility and the themes of the house. This aspect can amplify feelings of insecurity or doubt, making it difficult to trust your efforts or see the progress you're making. You might feel that no matter how hard you work, things don't turn out as expected, leaving you questioning whether the house's topics are worth pursuing.

Timing can be a major challenge with this aspect. You may feel perpetually out of sync, as if the right opportunities always come too late or too early. This mismatch can make you second-guess your decisions or hesitate to commit fully, reinforcing a cycle of doubt.

The key to working with this aspect is learning to see the unintended benefits of hard work, even when the results aren't immediately obvious. Saturn's lessons take time, and with patience, you can begin to appreciate the value of persistence and resilience. Recognizing small wins and reframing your efforts can help shift your perspective and reduce frustration.

Over time you'll find creative solutions to the house's challenges. By answering Saturn's call for steady effort and learning to trust your process, you can turn this aspect's discomfort into undeniable progress and unexpected rewards.

Saturn Quincunx (Inconjunct) the Descendant

When Saturn is quincunx the Descendant, relationships can stir up persistent uncertainty, as if you're never quite sure whether you're doing enough or if the partnership is truly working. You might question your role, feel like you're falling short, or wonder whether commitment and connection can coexist. This aspect can create friction that doesn't have a clear cause, just a vague sense of insecurity. The challenge is learning not to let doubt drive disconnection. Over time, you develop a deeper kind of maturity: the ability to stay present through discomfort, honor your emotional limits, and build stability that's flexible, not rigid.

Saturn in Opposition to a House Ruler

An opposition between Saturn and a house ruler creates a tension between your sense of responsibility and the themes of the house. This aspect often feels like a balancing act, where the demands of one area of life seem to conflict with the needs of another. Saturn's influence can make this tension feel heavy, as if you're constantly being tested to find a way to meet the expectations of both sides.

As with Mars, it's common to project Saturn's energy outward. You might see the house's themes as something others control or as obstacles imposed by external forces. For example, you could experience authority figures or societal structures as roadblocks to achieving success in the house's topics. This can bring feelings of limitation, but it also holds a mirror to the boundaries you need to establish for yourself.

The opposition challenges you to find compromise between the competing demands. Success comes when you learn to work with Saturn's discipline and create structures that allow both sides of the opposition to coexist. This process takes time and effort but leads to a stronger sense of self and greater understanding of the house's themes.

Saturn in Opposition to the Descendant

When Saturn opposes the Descendant, relationships often become the arena where you're pushed to confront your deepest fears about commitment, rejection, and responsibility. You may attract partners who challenge your boundaries, highlight your insecurities, or reflect the parts of you that you've avoided owning. This dynamic can also pull early father or authority figure themes into your partnerships, making it easy to project old expectations onto someone who isn't actually responsible for them. This aspect can create a push-pull dynamic: wanting connection but bracing for disappointment, or taking on too much responsibility while feeling unappreciated or unseen. Saturn asks you to grow up in relationships: to set clear boundaries, communicate your needs directly, and stop assuming you have to carry the weight of the relationship alone. Over time, this aspect helps you build partnerships that are authentic and honest, not fear-based. But the work begins with owning your authority and learning that real commitment doesn't require self-sacrifice; instead, it requires clarity, maturity, and mutual commitment and effort.

What's Love Got to Do with the Outer Planets?

The outer planets—Uranus, Neptune, and Pluto—operate on a collective level, representing forces that shape generational shifts and societal trends. When these planets are prominent in your chart or when they aspect a house ruler or the Descendant, they bring bigger universal energy to personal themes. Their influence often introduces larger-than-life challenges or opportunities that stretch beyond individual concerns, connecting your experiences to broader collective movements.

Aspects with Uranus (or Uranus in a Relationship House)

When Uranus is in a house or aspects a relationship house ruler or the Descendant itself, it introduces themes of independence, individuality, and unpredictability to the house's topics. Uranus's influence disrupts the status quo, encouraging you to break free from traditions and embrace new, unorthodox ways of relating to the house's themes. This planet pushes you to grow by challenging any need for social norms and stability in relationships and partnerships. Notably, Uranus is closely tied to technology and innovation, making it a key factor in forming connections through online platforms or unconventional means. Without strong Uranus influences in these areas, meeting someone via the internet becomes unlikely.

Uranus Sextile or Trine to a House Ruler or the Descendant

In easy aspect, Uranus brings excitement and originality to the house's themes. These aspects make it easier to experiment and explore unconventional ideas or relationships without the chaos that harder aspects might bring. You're likely to feel inspired to embrace your individuality and seek connections with those who respect freedom and authenticity. Uranus in easy aspect often feels liberating, encouraging healthy detachment and a progressive approach to the house's topics.

Uranus in Conjunction, Square, Quincunx, or Opposition to a House Ruler or the Descendant

In hard aspect, Uranus's energy can be disruptive, creating tension between the need for change and excitement and the desire for stability and convention. In relationships or situations tied to the house's themes, you may experience sudden upheavals or unexpected shifts that test your ability to adapt. These aspects often demand that you confront where you feel stuck or too reliant on tradition and push you to welcome personal freedom, even if it's uncomfortable.

Hard Uranus aspects can also bring restlessness or instability, making it challenging to maintain long-term commitments. They do offer powerful opportunities for development by teaching you how to balance independence with connection and how to navigate the house's themes without losing your originality.

When Uranus directly aspects the Descendant, relationships become a catalyst for personal awakening. This placement often signals a need for freedom, individuality, and authenticity within partnership—or a tendency to attract partners who embody those qualities. Whether through sudden beginnings, breakups, or shifts in dynamic, Uranus aspecting the Descendant disrupts static patterns and invites you to challenge conventional ideas about what a relationship *should* be. The impact can be exhilarating, destabilizing, or both—but over time, it teaches you how to cultivate connection without compromise and to embrace change as an essential part of love's evolution.

Overall, Uranus aspects challenge the status quo and require flexibility and openness to surprising possibilities. When you adapt and embrace change, these aspects can lead to dynamic relationships and experiences that redefine how you approach the themes of the house(s) involved.

Aspects with Neptune (or Neptune in a Relationship House)

Neptune represents the realms of imagination, spirituality, and dreams. It dissolves boundaries, connecting us to the intangible and the mystical. Neptune's energy can inspire profound compassion, creativity, and a longing for something greater, but it can also blur reality, leading to confusion, escapism, or disillusionment.

In relationships, Neptune highlights the potential for deep spiritual connections and idealism, but it can also introduce themes of fantasy, illusion, martyrdom, and unmet expectations. Its influence asks us to balance dreams with practicality and navigate the fine line between unconditional love and losing ourselves. Neptune aspects to the rulers of relationship houses or the Descendant (or other relationship planets) are major culprits in a person being attracted to potential instead of reality.

Neptune Sextile or Trine to a House Ruler or the Descendant

In easy aspect, Neptune brings a sense of or a desire for spiritual connection, creativity, and inspiration to the house's themes. These aspects encourage imagination and idealism, making it easier to dream big and infuse your relationships or experiences with a sense of magic and wonder. You're likely to feel drawn to the beauty, mystery, or artistic side of the house's topics. Neptune in easy aspect supports compassion and empathy, creating opportunities for deep and meaningful connections.

However, in easy aspect, Neptune can blur boundaries and foster escapism, so it's important to stay grounded and avoid overidealizing relationships. With awareness, these aspects help you align your visions with reality and create relationships or experiences that feel mystical.

Neptune in Conjunction, Square, Quincunx, or Opposition to a House Ruler or the Descendant

In hard aspect, Neptune's energy can create confusion, unrealistic expectations, or a tendency to see what you want to see rather than what's real. Relationships or situations tied to the house's themes may involve illusion, escapism, or a struggle to materialize your dreams. These aspects often challenge you to confront where you've lost touch with reality or allowed fantasy to overshadow practicality.

Neptune's hard aspects can bring disillusionment, especially when the reality of the house's topics doesn't match your hopes. There's also a risk of dependency or martyrdom—giving too much without receiving the support you need in return. But these challenges offer rich opportunities to develop discernment, resilience, and a stronger connection to your inner truth. And sometimes the gentle delusion Neptune brings is exactly what saves a long-term relationship when reality gets hard.

Overall, Neptune aspects require you to balance dreams and reality while you navigate the tension between fantasy and what's in front of you. These aspects challenge you to look honestly at a person or situation while maintaining the compassion, creativity, and spiritual depth that Neptune offers. Neptune aspects can lead to profound insights and connections that rise beyond the ordinary and can align you with higher ideals and soulful experiences.

Aspects with Pluto (or Pluto in a Relationship House)

Pluto delves into the unconscious, bringing hidden fears, desires, and power dynamics into the light. Its energy compels us to confront what lies deep beneath the surface, whether that's personal fears, buried emotions, or unspoken truths. Pluto's influence can feel intense or even overwhelming, often pushing us to face situations that seem out of our control.

In relationships, Pluto highlights themes of control, vulnerability, possession, and profound emotional bonds. It reveals where power struggles or deep attachment issues can emerge and where we're drawn to intense and magnetizing connections. Pluto aspects ask us to brave the shadow side of relationships: trust, fear of betrayal, and the need to let go of old patterns or control tactics. Pluto doesn't just expose; it demands engagement with what's discovered. Working with Pluto is about navigating these depths with courage, allowing you to uncover strength and empowerment within the house's themes that it touches.

Pluto Sextile or Trine to a House Ruler or the Descendant

A sextile between Pluto and a house ruler can bring opportunities to engage deeply with the house's themes, fostering emotional complexity and profound connections. In relationships, the easy aspects can create a compulsion to go deep with people you meet in the context of the house's topics. This can show up as an innate grasp of power dynamics or a natural ability to address hidden fears and vulnerabilities.

The ease of the sextile and trine can present opportunities for meaningful transformation, but it can also become a crutch. You might lean too heavily on familiar dynamics, such as bonding through shared emotional struggles or relying on others to help you rebuild. Recognizing these patterns allows you to use Pluto's gravity more purposefully, turning natural intensity into strength.

A trine between Pluto and a house ruler can feel magnetic, drawing you toward situations or relationships where going deep feels both compelling and effortless. With the trine, cycles of destruction and rebuilding can present themselves as opportunities for personal empowerment rather than crises, helping you grow through these experiences.

While the trine brings ease, it can also lead to patterns of destruction and rebuilding. There's a risk of relying on shared trauma or intense (obsessive) attraction as a default rather than exploring other ways to relate. With awareness of this tendency, you can work with Pluto's energy as a tool for development and healing instead of the basis of a relationship.

Pluto in Conjunction, Square, Quincunx, or Opposition to a House Ruler or the Descendant

Hard aspects between Pluto and a house ruler throw you headfirst into the shadow side of the house's themes. These aspects create intense power struggles, control issues, and emotional upheaval in relationships or situations tied to the house. You're often compelled to confront hidden fears, betrayals, or obsessions, whether you want to or not. There's no escaping the intensity; Pluto doesn't ask—it demands.

The square and opposition in particular can bring cycles of destruction and rebuilding that feel like an emotional battlefield. You might attract relationships or scenarios that force you to face your deepest vulnerabilities, exposing fears of loss, abandonment, or betrayal. These patterns can feel relentless, as if you're stuck in a loop of pain and reconstruction.

The quincunx adds another layer of dissonance, creating a sense that no matter how hard you try, the pieces don't fit. Trust feels impossible, and you might grapple with phobias or anxieties that seem irrational yet unshakable. Pluto's grip can feel overwhelming, driving you to try to control the house's themes to avoid facing what's underneath it all.

Hard Pluto aspects don't leave you broken, but they can leave you dismantled and vulnerable, clearing the way to rebuild with greater clarity and strength. These aspects demand that you look your demons in the eye, confront the unspoken truths, and release what is no longer relevant to you. Success lies in letting go of a need to control everything and learning to trust the process, even when it feels like everything is falling apart.

When Pluto directly aspects the Descendant, relationships become the arena where transformation unfolds. You can attract intense, magnetic partners who challenge you to confront your deepest fears around power, control, and vulnerability. Power struggles, jealousy, or emotional enmeshment can arise, not necessarily because of the other person but because of the way Pluto reveals what you've buried. These partnerships often feel fated, consuming, or impossible to forget. Over time, you're asked to let go of power struggles, release what you can't control, and reclaim your personal power.

With Pluto, there's always a choice: stay buried under the rubble or rise stronger than before. These hard aspects are a test that refine you into someone capable of traveling to the depths of the house's themes and emerging with purpose and greater resilience.

So What Does It All Mean for Love?

When planets occupy a relationship house or aspect its ruler, they become important guides to help you navigate love, intimacy, and connection. Each planetary influence adds a layer that shapes your experiences, beliefs, challenges, and opportunities in relationships. Whether they bring ease, tension, or profound lessons, these energies ask you to explore your relationship with others *and* with yourself.

Another important consideration is whether the 5th, 7th, and 8th houses connect—and while this does happen, it's not as common as you might think. Socially we're taught that relationships follow a predictable path: meet, date, and enjoy romance (5th house), then commit (7th house), and finally deepen intimacy (8th house). But for many, these houses don't naturally align. If your 5th house doesn't connect with your 7th house, you're less likely to meet someone, experience a magical romance, and then check all the traditional relationship boxes that society expects.

If this is the case for you and you keep trying to date with the expectation that it will lead to marriage, you might find yourself stuck in a pattern of first and second dates that don't go anywhere. That's why it's essential to know what you're looking for before you even begin. If your goal is a committed partnership, then focusing on 7th house activities is where you'll have the most success.

This doesn't mean your marriage or partnership won't have romance. The right person can still activate your 5th house or Venus, bringing romance into your relationship in their own way.

Understanding these dynamics isn't just about decoding your chart; it's about recognizing patterns, owning your strengths, and facing your vulnerabilities. The planets and their aspects show where you can grow, how you can align with your values, and where your relationships can bring out the best in you.

Your Relationship Rulers in Action

Here are some exercises to help you apply what you've learned and deepen your understanding of how these planetary energies show up in your life.

Ruler of Your 5th House

Ruling planet of your 5th house: __________

Planets making easy aspects (sextile, trine) to your 5th house ruler: __________

Planets making challenging aspects (conjunction, square, quincunx, opposition) to your 5th house ruler: __________

Reflection:
What or how do the easy aspects encourage or support you when it comes to love, joy, or creativity?

What challenges, patterns, or lessons do the harder aspects ask you to face?

Ruler of Your 7th House

Ruling planet of your 7th house: __________

Planets making easy aspects (sextile, trine) to your 7th house ruler: __________

Planets making challenging aspects (conjunction, square, quincunx, opposition) to your 7th house ruler: _________

Reflection:
How might the easy aspects help you with building partnerships?

What can the challenging aspects reveal about your commitment patterns?

Ruler of Your 8th House

Ruling planet of your 8th house: _________

Planets making easy aspects (sextile, trine) to your 8th house ruler: _________

Planets making challenging aspects (conjunction, square, quincunx, opposition) to your 8th house ruler: _________

Reflection:
What strengths or vulnerabilities do you notice in how you navigate intimacy, trust, or emotional depth?

Descendant Analysis

Planets aspecting the Descendant: _________

Nature of the aspects (easy or challenging): _________

Reflection:
How might these influences shape your overall experience in one-on-one relationships?

8
Where to Find Love
You've Got Places to Go and Things to Do

To find love, it's important to know where your energy naturally aligns with opportunities for connection. We've already explored how the rulers of the 5th, 7th, and 8th houses—through their planet, sign, and house placements—shape your romantic, partnership, and intimate experiences. Now it's time to turn those insights into practical guidance and identify the spaces and environments that represent your personal relationship blueprint.

There are plenty of "typical" places people expect to meet a partner, but that doesn't mean they're right for everyone. Not all of us are wired to follow the same path to connection, and our charts show us that relationships don't have to unfold according to a conventional script. Some people thrive by building friendships first, while others might skip the step-by-step journey from romance to commitment to intimacy altogether. And let's not forget that not everyone even wants a traditional partnership. Aligning with *your chart* instead of society's expectations of what a relationship should look like is the key to finding fulfilling, self-affirming connections.

Where Are the Rulers of Your 5th, 7th, and 8th Houses?

The house placements of your 5th, 7th, and 8th house rulers point to where these connections are most likely to show up. Whether it's finding romance through shared creative passions, forming a committed partnership through a collaborative project, or exploring deep intimacy in private, reflective spaces, these house placements reveal the environments that align with the relationship energy in your chart.

Relationship House Ruler in the 1st House

When the ruler of your 5th, 7th, or 8th house is in the 1st house, romantic connections often come through activities where you're front and center. The 1st house emphasizes you, especially the *you* people meet first—meaning the more you embrace being unapologetically yourself, the more magnetic you become. Love finds you when you're putting your energy into personal projects and spaces that let your natural personality shine and places where you're focusing on helping yourself be the best version of *you*.

Where You're Likely to Meet:

- **Fitness Classes or Gyms:** Spaces focused on self-improvement and personal health—like yoga, cycling, or weightlifting classes—are prime places for you to connect. These environments allow you to showcase your energy and vitality while meeting others who are equally focused on bettering themselves.
- **Public Speaking Events or Workshops:** Any time you're in front of an audience—whether at a seminar, event, or skills-based workshop—your confidence and ability to communicate can stand out. These environments make it easy for people to notice and appreciate who you are and can spark connections that feel natural and aligned.
- **Social Media and Personal Branding:** If you're active on social media, your authentic posts about your interests, achievements, or daily life can attract admirers. Engaging with others who share your passions can lead to meaningful online interactions that might even turn into something more.
- **Creative or Artistic Pursuits:** Whether you're performing in a community play, showcasing art at a gallery, or leading a creative class, these spaces highlight your individuality. Romantic opportunities come naturally when you're expressing yourself and enjoying what you do.

- **Solo Adventures:** Romantic connections may also find you while you're exploring independently—traveling solo, taking yourself out to dinner, or diving into a new hobby. These moments of independence showcase your confidence and create opportunities for others to approach you.
- **Self-Improvement Events:** Any event where you're doing something with the intention to work on or improve yourself, such as a workshop, retreat, or spa, is considered a 1st house place.

Why It Works

With the ruler of the 5th, 7th, or 8th house in the 1st, relationships often begin with someone noticing your authenticity and energy. You're not just looking for love; love often comes looking for you when you're immersed in your own passions and pursuits, especially when you're putting yourself first. So focus on activities that make you feel confident and allow you to be unapologetically yourself, and connections will naturally follow.

Relationship House Ruler in the 2nd House

When the ruler of your 5th, 7th, or 8th house is in the 2nd house, opportunities for connecting are tied to what you value, both materially and emotionally. This placement highlights environments that reflect your focus on security, comfort, and quality. Love for you often connects to shared interests in resources or the finer things in life. The 2nd house also invites you to seek out places where people share your appreciation for what's truly worth investing in, whether that's relationships, experiences, literal material items, or *you*. The 2nd house is still in the *self* quadrant of the chart, and with its link to valuing the self, a situation you consider to be an investment in yourself is ripe with potential for meeting someone.

Where You're Likely to Meet:

- **Financial Workshops or Investment Clubs:** Spaces like wealth-management seminars, budgeting workshops, or investment groups/memberships can align perfectly with this placement. These settings attract people who value financial security and growth, making it easier to bond over shared goals.

- **Luxury Stores or Art Galleries:** Whether you're admiring a stunning piece of jewelry or browsing an art exhibit, these environments attract people who share your appreciation for a particular thing. Shared admiration for something exquisite can easily spark a conversation.
- **Farmers' Markets or Craft Fairs:** Markets that feature handmade goods, fresh produce, or sustainable products are great spaces to connect with people who prioritize value, quality, and a sense of community. These relaxed settings make it easy to strike up a conversation.
- **Cooking Classes or Wine Tastings:** If you value good food and wine, engaging in experiences that involve indulgence and enjoyment, such as gourmet cooking classes or wine-tasting events, can allow you to connect with others who appreciate comfort and good taste.
- **Home and Design Stores:** Spending time in home stores, antique shops, or places that reflect your taste in aesthetics could lead to meeting someone who shares your tastes.
- **Charity Auctions or Fundraising Events:** Attending events where people are supporting an organization aligned with your values can introduce you to like-minded people.

Why It Works

With the ruler of your 5th, 7th, or 8th house in the 2nd, love can blossom in environments that reflect your core values. Whether it's through shared financial goals, a mutual love of quality, or an appreciation for sustainability, these spaces align with your natural energy and priorities. By leaning into what you value most, both materially and emotionally, you're more likely to attract someone who values you in the same way.

Relationship House Ruler in the 3rd House

When the ruler of your 5th, 7th, or 8th house is in the 3rd, love and connection are closely tied to communication, your community, hobbies, and the people you interact with daily. This placement emphasizes meeting people through conversations, shared learning experiences, and neighborhood activities. With this placement, relationships can feel casual and natural, often growing out of friendships or shared interests. Don't overlook introductions from siblings—they can play a surprising role in your relationship story!

Where You're Likely to Meet:

- **Community Classes or Workshops:** Local cooking classes, photography workshops, or DIY sessions bring people together around shared hobbies and interests. These settings are perfect for striking up casual conversations and connecting with others in a natural way.
- **Bookstores and Libraries:** Book stores and libraries in general are associated with the 3rd house, and they don't need to be in your specific community for you to meet someone. Places where people gather to read or study are ideal with this placement, as these environments offer relaxed opportunities to meet people who appreciate thoughtful conversations.
- **Cafés:** Neighborhood spots where people gather to talk and enjoy community are great places with the potential to meet someone in.
- **Neighborhood Events or Social Gatherings:** Block parties, local fairs, or events organized by community centers/leagues are great ways to meet people who share your love of local culture and connection. These events foster an easygoing atmosphere where new relationships can take root.
- **Writing Workshops or Book Clubs:** Spaces that encourage intellectual and creative exchanges—like writing groups or book clubs—are perfect with this placement. They're also a great way to meet people who share your interest in reading, self-expression, or learning.
- **Language Classes:** Taking a class to learn a new language not only expands your horizons but also connects you with people

who are curious, interested in languages, and invested in personal growth.

- **Community Volunteer Programs:** Engaging in local volunteer work lets you make a positive impact while meeting like-minded people who share your values and commitment to get involved.
- **Car Shows or Auto Clubs:** If you're a car enthusiast, car shows and auto clubs provide an engaging way to meet others who share your interests. These situations offer a fun, low-pressure space to build connections.

Why It Works

With the ruler of the 5th, 7th, or 8th house in the 3rd, relationships grow naturally from shared conversations and interests. Your local environment becomes a rich source of opportunities to connect, whether it's through casual chats, mutual hobbies, or community involvement. Staying curious and engaged with the world around you can open doors to meaningful relationships.

Relationship House Ruler in the 4th House

When the ruler of your 5th, 7th, or 8th house is in the 4th, love and connection are tied to themes of home, family, and your roots. This placement emphasizes meeting people through environments or activities connected to your private world, whether that's your physical home, your family, or your cultural heritage. Relationships often grow in comfortable, familiar settings, where trust and shared values can grow organically.

Where You're Likely to Meet:

- **Family Gatherings or Reunions:** Whether it's a big family reunion, a holiday dinner, or a casual barbecue, these settings bring together people who share or respect the idea of close-knit relationships. With this placement, introductions from relatives can lead to meaningful connections—so don't ignore that suggestion from your mom or aunt about someone "nice."

- **Home Improvement Stores or DIY Workshops:** Spending time in places like hardware stores or attending workshops on DIY home projects can bring you into contact with people who share your appreciation for creating a comfortable, welcoming home.
- **House Parties or Casual Gatherings:** Love can show up at house parties, dinner parties, or informal get-togethers hosted by friends or family.
- **Real Estate Open Houses or Networking Events:** Whether you're house-hunting or attending a real estate–related event, these settings provide opportunities to meet people who share your interest in homes, property, and creating a sense of stability.
- **Cultural Festivals and Heritage Celebrations:** Events that celebrate your cultural roots or traditions are perfect spaces for connection. Whether it's a heritage festival, food fair, or performance, these events bring together those who value their history and community.
- **Local History Tours or Historical Society Meetings:** If you're drawn to learning about your local history or preserving local cultural traditions, these activities offer a shared interest that can spark connections with like-minded folks.

Why It Works

With the ruler of the 5th, 7th, or 8th house in the 4th, love often feels most natural when it's grounded in shared values around home and family. These placements encourage you to look for connections in familiar, intimate settings that reflect your appreciation for home, family, and your culture. By hanging out in spaces that align with your roots or reflect your feeling about houses and homes, you're more likely to find relationships that feel authentic and meaningful.

Relationship House Ruler in the 5th House

When the ruler of your 5th, 7th, or 8th house is in the 5th, you're naturally aligned with the energy of romance, creativity, and joy. This placement suggests that love can bloom in places where people gather to express themselves, have fun, and enjoy life's pleasures. The 5th house thrives on playfulness and passion, so your best romantic opportunities are likely to arise in settings that emphasize fun, performance, sport, gambling, or shared creative pursuits. This placement also highlights connections through activities involving children, offering a unique way to meet someone special.

Where You're Likely to Meet:

- **Art Galleries or Creative Workshops:** Whether you're checking out an art exhibit, attending a painting class, or joining a photography workshop, these spaces attract people who share your appreciation for creativity and beauty. Romantic sparks can fly in environments that promote inspiration and self-expression.
- **Theater Productions or Music Concerts:** Love the buzz of a live performance? Attending theater, improv, or concerts provides vibrant energy and a shared love of creativity and entertainment—perfect for meeting someone who enjoys life as much as you do.
- **Social Clubs or Dance Classes:** From salsa and swing nights to community theater or pottery groups, these activities bring people together for shared joy. Joining a club or class geared toward creativity not only sparks joy but also creates opportunities to connect with those who share your interests—not to mention, the two of you are potentially both operating outside your comfort zones, which in itself can foster connection.
- **Music Festivals or Outdoor Events:** Music festivals, open mic nights, or even outdoor movie screenings can create an electrifying atmosphere where you can bond over shared tastes and a love of entertainment.
- **Sports Leagues or Recreational Teams:** If you enjoy physical activity, joining a sports league or recreational team is a great way to meet someone. Activities like tennis, soccer, or even a frisbee game offer the perfect mix of teamwork and playful competition.

- **Places Where One Gambles:** Gambling is associated with the 5th house, so casinos, casino nights, poker tournaments, or situations that involve gambling have great potential for making a connection (as long as you or whoever you meet are not feeding an addiction).
- **Activities with Children:** For those involved in activities centered on kids—like volunteering at a school event, attending a child's soccer game, or joining a parenting group—romantic opportunities can naturally arise while bonding over shared family-oriented values.

Why It Works

With the ruler of the 5th, 7th, or 8th house in the 5th, romance thrives in environments full of joy, energy, and creativity. These settings support your natural ability to connect through fun and creativity. Whether it's performing, playing, gambling, or creating, love is most likely to find you when you're fully embracing your passions and enjoying life.

Note: If you have the ruler of the 5th house *in* the 5th house, read the special section at the end of this chapter.

Relationship House Ruler in the 6th House

When the ruler of your 5th, 7th, or 8th house is in the 6th, romantic opportunities are closely tied to daily routines, work environments, and activities focused on health, service, and small animals. Love is likely to find you in places where people are prioritizing well-being, productivity, improving habits, or caring for others. This placement suggests that connections can grow naturally out of shared habits or a mutual commitment to improving daily life, whether through work, fitness, diet, or acts of kindness.

Where You're Likely to Meet:

- **Pet Stores, Dog Parks, or Animal Shelters:** These spaces bring together fellow animal lovers, making it easy to connect over shared experiences and a mutual appreciation for pets. Volunteering at shelters, attending pet-friendly events, waiting at the groomers, or even simply shopping for pet supplies can open the door to meeting someone special.

- **Healthy Habit-Building Workshops or Memberships:** Workshops or memberships focused on creating healthier routines—such as mindfulness programs, meal-prepping groups, or self-improvement challenges—are great for meeting like-minded people who value growth and wellness.
- **Group Fitness Challenges or Classes:** Join a boot camp, running club, or spin class to bond with others who share your commitment to health. These activities foster teamwork and fellowship and can be the perfect environment for sparks to fly.
- **Healthy Cooking Classes or Meal Prep Groups:** Cooking classes focused on nutritious meals or organized meal-prepping sessions are interactive and fun, offering an excellent opportunity to connect with someone who shares your interest in creating better eating habits.
- **Workplace or Professional Events:** Don't underestimate the potential for romantic connections at work. Professional conferences, networking events, or even casual workplace interactions can lead to connecting with people who have things in common.
- **Yoga Studios or Wellness Retreats:** Wellness-focused spaces such as yoga studios or weekend retreats (focusing on your ongoing wellness) offer a calming, health-centered vibe that's ideal for meeting potential partners who share your mindful approach to life.
- **Farmers' Markets or Health Food Stores:** These settings can naturally attract health-conscious individuals. Whether you're picking up produce or browsing organic snacks, casual conversations about healthy choices can spark something deeper.

Why It Works

With the ruler of the 5th, 7th, or 8th house in the 6th, love often comes through the steady (or not so steady) flow of daily life. Whether it's through shared routines, care for furry family members, or a commitment to health and service, these connections can be grounded and supportive. By exploring activities that align with your everyday priorities, you're likely to meet someone who shares your standards and complements your lifestyle.

Relationship House Ruler in the 7th House

When the ruler of your 7th house is in the 7th itself, relationships and partnerships are central themes in your life. Love and connection come naturally to you, often through activities that emphasize one-on-one interactions, formal partnerships, or shared commitments. This placement prefers environments where mutual respect, collaboration, and balance are key. Interestingly, the 7th house also governs open enemies—so for you, there's always the possibility a spark of love could come from a surprising rivalry or resolving a conflict.

You're likely to have luck in spaces that focus on partnership dynamics, whether through traditional dating, professional matchmaking, or situations where meaningful connections can develop organically.

Where You're Likely to Meet:

- **Diplomatic or Mediation Events:** Attending events or workshops focused on diplomacy, conflict resolution, or mediation can hold opportunities. These places attract people who likely value partnership, harmony, and the ability to work together—key qualities for building a strong partnership.
- **Legal or Contract Meetings:** Whether it's negotiating business deals, signing contracts, or even meeting with legal professionals, these interactions can provide opportunities to connect with those who are serious about commitment and mutual benefit.
- **Matchmaking Services or Dating Sites:** You'll likely find success using matchmaking services or dating apps that emphasize quality over quantity. With this placement, you're aligned with anything related to meaningful, direct, one-on-one interactions focused on commitment rather than casual encounters.

- **Networking or Professional Events:** If you are in a 7th house profession (anything to do with working one-on-one with people), then formal networking settings allow you to meet people who value partnership, whether romantic, business-related, or collaborative. A professional atmosphere might provide just the right balance of structure and personal connection.

Why It Works

With the ruler of your 7th in the 7th, you're naturally drawn to partnerships. Love can find you in any environment that emphasizes commitment to another, contracts, cooperation, and respect. By focusing on activities and spaces where a one-on-one connection is a priority, you're likely to form relationships that connect to your appreciation for partnership and shared growth.

Note: If you have the ruler of the 7th house *in* the 7th house, read the special section at the end of the chapter.

Relationship House Ruler in the 8th House

When the ruler of your 5th, 7th, or 8th house is in the 8th, love and connection are deeply tied to themes of intimacy, shared resources, and profound emotional experiences. This placement emphasizes meeting people in environments where vulnerability, mysticism, transformation, and depth are at the forefront. The 8th house thrives on the exploration of life's hidden layers, whether through finance, psychology, or even esoteric and/or metaphysical subjects. With this placement, relationships can form in places that encourage trust and the merging of energies—emotionally, physically, psychically, or financially.

Where You're Likely to Meet:

- **Financial Planning Seminars or Investment Groups:** Spaces focused on wealth management, joint ventures, or long-term financial planning are a natural fit with this placement. These settings provide opportunities to connect with people who value shared goals and commitment.

- **Therapy Sessions or Support Groups:** Participating in counseling workshops, support groups, or group therapy settings can lead to deep emotional connections. These environments create a safe space for vulnerability and often attract people looking to grow emotionally.
- **Intensive Workshops or Transformational Retreats:** Workshops or retreats that focus on personal growth, shadow work, or transformative experiences are excellent places for you to connect with like-minded individuals who value introspection and emotional depth.
- **Occult Workshops or Metaphysical Stores:** Whether you're attending a tarot reading, exploring astrology at a metaphysical shop, or participating in an alchemy workshop, these spaces draw individuals who are curious about life's mysteries and the hidden things that connect us.
- **Mystery or Crime Book Clubs:** For the intellectually curious, joining a mystery or crime book club offers a novel setting to connect with others who are drawn to exploring the darker themes of life. These groups encourage thoughtful discussions and foster connections over shared interests.
- **Places of Sexual Exploration:** For those open to it, environments that emphasize sexual expression and exploration may align with this placement. From workshops and retreats to private clubs, these spaces provide opportunities to connect with others in a deeply intimate and authentic way.
- **Financial Institutions or Tax Season Opportunities:** Even practical spaces such as your accountant's office, a bank, or a tax seminar can create opportunities for connection. These settings emphasize shared resources and the collaboration needed to navigate finances.

Why It Works

With the ruler of the 5th, 7th, or 8th house in the 8th, relationships are anything but surface-level. Love finds you in places that encourage trust, emotional depth, and shared transformation. By leaning into spaces where people explore life's complexities—whether emotional, financial, or mystical—you're likely to meet someone who matches your need for deep, meaningful connections.

Note: If you have the ruler of the 8th house *in* the 8th house, read the special section at the end of this chapter.

Relationship House Ruler in the 9th House

When the ruler of your 5th, 7th, or 8th house is in the 9th, love is deeply connected to exploration, learning, and broadening your horizons. This placement highlights romantic opportunities tied to travel, higher education, cultural exchange, and spiritual or philosophical pursuits. Relationships often form in settings that encourage personal growth and expose you to new ideas, perspectives, and adventures. There's also a strong potential for romance with someone from a different cultural, social, or religious background, adding an element of excitement and discovery to your connections.

Where You're Likely to Meet:

- **Travel and Adventure:** Whether you're on a vacation abroad or a backpacking trip or participating in a cultural exchange program, these experiences open doors to new people and perspectives. Travel helps you meet someone who shares your love of adventure and exploration.
- **University or Educational Settings:** Enroll in courses, attend lectures, or participate in workshops and seminars. Higher education environments naturally align with this placement, offering opportunities to connect with individuals who value learning and intellectual curiosity.
- **Cultural or International Events:** Attend events that celebrate diversity, such as cultural festivals, international film screenings, or global conferences. These spaces attract people from varied backgrounds, creating the perfect setting for meaningful and dynamic connections.

- **Philosophy or Study Groups:** Join a philosophy club, a study group, a church group, or even a book club focused on topics such as culture, personal growth, or spirituality. These gatherings foster deep conversations and a shared passion for big ideas, providing a strong foundation for connection.
- **Language Classes or Cultural Exchange Programs:** Learning a new language in an immersive situation or participating in programs focused on cultural exchange can create natural opportunities for connection. These settings emphasize mutual learning and the joy of discovering new perspectives.
- **Spiritual Retreats or Religious Gatherings:** Attend retreats, workshops, or gatherings focused on spiritual or philosophical discussions. These settings attract people seeking meaning and understanding, offering a great place to potentially form heartfelt and purposeful relationships.
- **Adventure Sports or Outdoor Activities:** Things like hiking, rock climbing, or group tours focused on outdoor exploration align with the 9th house themes of adventure and personal growth.

Why It Works

With the ruler of the 5th, 7th, or 8th house in the 9th, love grows in environments that push boundaries and encourage exploration. Whether it's through travel, education, or cultural exchange, relationships thrive when they're built on a shared love of adventure and discovery. By seeking out spaces that inspire growth and broadening your worldview, you're likely to find connections that are both meaningful and fulfilling.

Relationship House Ruler in the 10th House

When the ruler of your 5th, 7th, or 8th house is in the 10th, love and connection are tied to your career, public presence, and social status. This placement highlights opportunities for romance through professional settings, ambition-driven activities, and events connected to your public life. Considering the 10th house's association with the dominant parent, there's even the potential to meet someone through parental introductions or connections. With this placement, relationships often revolve around shared goals, respect for each other's achievements, and a mutual appreciation for success.

Where You're Likely to Meet:

- **Professional Conferences or Networking Events:** Industry conferences, professional association meetings, and networking events are prime locations for you to connect with people who share your career aspirations.
- **Mentorship Programs or Career Development Workshops:** Joining mentorship programs or career-focused workshops allows you to connect with mentors, mentees, or peers who are equally committed to professional growth.
- **Workplace or Corporate Functions:** Company retreats, team-building activities, or even office parties provide a relaxed setting to engage with colleagues and peers. These events are ideal for forming connections outside of the usual work environment, making it easier for a different type of relationship to bloom.
- **Public Speaking Engagements or Award Ceremonies:** Attending or participating in public-facing events—such as giving a speech, receiving an award, or showcasing your accomplishments—puts you in the spotlight. These settings naturally attract people who admire your drive and success, offering an organic way to connect.
- **Parent-Linked Social Circles:** With the 10th house's connection to the dominant parent, introductions through a parent's social or professional circle could lead to significant connections. Keep an open mind when family suggests potential introductions—there's a chance they see something you don't!
- **Charity Events or Fundraisers:** High-profile charity galas or fundraising events offer opportunities to meet people who align with your values and share a commitment to making an impact.
- **Public-Focused Volunteer Work:** Engaging in community service or volunteering for public initiatives can introduce you to individuals who are equally driven to contribute to society.

Why It Works

With the ruler of the 5th, 7th, or 8th house in the 10th, love often comes through shared professional goals, mutual respect for achievements, and public interactions. By placing yourself in environments that emphasize reputation, career, ambition, and public presence, you're likely to meet someone who not only admires your drive but also complements your vision for success. With this placement, any situation where you're potentially visible to the world can hold the potential for meeting someone special.

Relationship House Ruler in the 11th House

When the ruler of your 5th, 7th, or 8th house is in the 11th, love and connection are deeply tied to organizations, your social circles, friendships, and group activities. This placement emphasizes meeting people through shared goals, community involvement, and collaborative projects. The 11th house often bridges the gap between friendship and romance, suggesting you may meet a romantic partner through mutual friends or even become romantically involved with someone already in your friend group. Love for you thrives in spaces that foster camaraderie and a shared sense of purpose.

Where You're Likely to Meet:

- **Clubs or Group Activities:** Whether it's an in-person hobby group, an online community, or a local club for special interests, these spaces offer opportunities to connect with like-minded individuals. By participating in activities that align with your passions—like book clubs, gaming groups, or fitness classes—you create natural openings for potential relationships.
- **Volunteer Organizations or Charity Events:** Engaging in volunteer work or participating in charity events (especially if the 12th house is also involved) is a great way to meet people who value giving back. Whether you're helping out at a food drive, fundraising for a cause, or volunteering on the board of a special interest group, these activities attract people who share your interests.

- **Networking Events or Meetups:** Attending professional networking events, social meetups, or gatherings centered around shared goals can connect you with potential partners. These environments encourage collaboration and provide opportunities for connecting through mutual interests.
- **Social or Political Activism:** Getting involved in social or political activism, protests, or advocacy work aligns perfectly with this placement. These spaces often attract passionate individuals who share your drive to create positive change, offering a unique foundation for connection.
- **Collaborative Projects or Team Efforts:** Joining a team for a group project, a community initiative, or even a collaborative artistic activity can introduce you to people who value teamwork and shared goals. Love can blossom naturally in environments where you're working together toward something meaningful.
- **Friend Introductions:** With this placement, your friends can be the key to meeting potential partners. Be open to invitations to social events or setups, as someone in your extended social circle may be your next romantic connection.

Why It Works

With the ruler of the 5th, 7th, or 8th house in the 11th, love is woven into the fabric of your social life. By leaning into group activities, volunteer work, or collaborative efforts, you're likely to find romantic connections that grow out of shared passions and mutual goals. This placement thrives on the energy of friendship and collective purpose, making relationships meaningful and fulfilling.

Relationship House Ruler in the 12th House

When the ruler of your 5th, 7th, or 8th house is in the 12th, love and connection often unfold in quiet, introspective, or hidden spaces. This placement emphasizes romantic opportunities tied to solitude, spiritual growth, and compassionate service. Relationships here can begin in places where reflection, empathy, and healing are the focus. Additionally, the 12th house governs large animals, suggesting that settings dedicated to their care may also open the door to meaningful romantic connections.

Where You're Likely to Meet:

- **Spiritual Retreats or Meditation Centers:** Retreats, meditation groups, or yoga classes provide introspective environments ideal for connecting with like-minded individuals. These spaces can encourage deep, meaningful interactions with people who value inner growth and spiritual connection.
- **Hospitals or Care Facilities:** Volunteering or working in hospitals, care homes, or support organizations can introduce you to compassionate and empathetic people. Shared dedication to helping others can create a strong emotional foundation for a relationship.
- **Charity Work or Nonprofit Organizations:** Engaging in charitable activities or volunteering for nonprofit organizations focused on selfless service aligns well with this placement. These spaces usually attract people who share your desire to give back and make a difference, creating fertile ground for romantic connections.
- **Animal Sanctuaries or Equestrian Centers:** With the 12th house's connection to large animals, volunteering or participating in activities at sanctuaries, equestrian centers, or large animal care facilities can lead to meeting people who share your love for animals and dedication to their well-being.
- **Creative or Healing Workshops:** Join art therapy sessions, music workshops, or other healing-focused activities. These behind-the-scenes, creative spaces foster vulnerability and emotional depth, offering opportunities to bond over shared interests and a desire for self-reflection.
- **Libraries or Quiet Public Spaces:** Quiet, reflective environments provide opportunities for subtle, meaningful connections. These settings attract individuals who appreciate calm, introspection, and thoughtful interaction.

- **Retreats Focused on Compassion or Service:** Attend retreats or workshops centered on themes of compassion, healing, or altruism. These experiences draw people who are open to deep emotional and spiritual exploration, aligning with 12th house themes.

Why It Works

With the ruler of the 5th, 7th, or 8th house in the 12th, love often feels deeply connected to purpose, reflection, and service. Relationships born in these environments are typically characterized by emotional depth, mutual compassion, and shared commitment to growth or healing. By leaning into spaces that nurture introspection and selflessness, you're likely to find connections that are profound, meaningful, and lasting.

When It's Coming from Inside the House

When the ruler of a house is placed in that house, this area of life becomes especially emphasized in your life. This concept isn't specific to the relationship houses; it's true for all the houses. These placements create a natural alignment with the house's themes, making the experiences and opportunities associated with it central to your life in some way. This isn't inherently good or bad—it simply places more focus on that particular part of life for you.

If the ruler of the house is in that house and also in a sign it rules, the themes of the house are likely to feel clear and natural to you. For example, if you have Leo on the 5th house cusp and the Sun is in that house, the Sun can be in Leo, Cancer, or Virgo (the signs on the 5th, 7th, and 8th house cusps, respectively), depending on the house system you're using. However, if you're using a quadrant system and the ruling planet is in the house but *not* in a sign it rules, then you may spend significant time trying to understand this area of life. In these cases, you might find yourself in situations where you struggle to fit into situations connected to the house's themes. If this is true for you, there's usually some learning about yourself to do before you find relationships that honor who you are.

Let's explore how the rulers of the 5th, 7th, and 8th houses can manifest in their respective houses, shaping your romantic and relationship experiences.

Ruler of the 5th House in the 5th

When the ruler of your 5th house is in the 5th, joy, creativity, and romance may take center stage in your life. You're naturally magnetized to creativity and self-expression, making you someone who thrives in environments that encourage playfulness, artistic pursuits, and even performing. Romantic connections may feel like an extension of your own creativity and zest for life.

This placement suggests that love comes easily when you're fully embracing your passions, whether through art, hobbies, or social events. You're drawn to people who celebrate your individuality and share your interests and creative spark. Children and activities centered around them may also play a significant role in your romantic story.

However, with this astrological scenario—and depending on the rest of your chart, as well as the planet and sign involved—it can sometimes lead to chasing romantic love for its own sake or being in love with the idea of love. If you notice this pattern in yourself, exploring it can help you break the cycle and move you toward more authentic connections. Experimenting with other 5th house activities and places can offer a simple, effective way to shift this dynamic.

Ruler of the 7th House in the 7th

With the ruler of your 7th house in the 7th, partnerships are a defining theme in your life. You're naturally attuned to one-on-one connections, and forming meaningful relationships often comes effortlessly to you. Love for you is about mutual respect, harmony, and collaboration, and you're likely to seek partners who you feel can balance and complement you.

This placement highlights a strong ability to attract and maintain partnerships, whether romantic, business-related, or platonic. There's a deep understanding of the dynamics of commitment and the importance of shared goals. This is a common placement for those who work in a client-based business of any kind. In any case, it's essential to maintain your individuality to avoid losing yourself in partnerships.

The danger with having the 7th house ruler in the 7th is the potential for there to be a strong pull toward being in a partnership just for the sake of it. If you've noticed a pattern of entering committed relationships because it feels like the "right" thing to do or because it fills a need rather than being with someone who truly fits you, consider exploring other types of partnerships or collaborations. This approach can help satisfy that need for connection while giving you the space to discover *your* right person for a deeper commitment.

Ruler of the 8th House in the 8th

When the ruler of your 8th house is in the 8th, your relationships are likely steeped in intensity, intimacy, and transformation. You're naturally drawn to connections that challenge you to grow and explore life's hidden layers. This placement emphasizes trust, shared resources, and emotional bonding as key themes in your partnerships.

Love for you isn't casual—it's about vulnerability and merging on an emotional and physical level, whether financially, emotionally, or physically. While this placement often brings transformative experiences, it also asks you to confront fears and embrace the power of true intimacy. Your relationships have the potential to create profound personal change for both you and your partner.

Having the ruler of the 8th house in the 8th can create intense cycles of death and rebirth in your intimate relationships or repeated patterns such as pursuing sexual connections for the sake of a physical relationship alone. If you find yourself caught in these patterns, exploring other 8th house themes—such as deep emotional healing through psychotherapy or delving into metaphysical or psychological interests—can help fulfill your 8th house needs in more rewarding ways. Doing so can also open the door to a different kind of connection, one that is more emotionally enriching and built on trust, true intimacy, and mutual growth.

Taking the Technique Further

This approach of tracking the house placement of a house ruler isn't just for relationships; you can reverse-engineer it to learn more about yourself or reconnect with aspects of yourself that feel unfamiliar or unexplored.

Here's one way to do this.

Let's say you don't feel connected to your Sun sign—the sign your Sun was in when you were born (the answer to "What's your sign?"). This is more common than you might think and can happen for several reasons, such as the following:

- You have important placements in your 1st house that others notice before your Sun sign traits emerge.
- The sign on your Ascendant is more dominant (for example, you have many planets in that sign, etc.).
- The ruler of your Ascendant is much stronger (in its own sign or in a more prominent, outgoing sign or house).
- Your Sun is in a quieter house, like the 6th or 12th, while other placements are in more visible areas of the chart.

This list could go on, but the point is that if your Sun feels distant or overshadowed, you can use this technique to engage in activities associated with its house placement to develop that part of yourself.

For example, if your Sun is in the 6th house in Virgo, but its ruler, Mercury, is part of a Leo stellium (three or more planets in the same sign), people might perceive you as more Leo-like. However, Virgo is still central to who you are. To connect with it, you could explore 6th house activities, such as adopting a pet to help you build more routine into your daily life.

You can apply this same technique to any planet. If you want to understand your Venus better, engage in activities tied to the house it's in and observe how you feel and respond. The house activities serve as a gateway to understanding the planet's role in shaping who you are.

Finding Your Love Spaces

Let's map out the core relationship themes in your chart by identifying which houses the rulers of your 5th, 7th, and 8th houses fall into.

Step 1

List the rulers of your 5th, 7th, and 8th houses:

5th house ruler __________ (planet) is placed in the _____ house

7th house ruler __________ (planet) is placed in the _____ house

8th house ruler __________ (planet) is placed in the _____ house

Step 2

Write down some places connected to the house placement of each of your relationship house rulers. For example, 9th house = travel, higher learning, cultural events.

Step 3

Pick one environment you feel excited to explore or reconnect with over the next thirty days. Which one feels the most natural or fun? (No pressure, just curiosity.) Is there a place you've been resisting that now feels worth another look? What qualities or experiences are you hoping to find there?

9
The Importance of Timing in Finding Love
Transits, Profections, and Progressions

Timing is everything, especially when it comes to love and relationships. While your natal chart reveals the foundation of who you are and what you're drawn to, timing techniques show when certain themes, opportunities, or challenges are most likely to come up in your life. Whether you're navigating a new romance, considering a commitment, or reflecting on past experiences, understanding the astrology of timing can provide clarity and insight.

In this chapter, we'll briefly look at three essential timing tools: transits, progressions, and annual profections. These techniques help us see how the cosmic clock interacts with our personal chart, illuminating moments of growth, change, and alignment. Each tool offers a unique perspective, and together they create a fuller picture of how astrological timing can shape your relationships and connections.

Let's take a brief look at these techniques and discover how they reveal the ebb and flow of your love life.

Transits: The Current Influence of the Planets

Transits occur when the planets in the sky form connections to your natal chart, activating specific areas of your life. Think of transits as the way the current cosmic energy interacts with the blueprint of your chart. While your natal chart is fixed, transits bring the dynamic, changing energy of the planets that reflect the timing of events, feelings, and opportunities.

Each planet carries its own energy and influences the areas of your chart that it touches, but it's also essential to consider your personal ruling planets. Understanding transits helps you make the most of opportunities while navigating periods of tension with greater awareness. Timing matters, and transits reveal when the universe is encouraging action—or inviting you to pause and reflect.

When it comes to meeting someone significant, it's rarely a single transit that triggers a meaningful event; it's the combination of several influences working together.

That said, tracking the moving planets can be a powerful way to learn more about yourself and your relationship patterns. For example, following the Sun as it moves through your 5th, 7th, or 8th house can inspire activities connected to those houses, leading to insightful experiences—and maybe even some fun! Even the Moon's quick journey through your chart can provide meaningful discoveries. Watching its movement through the relationship houses or its connections to house rulers offers small but powerful windows of insight into your personal story.

Venus, Jupiter, or House Rulers Moving Through the Desired House

First, decide what type of relationship you're looking for. While the 7th house is traditionally associated with marriage, not all committed relationships follow that structure; but whether you're seeking a long-term partnership, cohabitation, or a different kind of commitment, the 7th house and its ruler will play a key role in timing. Even if you decide to work with the 5th or 8th house as your starting point, keep an eye on the 7th house when you're working with timing techniques.

Tracking the movement of Venus, Jupiter, and your relationship house rulers throughout the year can help you recognize when relationship opportunities are most active in your chart. The Sun and Moon also provide windows of activation and are usually part of the meeting story of long-term relationships. When the Sun moves through one of your relationship houses, it can illuminate those themes and bring attention to them. The Moon's movement through these houses happens monthly, offering short-lived but insightful emotional triggers or moments of emotional connection.

By keeping an eye on these planetary transits, you can anticipate when relationship energy is strongest, giving you the opportunity to be intentional about the experiences you engage with and the connections you cultivate.

Eclipses in the Relationship Houses

Eclipses bring fated events, revelations, and turning points. When they occur in your 5th, 7th, or 8th house, they can coincide with significant shifts in your romantic relationships, dating life, or intimate connections. These periods may mark the beginning or end of a major relationship, a deepening commitment, or a powerful realization about what you truly want in love and intimacy.

Every eclipse occurs near the lunar nodes, the North Node or the South Node, and knowing which one is involved adds important insight. A North Node eclipse occurs when the Moon is close to the North Node, bringing new opportunities, attraction, and an influx of energy into the house it activates. A South Node eclipse happens when the Moon is near the South Node, often signaling release, endings, or a shift away from what is no longer working for you. While North Node eclipses in the relationship houses may bring important new connections or pivotal moments in existing partnerships, South Node eclipses can indicate the closing of a chapter, whether through a breakup, a change in circumstances, or a transformation in how you relate to others.

Since eclipses accelerate change, they can feel unexpected or dramatic, even if the shifts have been building beneath the surface for a while. In some cases, they bring external events—a sudden attraction, a breakup, or a change in a partner's circumstances—that push you toward growth. Whether you're meeting someone new, letting go of an old connection, or redefining your desires, eclipses through the relationship houses ask you to pay attention to what's being revealed and trust the shifts happening in your life.

A Note on Saturn

The Saturn cycle lasts 29 years, and once we move through our Saturn return (around age 29), we begin a new cycle of growth and maturity. Starting a relationship in the early years of this cycle (after the return) can bring a built-in sense of commitment, as the relationship becomes tied to a long-term process of personal and relational development.

When relationships align with the Saturn cycle, they also follow major Saturn aspects to itself—the squares, opposition, and return—which provide checkpoints throughout the relationship. These aspects bring challenges, but they also offer opportunities for growth and deepening commitment. The stability of Saturn creates a level of predictability, structure, and endurance, but it also demands effort. Saturn loves hard work, and relationships formed under its influence often require perseverance, responsibility, and a willingness to evolve together.

For those who begin relationships in their twenties—before the Saturn return—the relationship is growing while Saturn is wrapping up its previous cycle. The Saturn return acts as a major life checkpoint, forcing us to evaluate where we're investing our time, energy, and commitment. Some relationships don't survive this transition, as individuals often realize they are growing in different directions. However, some do, and with effort and shared growth, couples who navigate the Saturn return together can emerge stronger. Those who endure this phase typically do so by putting in the work to realign their goals, responsibilities, and expectations as they step into this phase of adulthood.

Using Planetary Returns to Activate Relationship Energy

In addition to transits, planetary returns offer a powerful way to reset and refocus relationship energy. A planetary return happens when a planet returns to the exact degree and sign it was in at your birth, marking a new cycle of development and opportunity in that area of your life.

If you're experiencing important transits to your relationship houses, paying attention to the return of the planet ruling that house can help you make the most of the timing.

- Venus return (occurs every 10–14 months)—A natural time to refresh romantic desires, attract new connections, or redefine what you value in life and love. If Venus rules your 7th and is returning, it's an ideal time to put yourself out there, especially if you're experiencing other relationship-related transits.
- Mercury return (occurs every year)—Can signal shifts in communication patterns in relationships. This can be an excellent time to clarify what you want, connect with new people, or revisit past discussions with a fresh perspective.
- Mars return—Brings renewed energy for pursuing relationships or deepening physical connections. If your relationship houses are highlighted by transits, a Mars return can be the perfect time to take action.
- Solar return (around your birthday)—If your Sun rules a relationship house, its return each year can illuminate themes around partnerships, making it a strong period for relationship developments.

These returns act as mini reset points, aligning with existing transits and giving you clear markers for when to take action. By tracking them, you can work with the natural cycles of your chart to time relationship decisions in ways that feel aligned and productive.

You can run return charts for any planet, and when the 7th house is emphasized—especially in the solar return or the return of the ruler of your 7th house—it's a great time to actively engage in activities or visit places that connect with your relationship houses. (See appendix B for ideas.)

Boosting the Energy with Fast-Moving Planets

If you're experiencing a major relationship transit but feel like nothing is happening, you don't have to wait passively. Timing the faster-moving planets can help activate the energy. The Sun, Moon, Mercury, and Venus move quickly and can act as triggers for bigger transits.

When we look at the transits around the time someone meets a significant other, each chart will typically be experiencing longer-term influences from slower-moving planets—transits that may have been active for weeks or months. But at the time of meeting, the fast planets have usually joined the party. The more planets being activated, the more areas of life are being touched by the event—something a meaningful relationship is likely to do.

You can start with something as simple as tracking the Moon phases. A New Moon in a relationship house can be a powerful kick start to that area of life.

For example, if Jupiter is moving through your 7th house (bringing relationship opportunities) while Pluto is aspecting your natal Sun (signaling major personal transformation), you might watch for a New Moon in your 7th house or one that conjuncts the ruler of your 7th house. You can also track Venus transits through your 5th or 7th house, or aspecting the house rulers, to enhance romantic opportunities.

Even the Moon's monthly cycle outside of its phases can provide insight and helpful energy or trigger slower transits into action. When the Moon moves through a relationship house or aspects a house ruler, it's a great time to be intentional about socializing, going on dates, or having important conversations.

By using transits consciously, you can align your actions with planetary energy, giving yourself the best chance to meet new people, deepen existing relationships, or navigate challenges with awareness. Timing matters—and knowing when to engage can make all the difference.

Transit Summary

Transits activate different areas of life, shaping experiences and opportunities as the planets move through your chart. Long-term transits, such as those of Saturn, Jupiter, or the outer planets, set the stage for major shifts, while faster-moving planets, like the Sun, Moon, Mercury, and Venus, bring immediate but likely temporary influences. When relationship houses are activated by transits, they create windows of opportunity for romance, commitment, or deeper intimacy. However, a single transit is rarely enough to bring lasting change—it's the interplay of multiple alignments that creates significant moments in life.

Annual Profections

Annual profections are a traditional timing method that highlights a specific house in your chart each year, showing where major life themes and developments will unfold. Starting from your Ascendant (1st house cusp) at birth, each year of your life activates the next house in order, cycling through all 12 houses every 12 years. The planet in charge of the house you move into on your birthday becomes the "lord of the year."

Note: This technique requires the use of Whole Sign houses. I've worked with annual profections in Placidus, and it doesn't provide the same quality of information. The inverse is true for transits.

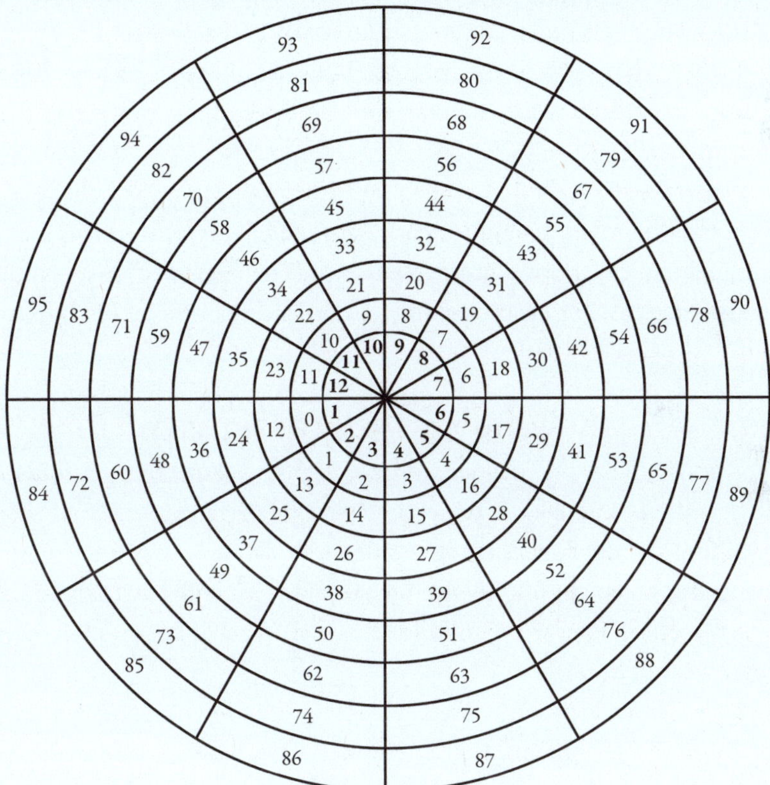

Annual Profections Wheel

When it comes to relationships, profections help pinpoint when the relationship areas of your life (and which planetary rulers) are active each year. As you can see in the annual profections wheel, the sets of numbers represent ages. We are in a 1st house year during the 1st year, 12th year, 24th year, etc. of our lives. The first age at which we have our 5th house profection year is between 4 and 5 years old, and every 12 years thereafter.

To use this technique for timing, look at the ruler of your profected house—where it's placed in your natal chart and what transits it's receiving. If you're in a 7th house year and Venus is your 7th house ruler, then Venus transits and returns will be important overall but especially for relationship timing.

Another way to work with profections is to track the movement of your natal relationship house rulers and use the timing of when the relationship ruler moves through your annual profected house. For example, if Mercury rules your 7th house and you're in a 9th house profection year, the period when Mercury transits your 9th house could serve as a key timing indicator—especially when it aligns with other significant transits or timing techniques.

In the annual profection wheel, you can easily track which house is activated and use this insight to work with the energy of the year, making intentional choices in love and partnerships. The beauty of this technique is that it's the same for everyone, so you don't need a time of birth to work with it.

Secondary Progressions

Progressions give us a deeper, more internal perspective on personal growth and life changes. Unlike transits, which reflect external events and shifting circumstances, progressions reveal how your inner world is evolving. The most commonly used technique—secondary progressions—moves the chart forward symbolically, where each day after birth represents a year of life.

Changes in progressed planets, especially the Sun, Moon, Venus, and Mars, can indicate shifts in desires, emotional needs, and relationship patterns. Changes to the angles and house cusps can show us changes in what we want from the world around is. When relationship planets or house rulers change signs, form new aspects, or progress into key houses, they can signal turning points in how you connect with others and what you look for in love and commitment.

The progressed Moon phase is also a factor to take into consideration. Each phase marks a different stage of emotional development, from new beginnings in the progressed New Moon to deep reflection during the progressed Balsamic Moon. When we look at progressions, it's important to see how they're moving through the natal houses, too, and if the progressed planets are making aspects to the natal chart and which houses the progressed planets are moving through.

The progressed Moon cycle is roughly the same length as the transiting Saturn timing—28 to 29 years—so we can look to either the lunar phase return (when the Sun and Moon are in the same relationship to each other as they were in your natal chart) or a progressed New Moon phase as potential relationship beginning times as well. Noticing where you are in your progressed Moon cycle can provide clarity on whether you're in a season of building new connections or focusing inward.

By understanding these timing techniques, you can work with the natural flow of your chart rather than against it. Whether you're actively looking for love or just curious about what's unfolding in your relationship story, these tools can help you recognize when the universe is opening doors—and when it's time to walk through them.

10

Putting It All Together

A Step-by-Step Guide to Exploring Your Own Story

This is where everything comes together. Throughout this book, we've explored the different layers of your chart that are responsible for shaping your experiences of love and relationships: Venus and Mars, the 5th, 7th, and 8th houses and their rulers, and the aspects that tie it all together. Now it's time to take what you've learned and apply it to your own story. This chapter is designed to guide you through these areas of your chart step-by-step, helping you uncover the themes, patterns, and opportunities that define your special approach to human connection. Whether you're seeking clarity, insight, or a deeper understanding of yourself or you're learning how to explore these areas of life through the lens of astrology, this is your chance to weave everything into a personal narrative that reflects who you are and how you love. Grab your journal and let's get started!

I'm going to supply a series of prompts to walk you though what we've looked at in each chapter of this book. Take your time and be honest (and gentle) with yourself. If you're feeling resistance to an idea, look at it before you discard it as untrue—it might be holding important information about patterns connected to these topics.

Step 1: Venus and Mars

What do your Venus and Mars placements say about your approach to relationships?

- Venus's sign and house: ____________________
- Mars's sign and house: ____________________
- Are Venus and Mars aspecting each other?
- What does their connection say about what you want and how you get it? (Go as deep with this as your astrological knowledge allows.)
- What relationship patterns have you noticed in your life and how might they connect to the placements of Venus and Mars in your chart?

Example

Here is an example of how to analyze Venus and Mars, using Louis XIV's chart (chart 3). This is a good example of a chart where Venus and Mars are compatible but are not talking to each other.

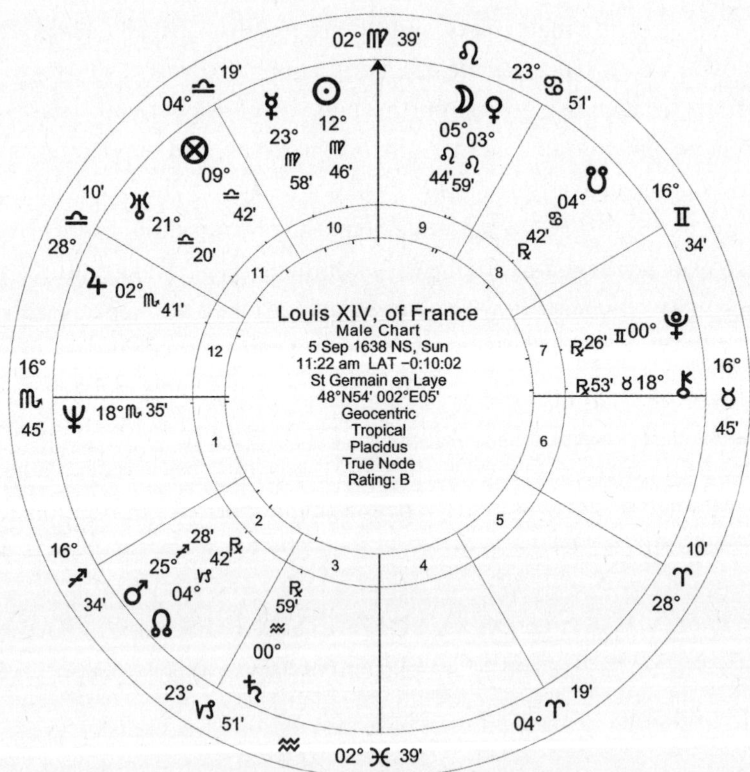

Chart 3: Louis XIV's Birth Chart

Venus in Leo, 9th House

What it says about how I love: Venus in Leo in the 9th house indicates that I'm bighearted and adventurous. I'm drawn to relationships that inspire me to grow, learn, or experience something new; love can feel like a grand quest or adventure. I'm generous with my affection and expressive about my feelings, and I value partners who match my enthusiasm for life.

The challenges: Venus's square to Jupiter in Scorpio can amplify my expectations in relationships. I have idealized love in the past, expecting it to be larger-than-life, or expected a deep connection, which can create tension between wanting excitement (Leo) and emotional depth or intensity (Scorpio). This has led to struggles setting realistic expectations or feeling like no relationship completely satisfies my need for both passion and profound connection.

Mars in Sagittarius, 2nd House

What it says about how I go after what I want: Mars in Sagittarius in the 2nd house says I'm bold and adventurous in pursuing my goals, but I also value tangible results. My drive is fueled by a love of freedom and exploration, but I aim to channel this energy into creating security or building resources. I tend to invest my time and energy in experiences or relationships that align with my personal values, and I'm willing to take risks to get what I want.

The challenges: I may struggle to balance my love of exploration with a need for stability, and in the past I've settled for one or the other. My adventurous streak could lead me to act impulsively, particularly with financial or material decisions, as I sometimes prioritize optimism over practicality.

Are Venus and Mars Aspecting Each Other?

Venus and Mars aren't aspecting each other, but their fire sign connection suggests a shared enthusiasm and boldness. This alignment between my values (Venus) and my drive (Mars) means I pursue love and desires with a sense of adventure, passion, and confidence. However, the lack of direct interaction could mean these energies sometimes operate independently, creating a disconnect between what I want and how I go about achieving it.

Venus in Leo Square Jupiter in Scorpio

While Jupiter amplifies my desires for meaningful and transformative relationships, the tension between Leo's need for recognition and Scorpio's intensity could lead to overindulgence or a tendency to overpromise or expect too much. Early in life, I might have been drawn to dramatic, all-encompassing relationships that seemed thrilling but left me feeling drained or overwhelmed. Over time, I think I've learned to balance my craving for excitement with a deeper understanding of what I truly need emotionally.

What Does the Connection Between Venus and Mars Say About What I Want and How I Get It?

With Venus in the 9th house and Mars in the 2nd, I want to explore situations that inspire me to grow, both spiritually and materially. I approach life with a sense of generosity and optimism, but I might also struggle to bridge the gap between the ideals I envision (9th house) and the practical steps needed to achieve them (2nd house). Mars in Sagittarius encourages me to take bold action, but the lack of a direct aspect to Venus means I sometimes go after desires that don't totally align with my values.

Relationship Patterns I've Noticed and How They Connect to Venus and Mars

I've noticed a pattern of wanting relationships that feel adventurous and all-encompassing, but I may have experienced moments where my ideals clash with the reality of what a partner can provide. This ties to Venus's square to Jupiter, which can amp up my expectations or create situations where I overextend myself. Mars in the 2nd house reminds me to stay grounded and focus on relationships that honor my values and provide mutual stability. Over time, I've learned to blend the fiery optimism of Mars with Venus's need for meaningful connections, creating a more balanced approach to life, love, and desire.

Step 2: Exploring the Houses of Relationships

What's the story of your 5th, 7th, and 8th houses?

- Identify the signs on the house cusps and write down their general themes.
- Note the ruling planets and their placements.
- Do these houses connect or operate independently? What does this tell you about your relationship dynamics?

Example

Let's continue with the analysis of Louis XIV's chart, focusing on the 5th, 7th, and 8th houses.

5th House: Aries, Ruled by Mars (Mars in Sagittarius, 2nd House)

With Aries on the cusp of my 5th house, I approach romance and creativity with boldness and spontaneity. I tend to want to take the lead in romantic situations and need some excitement and adventure in my relationships. Mars, the ruler, is in Sagittarius in the 2nd house, tying my romantic and creative passions to my personal values and resources. This might explain why I often invest time or money in adventurous dates, travel, or creative projects. However, with Mars square Mercury in Virgo in the 10th house, there's a tension between my values and how I communicate or express myself professionally. Sometimes I feel pulled between pursuing my passions and focusing on career responsibilities.

7th House: Taurus, Ruled by Venus (Venus in Leo, 9th House)

Taurus on the 7th house cusp suggests I value stability and loyalty in partnerships. With Venus (its ruler) in Leo in the 9th house, my relationships are influenced by a desire for shared learning, growth, and inspiration. I'm drawn to partners who encourage me to explore new perspectives, express my creativity, and bring a sense of optimism to experiences. With Venus in Leo, I have a flair for romance, and I was definitely attracted to drama when I was younger. I do enjoy grand romantic gestures and relationships that feel vibrant and fulfilling.

8th House: Gemini, Ruled by Mercury (Mercury in Virgo, 10th House)

With Gemini on the cusp of my 8th house, I'm drawn to mental connection and communication in intimate relationships. Mercury, the ruler, is in Virgo in the 10th house, suggesting that themes of intimacy may tie into my public life or career. However, the square between Mercury and Mars in the 2nd house can create tension. I sometimes struggle to reconcile my need for intellectual connection in intimacy with the more adventurous or expansive way I pursue my passions. This could manifest as feeling torn between financial independence and deeper emotional bonds.

Summary

Looking at these house rulers, I see that romance (5th house) and intimacy (8th house) are tied to my values (2nd house), while partnerships (7th house) connect to my public life (10th house). With Venus not aspecting Mercury or Mars, the connection between romance, commitment, and intimacy doesn't feel seamless. There have been situations of compartmentalization, where my partnerships exist in a separate space from other parts of my life. Learning about this placement can help me work on integrating the enthusiasm and exploration of the 9th house into my partnerships. Now that I can admit I'm ready to find a life partner, I also have to acknowledge that traditional romance and dating might not be the place to start, and exploring the 10th house activities and places may offer opportunities I hadn't considered.

Step 3: Analyzing the House Rulers

What do the rulers of the 5th, 7th, and 8th houses reveal about your relationship experiences?

- Describe the planet ruling each house: its sign, house, and aspects. (If you're ready, you can add an exploration of how the dignity of the house rulers plays a role, but it's not necessary, as there is plenty to work with already.)

- Ask yourself how the element and house placement of the ruler shape your relationship patterns.

Example

Let's return to our analysis of Louis XIV's chart, this time focusing on the rulers of the 5th, 7th, and 8th houses.

5th House: Aries, Ruled by Mars (Mars in Sagittarius, 2nd House)

Mars rules the 5th house of romance and creativity, and it's in Sagittarius in the 2nd house. This combination shows I approach romance and creativity with passion, adventure, and a desire for freedom. The fire element of Sagittarius says I like excitement in romance, but since Mars is in the 2nd house of values, things I pursue often tie into what I find personally meaningful or what enhances my sense of security.

But Mars is square Mercury in Virgo in the 10th house, creating tension between my adventurous romantic pursuits and how I communicate my needs. I often feel torn between taking risks in love and sticking to what feels practical or aligned with my ambitions. This square has brought frustration in how I process information and manage attention to detail, clashing with my tendency to struggle when choosing a direction. I've had to work on committing to a path and letting go of perfectionism. Over time, this aspect has likely made me more aware of balancing my need for freedom with my long-term goals.

7th House: Taurus, Ruled by Venus (Venus Leo, 9th House)

The ruler of my 7th house, Venus, is in Leo in the 9th house. This suggests that I look for partnerships that not only provide stability and loyalty (Taurus) but also expand my horizons—intellectually, spiritually, or even geographically. I find myself attracted to people who inspire me to explore new ideas, cultures, or philosophies. With Venus in Leo, I love to shine and be admired, but it's taken time and age to accept this about myself. Venus's placement in the 9th house highlights the fact that relationships for me are often tied to an adventure, learning, travel, or personal growth, or in some cases all four.

Interestingly, Venus doesn't form any major aspects to Mercury or Mars. This lack of connection between the 7th house ruler and the other relationship houses explains why my romantic and sexual relationships haven't always led to committed partnerships. The ones that have didn't start in a traditional way. It's something I've had to work on—finding ways to weave the excitement and depth of the 9th house into other areas of my relationship life. This also explains that the part of my dating history I've seen as failure or bad luck can be helped by approaching dating a little differently.

8th House: Gemini, Ruled by Mercury (Mercury in Virgo, 10th House)

Gemini on the 8th house cusp shows that I seek intellectual stimulation in intimacy and shared experiences. The ruler, Mercury, is in Virgo in the 10th house, which ties the themes of deep connection, psychological depth, and shared resources to my career or public life. This placement suggests I prefer intimate relationships where communication and shared goals are prioritized, but I feel more comfortable when I don't have to go too deep emotionally. I definitely need to write my emotions down in times of psychological stress. The square between Mercury and Mars introduces tension and explains why I sometimes feel angry when I'm pressed about my deeper issues or I have to look honestly at shared resources.

I often feel conflicted about my need to be free (Mars in Sagittarius) and the more detail-oriented, perfectionistic energy of Mercury in Virgo. This tension has shown up in relationships as a need to balance chasing the big picture with attending to boring details. At times I feel overwhelmed by a clash between my optimism and ideals versus reality in deep emotional connections.

Reflection

Looking at the rulers of my 5th, 7th, and 8th houses, I see a theme of balancing my adventurous, risk-taking side with my desire for stability and intellectual connection. Mars, Venus, and Mercury each bring something different to these areas, and the square between Mars and Mercury highlights a specific challenge I've faced in satisfying my passions with my partnerships and intimacy. I can also see why the traditional path to commitment and marriage hasn't been so straightforward.

Step 4: Where Can I Find Love?

Use the prompts below to help you reflect on where love, connection, or meaningful relationships are most likely to show up in your life.

- Where might you meet a potential partner or romantic connection?
- Reflect on the material on where to find love in chapter 8 (and appendix B) and consider the house placements of the relationship rulers.
- Make a list of environments or activities that you're interested in and that align with your chart. (See appendix B for ideas.)

Example

Let's take another look at Louis XIV's chart, this time focusing on the house placements of the rulers of the relationship houses.

Seeing the Connections in My Chart

When I look at my chart, I see a strong connection between my 5th and 8th houses. The ruler of my 5th house, Mars, is in Sagittarius in the 2nd house and is sextile Uranus in Libra in the 12th and square Mercury (the ruler of my 8th house) in Virgo in the 10th. This suggests that my romantic pursuits (5th house) naturally flow into deeper intimacy (8th house). For me, having fun and experiencing romance often leads to the more intense emotional connections of the 8th house, and that's okay! Knowing this can help me approach relationships with more clarity and intention.

Starting with Romance and Fun (5th House–8th House Connection)

Since my 5th and 8th houses are connected, exploring 5th house activities is a great way to open the door to both romance and intimacy. Mars in Sagittarius suggests I thrive in adventurous, lively environments aligned with my values (2nd house).

Places to Explore Romance (5th/8th House Focus)

- Cultural festivals or outdoor sports events (Mars + 5th house)
- Workshops, clubs, or courses (Gemini 8th house) to learn how to build financial (2nd house) freedom (Mars in Sagittarius)
- Trip to explore a culture (Mars in Sagittarius) and acquire cultural art (2nd house)
- A pottery class (5th + 2nd houses) teaching Japanese Raku pottery (cultural—Mars in Sagittarius)

Reflection

Looking at my chart, I can see that relationships are deeply tied to growth and self-discovery. By recognizing the natural flow between my 5th and 8th houses, I can embrace experiences that combine fun and intimacy without guilt or confusion. For long-term commitment, focusing on 7th house activities and environments will help me connect with someone who complements my emotional and creative energy. This process starts with knowing what I want and trusting my chart to guide me toward the right opportunities.

Finding a Partner or Spouse (7th House Focus)

For a committed relationship, I'll want to focus on my 7th house. Taurus rules my 7th house, and its ruler, Venus, is in Leo in the 9th house and is conjunct the Moon in the 9th and square Jupiter in Scorpio in the 12th. This suggests I might meet a partner through activities tied to travel, learning, or cultural exploration. Emotional warmth (Venus conjunct Moon) and creative self-expression (Leo) are key themes in how I approach relationships. With the square between Venus and Jupiter and Jupiter in the 12th house, I need to approach meeting a partner from a realistic point of view and not be overly optimistic. Because the Moon is also involved (conjunct Venus and ruling the 9th house), Cancer themes are also on the table.

Places to Look for a Committed Partner (7th House Focus)

- Take a trip to a foreign country (9th house) focused on cuisine (Cancer)

- A family (Cancer) vacation to a far-off destination (9th house)
- Volunteer for a humanitarian project, overseas or within a specific cultural group (9th house travel) that focuses on women and children (Cancer and Venus)
- Take a culturally specific (9th house) cooking class (Cancer)

Step 5: Layer in Aspects

Now it's time to reflect on how the planetary aspects shape your experiences in love and connection. The following prompts will help you notice where energy flows easily, where tension may arise, and how your patterns have evolved.

- What influences shape the story of your 5th, 7th, and 8th houses?
- List the aspects to your house rulers, to the Descendant, and to Venus or Mars (if they don't rule one of the relationship houses).
- Reflect on whether these aspects suggest flow, tension, or growth opportunities in your relationships.

For this step, focus on the house rulers to start, unless you feel there's Venus/Mars work you'd like to address first. If you've noticed patterns, you can start with "I used to…" or "In the past I…" and then add "Now I'm more interested in…" or something along those lines to acknowledge how you've grown and how your focus may have changed. Maybe you used to be very Venus-focused in a hedonistic way and now you're more interested in what you truly value or your focus has shifted to another planet's purview altogether.

Example

Here's an example from Louis XIV's chart.

- "In the past I was into free spirits who were not philosophical and who wanted to explore the world (Mars in Sagittarius ruling the 5th), but the romances never went past dating and sex (5th/8th houses). Now I want (Venus) a committed relationship (Taurus on the 7th), one where I'm adored and I feel special (Venus in Leo) and safe (Venus conjunct the Moon)."

Step 6: Synthesize Your Story

Now it's your turn. You've explored the pieces step-by-step in the previous sections, and now it's time to put it all together. The examples I've provided are guides. If you already have a rich astrological vocabulary, use your own words and knowledge to draw from. The only rule—if there are any—is to be honest with yourself.

- How do all these pieces come together to describe your approach to relationships?
- Write a short narrative that combines your Venus and Mars placements, the relationship houses, their rulers, and key aspects.
- What strengths and challenges do you notice?
- How do these elements play out in your relationship patterns?
- What goals or insights can you take away from this?

Here are two suggestions for how to write your personal narrative based on your chart:

- Start with step one and work your way through all the pieces you gathered to create a story using the astrological themes.
- Write a story about your love life—from what you wanted in the past and what you want now to past relationships and how they turned out. When you're done, go back through it and identify the astrological themes you find.

Step 7: What Are the Best Times for Me to Put Myself Out There?

Now that you've explored the story your chart tells about love and relationships, it's time to bring in the *when*. We looked at the tools to recognize timing windows that support connection, healing, and growth in chapter 9. Think of these timing techniques as invitations to engage, reflect, or shift course. Here are a few simple ways to work with timing right now:

- Track the Moon. Look at when the Moon moves through your 5th, 7th, or 8th house each month. These short windows offer insight into how you're feeling about connection and where your energy is focused.

- Pay attention to Venus and Jupiter. These two planets bring ease, attraction, and opportunity. When they transit your relationship houses or aspect your relationship house rulers, things often fall into place more naturally.
- Check for New Moons and eclipses in your relationship houses. New Moons = fresh starts. Eclipses = big shifts. These are not always gentle, but they're always revealing.
- Know your timing cycles. Annual profections and progressions can show you which themes are active this year and where your attention is being drawn internally and externally.

Use this information to support your next steps. If you're in a year that activates your 7th house or your Venus return is coming up, you don't need to force anything—but it might be the perfect time to be open, curious, and a little more intentional.

If nothing seems to be happening even when the astrology is active, try engaging the energy: go out, talk to someone new, revisit what you want in a relationship, etc. Transits respond to movement.

Just like the rest of your chart, timing isn't about fate—it's about flow. The more you work with it, the easier it becomes to notice the doors when they open.

Start a Transit Journal

To begin understanding your rhythms, try keeping a simple transit journal:

- Note what you feel when the Moon moves through your relationship houses.
- Jot down how you respond to Venus or Mars transits.
- Record any significant moments in your life (a date, a reconnection, an ending) and check what was happening in the sky.

Over time, you'll start to see patterns—and the more you notice, the easier it becomes to move in sync with your chart.

Explore Your 5th House Further

If you're feeling disconnected from the themes of your 5th house, doing 5th house things can bring joy and fun into your life beyond romance. To enhance your connection with this part of your life, consider using the current transits as a guide—specifically the Moon's movement—to light up your 5th house. The Moon's movement provides great opportunities to reconnect with the house's themes and energy.

For an even more personalized approach, try using a Moon tracker, astrology calendar, or Moon journal to find when the Moon moves through your 5th house. During this time each month, you can focus on doing activities that align with your 5th house themes, like creative projects, playful pursuits, or just embracing what brings you joy.

Astrology isn't about making things happen on command; it's about noticing the rhythms, trusting the timing, and staying open to what unfolds. The more you explore your chart, the more confidence you'll build in knowing when to move forward, when to pause, and when to leap.

Your birth chart isn't a set of rules or a list of flaws. It's a guide—a mirror reflecting your potential, your patterns, and your personal truth. It's here to help you understand your love story more clearly so you can live it more fully.

Exploring your birth chart is rarely a one-time thing. You can return to these prompts, exercises, and reflections any time you need clarity or feel a shift in what you're looking for. Each pass through will reveal something new. The more you engage with your chart, the more it can support you in creating the relationships that feel right for you—at your own pace and on your own terms.

Conclusion

Astrology offers a powerful lens for understanding ourselves: how we love, what we desire, and the patterns shaping our relationships. Throughout this book, you've explored multiple layers of your birth chart, including Venus and Mars, the 5th, 7th, and 8th houses, the planetary rulers that guide them, and the ways transits, progressions, and profections influence timing in love. The goal has never been to provide rigid answers but rather to offer tools for exploration, self-awareness, and reflection.

Relationships, like astrology, are dynamic—they evolve over time, shaped by experience, growth, and personal choices. Whether you're searching for love, deepening an existing connection, or simply learning more about yourself, your chart is a guide, not a rulebook. The more you engage with it, the more you'll see how its insights can empower you to move through life and relationships with clarity and confidence.

Astrology is a tool for awareness but not necessarily prediction. So this book isn't about predicting when or where you'll meet someone, but is meant to help you recognize patterns, cycles, and opportunities. The more self-awareness you have, the more intentionally you can engage with your life.

Your chart evolves with you. Just as you grow and change, so does your approach to relationships. Transits and progressions activate different themes at different times, and what you need in a partner or relationship can change dramatically. Understanding your chart allows you to work with these shifts rather than resist them.

You don't need every astrological factor to line up for love to happen. Let's face it—perfectionism is the killer of all types of dreams. While some people meet their significant partner under multiple, powerful astrological alignments, others may have just a few key activations. The important thing is to be open to recognizing the timing when it happens and, more importantly, to have fun and remain curious. Try not to let your past expectations stop you from moving forward.

Astrology provides a detailed road map, but ultimately you are the one driving. Use what you've learned to make empowered choices, trust your own timing and intuition, and build relationships that reflect who you are and what you truly want out of your life. And always be kind to yourself.

Appendix A
Understanding Your Birth Chart

Astrology is an incredible tool for self-discovery, but it can feel overwhelming at first. This appendix is designed to walk you through the process step-by-step so you can explore your distinct relationship story in a way that's approachable and clear. Here's how to get started.

Get Your Natal Chart

Start by generating your natal chart using free online tools such as the chart calculator at Astro.com, Time Passages, or ConsultTheSky.com/tools. All you need is the date, exact time, and location of your birth. I recommend using the Placidus house system. That's what I use and there's an extra layer of information you get using these calculations that you won't find if you use the Whole Sign house system.

Throughout this book, the examples you'll see are calculated in the Placidus house system. If you're already comfortable using a different house system for your chart, feel free to stick with what you know. However, if you're a student of astrology, already familiar with astrology, or diving deep into self-discovery and aren't overwhelmed by exploring multiple chart views, I encourage you to look at your chart in Placidus alongside any other house system you're using.

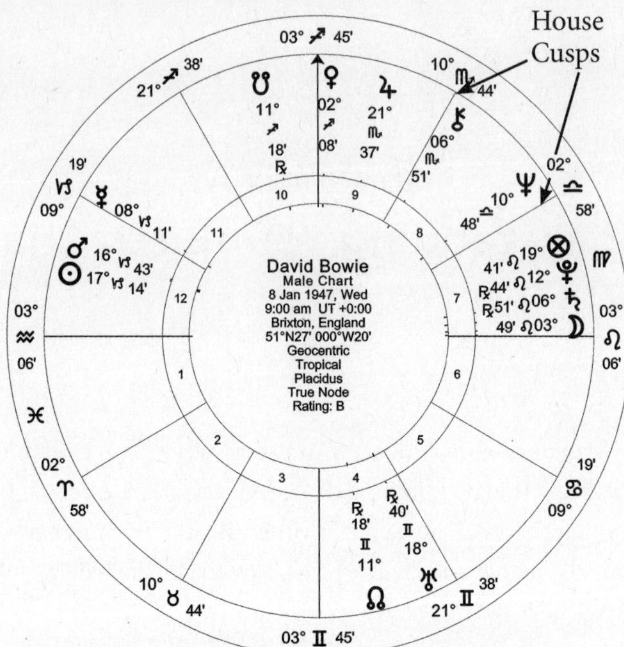

Chart 4: David Bowie's Birth Chart, Placidus Houses

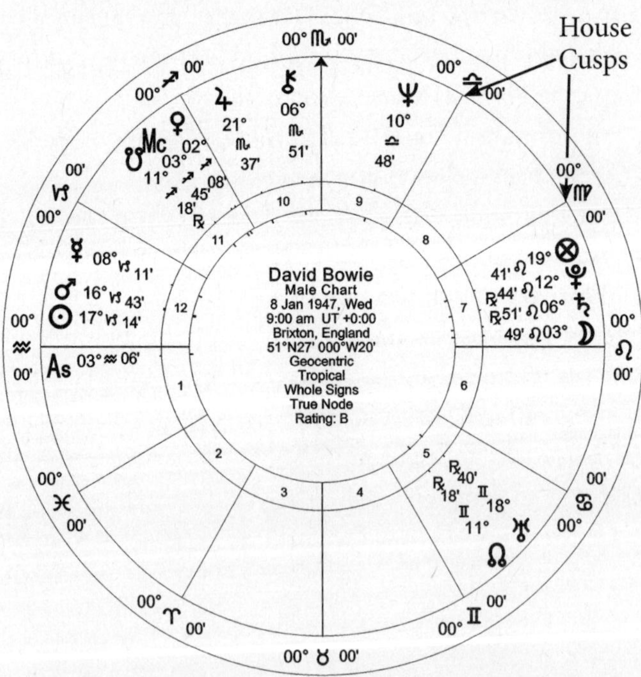

Chart 5: David Bowie's Birth Chart, Whole Sign Houses

I've included examples of David Bowie's chart in both Placidus houses (chart 4) and Whole Sign houses (chart 5) so you can see the difference between them. I primarily use Placidus houses, but I use Whole Sign houses for a few specific things. Remember, you must set your chart to Whole Sign houses when looking at what profection year you're in.

As you can see in the examples, in the Placidus chart, each house cusp has different numbers and signs. Because of how it's calculated, some signs don't have a house cusp (note Virgo floating in the middle of the 7th house and Pisces floating in the 1st house, which is called an interception or an intercepted sign) and some signs repeat, like Gemini and Sagittarius in the example.

The style of the chart will look different from platform to platform. I set my program so that all the houses are of equal proportion visually, but that's a personal preference. How you prefer to see a chart is something that develops over time, so feel free to check out your chart in all sorts of ways to see how your eye is drawn to the significant parts.

In charts 6 and 7 (on the next page), I've marked the difference between the houses and the house cusps with arrows. The house is the space in the middle, but its beginning is marked by the house cusp.

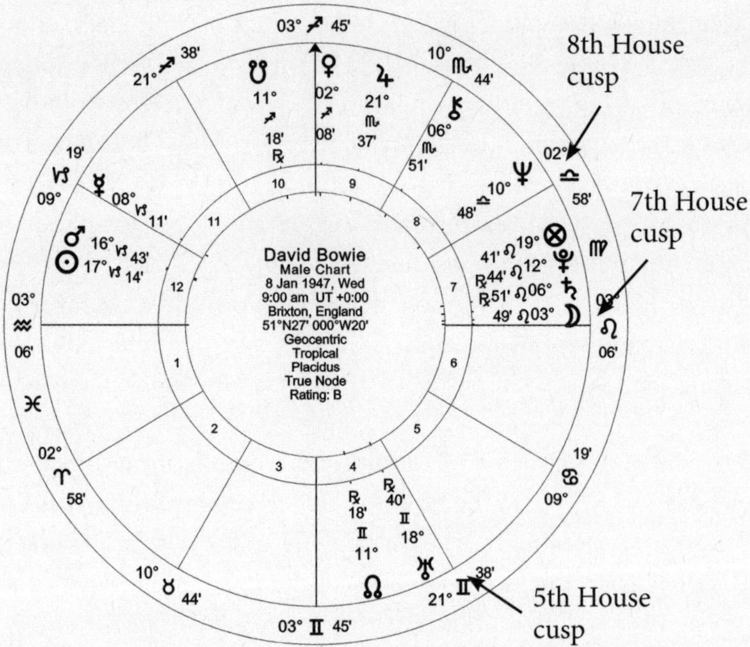

Chart 6: David Bowie, Relationship House Cusps with Placidus Houses

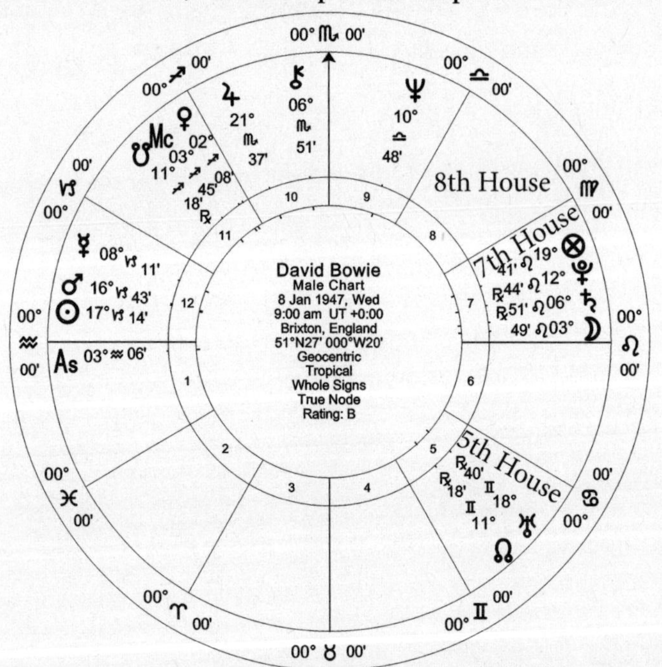

Chart 7: David Bowie, Relationship Houses with Whole Sign Houses

Familiarize Yourself with Astrology Basics

If you're new to astrology, don't worry! I've included a table of symbols (glyphs) for the planets, signs, and aspects on page 298, plus images throughout the book to show you where you need to be looking and what you need to be looking at.

Locate Key Areas in Your Chart

To explore your relationship story, start by identifying the following:

- Venus (♀) and Mars (♂): Find where these planets are located in your chart by sign and house.
- The 5th, 7th, and 8th Houses: These are the houses most associated with love, connection, and intimacy. Note the sign on the cusp (border) of each house.
- The Ruling Planets: Look at the ruling planets of the 5th, 7th, and 8th houses and note where they're placed in your chart. For example, if your 7th house cusp is in Taurus, Venus is the ruler.

In the chart examples, you can see that David Bowie has Venus in the sign of Sagittarius. If he were still on the planet and wanted to know about his Venus sign, he could look for the Venus glyph and see which sign glyph is beside it.

Once you have your chart, you can find the glyphs for the planets and signs in the table of symbols to find your specific placements—easy peasy! Keeping it simple and *not* getting ahead of yourself will help you avoid confusion.

Table of Symbols (Glyphs)

Planets		Signs		Aspects	
Sun	☉	Aries	♈	Conjunction	☌
Moon	☽	Taurus	♉	Opposition	☍
Mercury	☿	Gemini	♊	Sextile	⚹
Venus	♀	Cancer	♋	Square	□
Mars	♂	Leo	♌	Trine	△
Jupiter	♃	Virgo	♍	Quincunx	⚻
Saturn	♄	Libra	♎		
Uranus	♅	Scorpio	♏		
Neptune	♆	Sagittarius	♐		
Pluto	♇	Capricorn	♑		
		Aquarius	♒		
		Pisces	♓		

Work Through the Exercises

At the end of each chapter, you'll find short exercises to help you reflect on what you've learned and apply it to your own chart. For example, before reading about Venus, you'll be prompted to locate Venus in your chart and note its sign and house. When you get to the end of the chapter, you will have the opportunity to reflect on how its themes resonate with your experiences. I recommend starting a journal to work through the exercises in the book.

Reflect on the Bigger Picture

As you move through the book, start connecting the dots. How do Venus and Mars interact in your chart? What stories do the 5th, 7th, and 8th houses tell about how you approach love and connection? Use the final chapter of the book to bring everything together and reflect on your unique relationship story.

This book isn't just about finding where love might show up—it's about understanding your *whole* relationship story (or a lot of it), from what you value and what fulfills you to how to create relationships that feel authentic and true to who you are.

Here is the natal chart for Kurt Cobain calculated in the Placidus house system (chart 8). Each component discussed throughout the book is identified for you. Use this example to help you navigate your own chart.

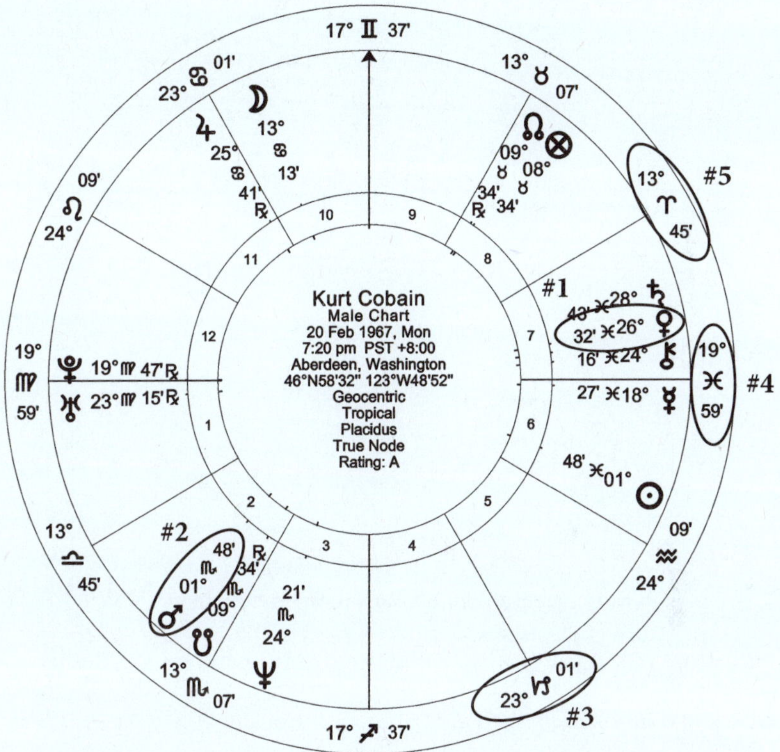

Chart 8: Kurt Cobain, Relationship Planet and Sign Placements

Marked are all the things you'll be looking at throughout the book:

1. Venus in Pisces in the 7th house
2. Mars in Scorpio in the 2nd house
3. Capricorn on the 5th house cusp
4. Pisces on the 7th house cusp
5. Aries on the 8th house cusp

In this example, the 1st house starts at 19 degrees 59 minutes Virgo (Ascendant).

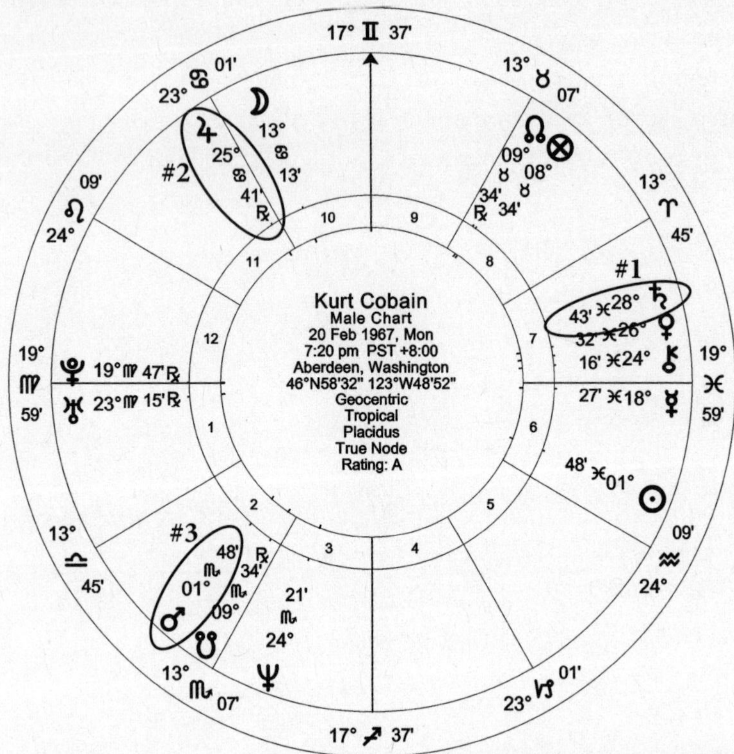

Chart 9: Kurt Cobain, Planets Ruling the Relationship Houses

In chart 9 you'll find the planets ruling the relationship houses circled:

1. Saturn in Pisces is the ruler of the 5th house.
2. Jupiter in Cancer is the ruler of the 7th house.
3. Mars in Scorpio rules the 8th house.

Next is an aspect grid for Kurt Cobain's natal chart (chart 10). An aspect grid is the easiest way to see the aspects being made between planets/points.

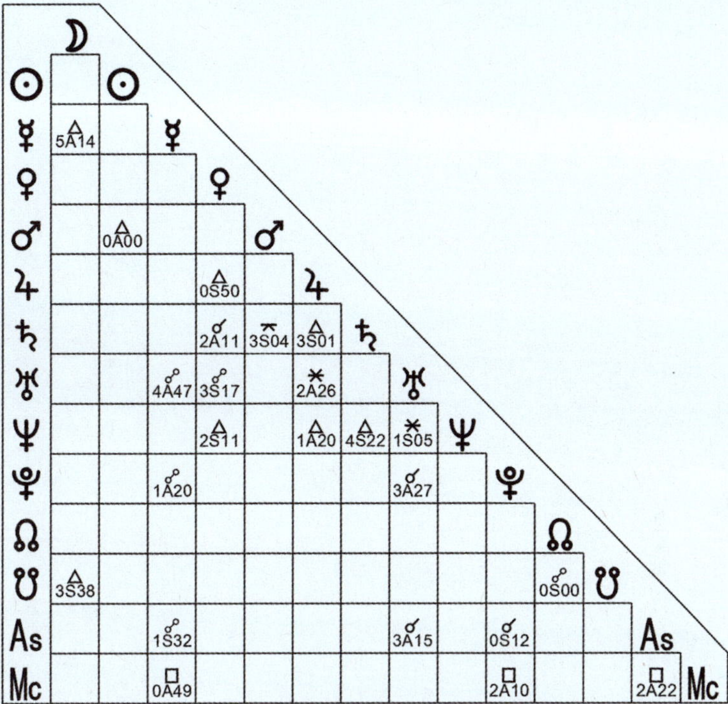

Chart 10: Kurt Cobain, Aspect Grid

Appendix B
Practical Tips and Locations for Each House

Use this guide to quickly find the best places, activities, and environments aligned with the house placements of your 5th, 7th, and 8th house rulers. Some entries may appear in more than one house list—that's intentional. Certain environments naturally support multiple types of connection or self-expression.

1st House Places

- Gyms
- Fitness classes
- Yoga studios
- Running clubs
- Public speaking venues
- Leadership seminars
- Networking events
- Art galleries (when showcasing your work)
- Theaters (as a performer or audience member)
- Solo travel destinations
- Hiking trails
- Rock climbing gyms
- Wellness retreats
- Self-help workshops
- Personal branding workshops

- Job fairs
- Any place where you're showcasing your skills
- Online platforms for personal achievements
- Local community fairs or festivals
- Entrepreneurial events or start-up expos
- Photography studios (your photo shoot)
- Personal growth summits
- TED talks (as an attendee or speaker)
- Self-defense classes
- Martial arts dojos
- Book signings (for self-help books)
- Dance studios
- Salons (any personal grooming space)
- Audition spaces
- Personal trainer sessions
- Coaching places

1st House Activities

1. Join a fitness class (like Zumba, spin, or boot camp).
2. Attend a self-discovery workshop or retreat.
3. Take a public speaking course or present at an event.
4. Start a personal blog or vlog to share your experiences.
5. Post regularly on social media about your hobbies or achievements.
6. Try out a new solo activity, like pottery or painting.
7. Engage in self-improvement workshops or self-help programs.
8. Sign up for one-on-one coaching sessions (personal training, life coaching, etc.).
9. Attend leadership seminars or workshops.
10. Audition for a local theater production or talent show.
11. Explore local hiking trails or outdoor fitness challenges.

12. Enroll in martial arts or self-defense classes.
13. Host a personal project showcase or art exhibit.
14. Compete in sports leagues or tournaments.
15. Attend networking events focused on personal growth.
16. Travel solo to a destination that excites or challenges you.
17. Participate in a fashion show.
18. Join a group that helps with personal branding or launching a side hustle.
19. Join a self-care retreat focused on personal reflection and growth.
20. Attend spa and salon events.
21. Attend any kind of event that focuses on all forms of self-improvement.

2nd House Places

- Banks
- Credit unions
- Financial planning offices
- Investment clubs
- Wealth management seminars
- Farmers' markets
- High-end boutiques
- Jewelry stores
- Antique shops
- Art galleries (focusing on valuable or collectible works)
- Auctions (art, antiques, or estate sales)
- Craft fairs
- Shopping malls
- Home décor stores
- Gourmet food shops
- Wine cellars or wine tasting events

- Cooking supply stores
- Health food stores
- Cheese or charcuterie shops
- Organic farms
- Health resorts
- Home improvement stores
- Kitchenware stores
- Sustainable living expos
- Charity fundraisers focused on wealth distribution
- Gem and mineral shows
- Workshops focused on personal finances
- Subscription box curations or pop-up events
- Boutique fitness studios
- Auction houses
- The spa
- Wellness retreats

2nd House Activities

1. Attend financial literacy workshops.
2. Take a budgeting course.
3. Join an investment club or stock market seminar.
4. Shop at farmers' markets or artisan fairs for handmade goods.
5. Most shopping is a 2nd house activity.
6. Browse or shop in art galleries.
7. Attend store and gallery openings.
8. Join and attend jewelry-making classes or workshops.
9. Explore antique shops.
10. Enroll in a wine-tasting class or attend a wine-pairing event.
11. Join a cooking class.
12. Take a workshop on sustainable living or eco-friendly home design.

13. Attend real estate open houses or home-buying seminars.
14. Volunteer for charity fundraisers focused on financial or material assistance.
15. Host or attend a dinner party featuring locally sourced ingredients.
16. Join a group focused on creating a vision board centered on financial and material goals.
17. Take a personal finance course to learn about investments or savings strategies.
18. Visit a gem and mineral show.
19. Participate in a home improvement or DIY project class.
20. Browse boutique shops.
21. Join a subscription service for artisan or luxury goods and attend related events.
22. Take up a hobby that teaches you to make something tangible, such as baking, pottery, or crafting.

3rd House Places

- Local libraries
- Bookstores
- Local cafés
- Community centers
- Adult education classes at local schools or colleges
- Writing workshops
- Language classes
- Local parks (especially those hosting local events)
- Neighborhood block parties
- Farmers' markets with a social vibe
- Car shows
- Auto repair workshops or garages
- Driving schools
- Sibling-organized gatherings or family reunions

- Neighborhood association meetings
- Local festivals or fairs
- Coffee shop open mic nights
- Poetry readings at local venues
- Bike shops or cycling groups
- Local coworking spaces
- Classes hosted in the community
- Hobby clubs (like photography or knitting groups)
- Local government meetings or town halls
- School reunions
- Tech repair shops or computer cafés
- Local grocery stores or gyms
- Shared transportation hubs (transit stops, rideshares, carpools, etc.)
- DIY classes at local hardware stores
- Newspaper or magazine offices for community publications
- Car dealerships or auto auctions

3rd House Activities

1. Take a creative writing class or joining a writing group.
2. Participate in or host a book club.
3. Attend language classes to learn a new language.
4. Join a local hobby group (such as photography, crafting, or knitting).
5. Volunteer to help organize a neighborhood block party or event.
6. Visit car shows or participate in car clubs.
7. Take a short road trip to explore nearby towns.
8. Enroll in a DIY or repair workshop (such as fixing bikes or small appliances).
9. Organize a sibling hangout or family game night.
10. Join a cycling or walking group in your neighborhood.
11. Attend open mic nights at local cafés or community centers.

12. Participate in community education classes on any topic of interest.
13. Explore local history through tours or small museum visits.
14. Engage in a town hall or local government meeting to discuss community issues.
15. Volunteer to teach or tutor in a subject you're passionate about.
16. Join a public speaking or Toastmasters group.
17. Help create or distribute a community newsletter.
18. Enroll in a local art or craft class.
19. Take part in a collaborative project with neighbors or a small group.
20. Plan a casual sibling get-together, like a hike, game night, or dinner.

4th House Places

- Family reunions
- House parties
- Cookouts/barbecue parties
- Ancestry or genealogy research centers
- Historical societies
- Museums showing local or national history
- National heritage sites
- Memorial parks
- Cultural heritage festivals
- Community centers hosting family events
- Family farms or homesteads
- Real estate open houses
- Home improvement stores
- Furniture stores specializing in cozy or vintage designs
- Kitchenware shops
- Estate sales or auctions
- Historic home tours

- Patriotic parades or celebrations
- Local history tours
- Libraries with genealogy sections
- Quilting or crafting groups focused on heirloom projects
- Farmers' markets that emphasize local produce and community pride
- Community potlucks or dinners
- Home goods expos or fairs
- Local historical landmarks
- Cemeteries (for family visits or history exploration)
- Cooking classes
- Events focusing on local traditions
- Church or temple gatherings that celebrate family
- Domestic-focused workshops (such as DIY home projects, canning, or sewing)
- Family-friendly parks or picnic areas
- Family matchmaking situations

4th House Activities

1. Attend a family reunion or organize one yourself.
2. Explore your family tree through genealogy research or visiting historical archives.
3. Tour heritage sites or take part in local history tours.
4. Participate in patriotic celebrations.
5. Spend time rediscovering your hometown.
6. Volunteer at a historical society or museum.
7. Host a potluck dinner for family and/or friends.
8. Decorate or renovate your home to reflect your personal history or culture.
9. Take a cooking class focused on traditional recipes.
10. Visit cemeteries to honor ancestors.
11. Join a quilting or crafting group to create family heirlooms.

12. Attend cultural festivals or events that celebrate your heritage.
13. Visit a farmers' market to support local traditions and agriculture.
14. Collect items for a family time capsule to share memories.
15. Research local historical landmarks and plan a day to explore them.
16. Join a class about creating a family cookbook or other crafts.
17. Join a local church or community group that emphasizes family connections.
18. Participate in a home improvement workshop to upgrade your living space.
19. Attend real estate events and classes.
20. Let your family (parents or extended family) set you up.

5th House Places

- Theaters (as a performer or audience member)
- Art galleries or art studios (2nd house is buying, 5th house is appreciating or creating)
- Music venues
- Dance studios or social dance events
- Amusement parks or carnivals
- Comedy clubs or improv shows
- Sporting events
- Children's museums or activity centers
- Music festivals
- Paint-and-sip events
- Craft workshops
- Casinos or gaming events
- Bowling alleys or arcade centers
- Open mic nights
- Community theaters or drama groups
- Summer camps (as a counselor or participant)

- Zoos or aquariums (especially with kids or family)
- Festivals celebrating arts or culture
- Children's sports games or recreational leagues
- Parks hosting picnics or outdoor movies
- Performance art spaces or dance showcases
- Storytelling festivals
- Farmers' markets with live entertainment
- Outdoor music events or local band nights
- Talent competitions or auditions
- Hobby stores catering to creative interests
- Workshops focused on crafts, painting, or sculpting
- Social clubs centered on games or creative hobbies
- Dating apps aimed at fun and flirting
- Ice skating rinks or roller-skating arenas
- Local talent shows or art exhibitions
- Family fun centers or adventure parks
- Speed dating events

5th House Activities

1. Attend or perform in a local theater production.
2. Take an art class to explore painting, pottery, or sculpture.
3. Go to live music concerts or open mic nights.
4. Join a dance class, such as salsa, ballet, or hip-hop.
5. Participate in a community sports league or recreational team.
6. Volunteer at children's events or activity centers.
7. Host or attend a themed party or celebration.
8. Try your luck at a casino or participate in a poker night.
9. Visit an amusement park.
10. Go dancing at a club.
11. Attend an event at a games café.
12. Play mini golf, bowl, or engage in other fun games.

13. Participate in a storytelling or improv workshop.
14. Organize a picnic or outdoor movie night.
15. Compete in a talent show or karaoke event.
16. Attend a summer festival or fair.
17. Join a painting and wine class or crafting session.
18. Coach or mentor a kids' sports team.
19. Watch or take part in a comedy or storytelling show.
20. Organize a creative hobby group, like a knitting circle or game night.
21. Take your children or nieces and nephews to a fun activity center.
22. Sign up for a photography or filmmaking workshop.

6th House Places

- Animal shelters
- Pet stores
- Dog parks
- Veterinary clinics (as a visitor or volunteer)
- Grooming salons for pets
- Pet adoption events
- Horse stables or equestrian centers
- Wildlife sanctuaries
- Zoos with conservation programs
- Animal training schools or obedience classes
- Fitness centers or gyms
- Yoga studios
- Health food stores
- Wellness retreats
- Cooking classes focused on healthy eating
- Farmers' markets with a focus on organic produce
- Community gardens

- Workplace or office events
- Cafeterias or shared office kitchens
- Group fitness classes, such as Pilates or spin
- Medical centers or clinics
- Physical therapy centers
- Pharmacies or health supply stores
- Volunteer events focused on healthcare or well-being
- Running clubs or local 5K events
- Parks with outdoor fitness equipment
- Dog-friendly cafés or restaurants
- Community service events for cleanups or habitat restoration
- Nutrition seminars or workshops
- Wellness expos or fairs

6th House Activities

1. Volunteer at an animal shelter or rescue organization.
2. Walk or exercise dogs.
3. Sign up for a group fitness challenge or boot camp.
4. Attend a yoga or Pilates class.
5. Cook or meal-prep healthy dishes at home or in a class.
6. Join a community garden to grow fresh produce.
7. Volunteer at a clinic or wellness center.
8. Participate in a workplace wellness program or fitness initiative.
9. Enroll in a physical therapy program or help someone through theirs.
10. Attend a pet training or obedience class.
11. Take part in a dog show or pet adoption fair.
12. Visit a wildlife sanctuary.
13. Run in a local charity 5K or marathon.
14. Take a workshop on herbal medicine or natural remedies.
15. Host a pet playdate or meetup.

16. Volunteer for a park cleanup or environmental project.
17. Take a nutrition seminar or workshop on mindful eating.
18. Start a workout routine in a group fitness class or with a fitness buddy or trainer.
19. Attend a seminar on productivity and stress management.
20. Care for foster animals in your home or through a local organization.

7th House Places

- Matchmaking services or offices
- Speed dating events
- Professional networking events
- Business conferences
- Contract negotiation meetings
- Doctor's office
- Cultural festivals with one-on-one activities (like paired cooking classes)
- Law offices
- Real estate offices for co-buying ventures
- Marriage officiant workshops or events
- Counseling centers
- Ballroom dance studios
- Coworking spaces with networking potential
- Workshops for small business partnerships
- Financial planning offices for joint ventures
- Partnered fitness classes, such as partner yoga or dance
- Small group cooking classes where you're partnered up
- Exclusive social clubs with one-on-one mentoring or interaction
- Specialized travel groups for couples or paired travelers
- Book clubs focused on relationship-building themes
- Weddings and all the events attached to a wedding, like rehearsal dinners, etc.

- Entrepreneurial workshops focusing on collaborative ventures
- Wine tasting sessions with pair-based games
- Couples retreats
- Wedding trade shows
- Specialty workshops (such as pottery or photography) for paired participants
- Partner-focused adventure activities, such as tandem kayaking or paired climbing classes
- Dating apps aimed at meeting a spouse

7th House Activities

1. Attend a matchmaking event or speed dating session.
2. Participate in a business networking event centered on partnerships.
3. Enroll in a self-improvement course centered on building healthy partnerships.
4. Join a paired cooking or wine tasting class.
5. Take part in a partner yoga or dance class.
6. Visit a real estate open house for co-buying opportunities.
7. Join a social club with a focus on partnerships.
8. Engage in a one-on-one mentoring program.
9. Plan a couples party where single friends bring a potential partner for someone else attending the party.
10. Volunteer for a partner-focused fundraiser.
11. Participate in a relationship-themed book club.
12. Take a workshop on co-leadership or teamwork.
13. Explore partnered fitness challenges or exercises.
14. Try tandem kayaking, rock climbing, or other activities that require a partner.
15. Host a small discussion group about partnerships or relationships.
16. Meet potential collaborators at a coworking space event.

17. Travel with a partner-focused tour group or cultural exchange program.
18. Attend a live event hosted by a dating site.
19. Join online forums geared toward meeting a partner.
20. If you work in a client-based business, any professional development event geared toward building clientele is fair game.

8th House Places

- Therapy or counseling offices
- Support groups for emotional growth
- Financial planning or tax seminars
- Tax advisor or accountant offices
- Wealth management workshops
- Estate planning events
- Insurance agency offices
- Bank branches
- Intimacy workshops
- Sexual health clinics offering education or services
- Metaphysical stores
- Occult workshops or gatherings
- Astrology conferences or classes
- Tarot reading sessions
- Transformational retreats
- Forensic or crime-solving clubs
- Mystery/occult-themed book clubs or events
- Escape rooms
- Sex clubs
- Crisis support centers
- Private investigation agencies
- Investment clubs
- Debt management counseling centers

- Funeral homes or grief support groups
- Cemeteries or memorial parks
- Research libraries with a focus on psychology or the occult
- Sexuality-focused art exhibits or galleries
- Stargazing groups or observatories
- Charity events focused on debt relief
- Specialized wellness retreats for emotional release
- Alchemy workshops

8th House Activities

1. Attend a sexual self-awareness workshop.
2. Join a support group for emotional healing.
3. Enroll in a financial literacy or investment workshop.
4. Attend a tax or estate planning seminar.
5. Take part in an intimate relationship-building workshop.
6. Explore an astrology or tarot class.
7. Attend a retreat focused on personal transformation.
8. Join a book club discussing mysteries or psychological thrillers.
9. Participate in a group focused on forensic science or crime-solving.
10. Visit an observatory for stargazing and nighttime discussions.
11. Plan a trip to a historical cemetery or memorial park.
12. Attend a gathering at a lifestyle club.
13. Host a passion party.
14. Take a class on alchemy or alternative healing practices.
15. Try an escape room activity with a group or partner.
16. Take a writing course on themes of trust and emotional connection.
17. Collaborate with others on an investment or resource-sharing project.

9th House Places

- Universities or colleges
- Lecture halls
- Study abroad programs
- Language schools
- Cultural exchange events
- International airports
- Travel agencies or tour operator offices
- Foreign embassies or consulates
- Religious temples or spiritual centers
- Pilgrimage sites
- Philosophy clubs
- Bookstores specializing in global or philosophical themes
- Adventure travel destinations
- International film festivals
- Cultural heritage museums
- Historical landmarks
- Retreat centers for spiritual growth
- Publishing houses
- Writers' workshops focusing on travel or philosophy
- Hiking trails in foreign countries
- Study groups for religious or philosophical texts
- Global food festivals
- Foreign language meetups
- Cruises or travel tours
- Libraries with a focus on philosophy or world history
- Debate clubs on philosophical or global topics
- International conferences or conventions
- Camps focused on global awareness or outdoor adventure
- Cultural festivals celebrating global diversity
- Expeditions to remote or adventurous locations

9th House Activities

1. Attend a university lecture or academic seminar.
2. Enroll in a foreign language class.
3. Participate in a cultural exchange program.
4. Plan a trip abroad or join a travel tour group.
5. Attend a spiritual retreat or pilgrimage.
6. Join a philosophy or debate club.
7. Take a workshop on global cuisines or cultures.
8. Volunteer for an international charity or humanitarian project.
9. Explore an adventure hiking or camping trip.
10. Attend a global film festival or cultural event.
11. Sign up for a course on world history or philosophy.
12. Host or attend a book club focused on travel writing or philosophical themes.
13. Engage in a guided tour of historical or cultural landmarks.
14. Participate in an international student exchange or study abroad program.
15. Join a local meetup group for expats or global travelers.
16. Take part in a yoga or meditation class with global influences.
17. Attend an outdoor adventure expo or global travel fair.
18. Explore a cultural food festival or cooking class featuring international cuisines.
19. Participate in an online course or forum with a global focus.
20. Join an outdoor adventure club or a global citizenship initiative.

10th House Places

- Professional networking events
- Industry conferences or expos
- Corporate retreats
- Leadership seminars
- Public speaking workshops

- Award ceremonies or galas
- Trade shows
- Coworking spaces
- Career development workshops
- Mentorship programs
- Executive dining clubs
- Professional associations or societies
- Job fairs
- High-profile charity events
- Exclusive business clubs
- Toastmasters or public speaking groups
- Board meetings (as a participant or guest)
- Real estate investment forums
- Business incubators or start-up hubs
- Political campaign events
- Entrepreneurial expos or summits
- Luxury hotel lounges during business trips
- Government offices during official events
- Networking mixers hosted by professional organizations
- Fundraising dinners with corporate sponsorships
- High-level sports events in VIP areas
- Cultural galas or public events featuring influential speakers
- Exclusive launch events for products or services
- Business-focused book signings or launches
- Social media platforms for professional branding, such as LinkedIn networking groups

10th House Activities

1. Attend a professional networking event.
2. Participate in a corporate retreat or team-building exercise.
3. Enroll in a leadership training program.

4. Deliver or listen to a keynote speech at an industry conference.
5. Sign up for a career development workshop.
6. Join a mentorship program, as either a mentor or a mentee.
7. Take part in a business panel discussion.
8. Attend an award ceremony or gala honoring professional achievements.
9. Volunteer to organize or host a trade show or expo.
10. Join a professional association or society for networking.
11. Attend a job fair to explore opportunities and connect with others.
12. Host or attend a high-profile charity fundraiser.
13. Participate in an exclusive business club meeting or dinner.
14. Attend a real estate investment seminar or forum.
15. Take a public speaking course to boost professional confidence.
16. Plan or join a political campaign event focused on leadership and community impact.
17. Attend an entrepreneurial expo or business summit.
18. Engage in a book signing or launch event for a business-focused author.
19. Explore coworking spaces to meet professionals from diverse industries.
20. Participate in a luxury brand launch or corporate-sponsored event.

11th House Places

- Social clubs or hobby groups
- Volunteer organizations
- Charity events
- Community centers
- Environmental or sustainability groups
- Political campaign offices or rallies
- Activist gatherings or protests

- Networking mixers for social causes
- Meetup events for shared interests
- Co-op markets or collective buying groups
- Community gardens
- Public town hall meetings
- Bookstores hosting discussion groups
- Group fitness classes, such as CrossFit or cycling clubs
- Shared coworking spaces with community events
- Online forums or virtual meetups for niche interests
- Local arts or music festivals
- Farmers' markets with community engagement activities
- Recreational sports leagues or team events
- Board game cafés or trivia nights
- Amateur theater or improv groups
- Coffee shops hosting open mic or live discussion nights
- Animal rescue organizations or group adoption events
- Makerspaces or community workshops
- Start-up incubators focused on collaboration
- Hackathons or tech meetups
- Group travel programs or guided adventure tours
- Cultural fairs or international exchange programs
- Alumni association events or reunions
- Collaborative creative projects or art installations

11th House Activities

1. Join a social club or community group centered on a shared interest.
2. Volunteer for a charity or nonprofit organization.
3. Attend a local activist meeting or rally for a cause you care about.
4. Participate in a community cleanup or environmental project.
5. Play in a recreational sports league or team event.

6. Organize or attend a neighborhood potluck or gathering.
7. Join a group fitness class, such as cycling or boot camp.
8. Sign up for a group art project or collaborative installation.
9. Participate in a group travel program or adventure tour.
10. Host or attend a board game night or trivia event.
11. Help organize a local festival or fair.
12. Take part in an alumni association event or reunion.
13. Attend a hackathon or tech meetup for innovation and collaboration.
14. Join a book club or study group focused on a shared topic.
15. Explore a makerspace or attend a DIY workshop.
16. Participate in a coffee shop's open mic night or discussion group.
17. Volunteer at an animal rescue organization or adoption fair.
18. Join a cultural exchange program or host an international guest.
19. Take part in a political campaign as a volunteer or supporter.
20. Plan or attend a community-building event, like a local movie night or picnic.

12th House Places

- Meditation centers
- Yoga studios focused on mindfulness
- Spiritual retreats
- Monasteries or ashrams
- Quiet libraries
- Hospitals or care facilities
- Wellness centers offering holistic healing
- Counseling or therapy offices
- Silent retreats
- Sacred temples or shrines
- Cemeteries or memorial parks

- Oceanfront or quiet beaches
- Secluded hiking trails
- Animal sanctuaries
- Equestrian centers
- Aquarium exhibits with tranquil settings
- Community healing circles
- Metaphysical bookstores
- Sound healing workshops
- Art therapy studios
- Isolation tanks or sensory deprivation centers
- Private art exhibits with calming environments
- Waterfall or river areas for peaceful reflection
- Sleep therapy clinics
- Music therapy sessions
- Hospice care or volunteer programs
- Small-group prayer circles
- Nature preserves or reserves
- Float spas or hydrotherapy centers
- Private home gatherings for meditation or spiritual discussion

12th House Activities

1. Meditate at a local center or join a mindfulness group.
2. Attend a yoga class focused on inner reflection.
3. Participate in a spiritual retreat or silent meditation weekend.
4. Volunteer at a hospital or care facility.
5. Join a sound healing or gong bath session.
6. Enroll in an art therapy workshop.
7. Take part in a group counseling or support session.
8. Explore a sensory deprivation or float therapy experience.
9. Visit an animal sanctuary and assist with caretaking.
10. Attend a small prayer circle or spiritual discussion group.

11. Walk along a secluded hiking trail or peaceful beach.
12. Join a private book club focused on spiritual or psychological themes.
13. Participate in a small-group music therapy session.
14. Host or join a meditation circle in a private home.
15. Assist at a hospice care program or grief support group.
16. Try a sleep therapy class or dream analysis group.
17. Enroll in a small class on astrology, tarot, or other esoteric practices.
18. Help organize a community healing or wellness circle.
19. Reflect and write at a tranquil library or peaceful café.
20. Explore equestrian therapy or help care for large animals at a ranch.

Wrapping It Up

So there you have it—a whole bunch of places and activities that align with the rulers of your 5th, 7th, and 8th houses. Think of these as a jumping-off point rather than a set-in-stone path forward. While these suggestions highlight where love might come into your life, they're not just about meeting someone; they're also about discovering more about yourself.

Every connection, whether it turns into romance or not, has something to teach you. Maybe you discover the type of environment where you feel most at ease or the qualities you value in a partner (or ones you'd rather avoid). These moments can help clarify what you're looking for and, just as importantly, what you need to feel fulfilled in a relationship.

Even if you don't meet "the one" at one of these places, you could end up forming meaningful friendships, gaining new skills, or simply learning more about who you are and what you want. That's just as important as the romance itself. The journey of finding love is also about loving yourself and aligning with the life you want to build.

So go out there, try new things, and keep an open mind. Love might be waiting for you—but just as importantly, you might find a deeper connection to yourself along the way.

Appendix C
Timing in Action

Let's look at an example of the astrological factors that were in play at the time of meeting of a couple—"Carl" and "Carolyn"—who met online in 2000, were married in 2004, and are still happily together.

Carl's Natal Chart and Transits

First let's look at a biwheel chart for Carl (chart 11). The inner wheel is Carl's birth chart and the outer wheel shows the transits on the day he met Carolyn.

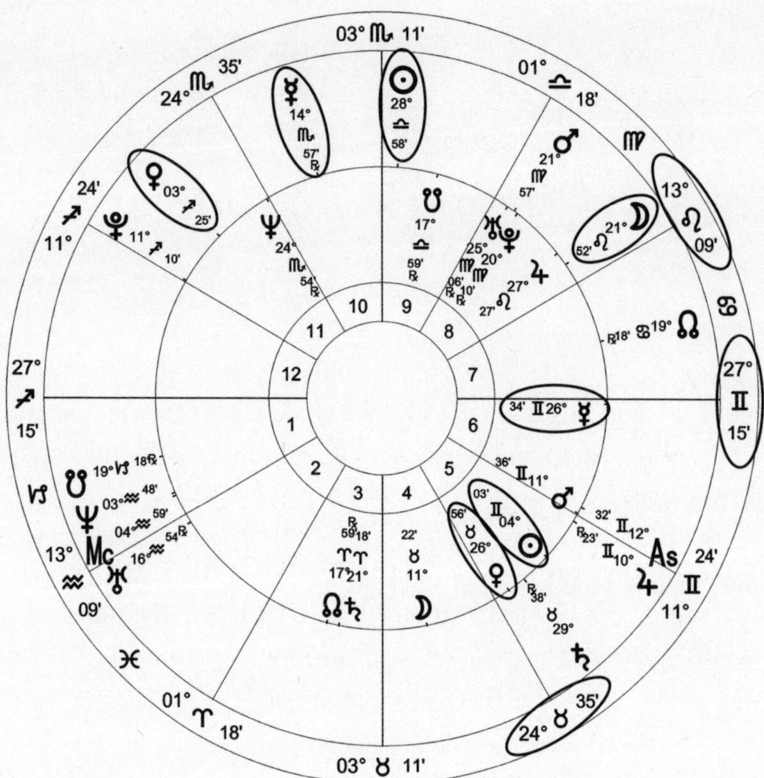

Chart 11: Carl Meets Carolyn: Carl's Natal Chart on the Inside, Transits on the Outside

Carl has Venus ruling his 5th house, placed in the 5th; Mercury ruling his 7th house, conjunct the Descendant; and the Sun ruling his 8th house, positioned in the 5th. This creates a strong connection between all three relationship houses.

At the time, Carl was actively looking for a long-term relationship and was ready to find someone to marry. He had been online dating but hadn't had much success. Given the interconnectedness of his relationship houses, traditional dating methods were all viable options for him. However, with Mercury playing a dominant role and both his 5th and 7th house rulers aspecting Uranus (Venus trine Uranus and Mercury square Uranus), meeting a partner online was a strong possibility.

Key Transits for Carl

Here are some key transits in Carl's chart on the day he met Carolyn. These transits highlight a significant activation of his relationship houses, reinforcing the likelihood of a major connection forming during this time.

- Venus opposing his natal Sun
- Mercury opposing his Moon
- The Sun trine his Mercury and Descendant
- Saturn moving through his 5th house
- Jupiter opposite Pluto, activating his Mars and forming an inconjunct with his Moon
- The transiting Moon, just coming out of his 7th house and now in his 8th, forming a trine to Saturn, a sextile to Mercury, a square to Venus, and a conjunction to Jupiter
- The North Node moving through his 7th house, potentially giving this time period a fated or karmic feel

Carolyn's Natal Chart and Transits

Carolyn wasn't looking for a relationship at the time, but a friend had been raving about a particular dating site, insisting that not only was the site entertaining but it was also a good time for her astrologically to meet someone. Even though she had no real interest in dating, Carolyn found herself with unexpected free time when a friend was running late for a study date. Annoyed and looking for a distraction, she decided to humor her friend and created a fake profile on the dating site.

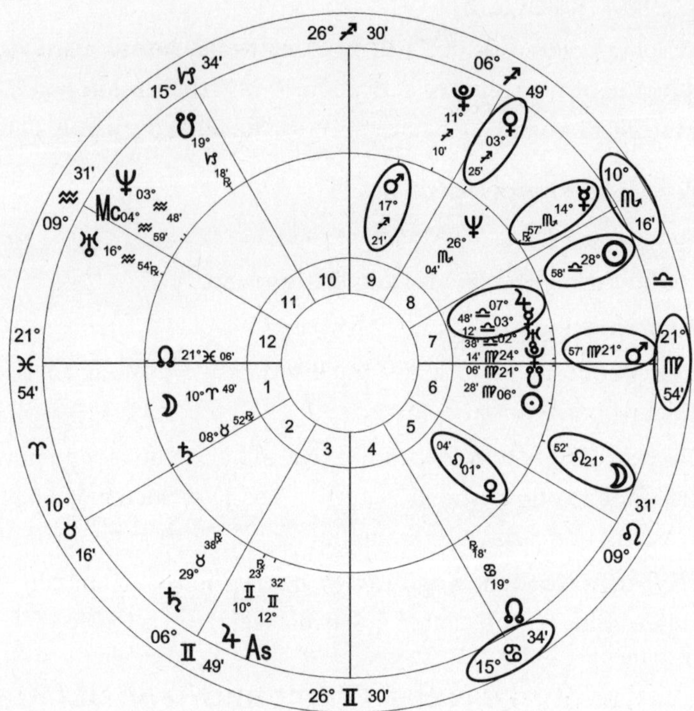

Chart 12: Carolyn Meets Carl: Carolyn's Natal Chart on the Inside, Transits on the Outside

Carolyn barely had time to finish setting up the profile before her friend finally arrived. Leaving her computer on with the dating site still open, she headed to the library. When she returned, she found a message from Carl.

Carolyn has the Moon ruling her 5th house, Mercury ruling her 7th, and Mars ruling her 8th (chart 12). With the ruler of her 7th in the 7th house and conjunct Uranus, she too has strong indicators for meeting a partner online. Her 5th house ruler was opposing her 7th house ruler while trining the ruler of her 8th, meaning all three relationship houses were connected. However, with the 5th house ruler opposing the 7th house ruler, she felt that her earlier relationships were primarily about self-discovery (1st house influence).

Key Transits for Carolyn

Here are some key transits in Carolyn's chart on the day she met Carl. With so much activity in her relationship houses, even though she wasn't intentionally looking, the timing was clearly ripe for a significant connection.

- Mercury transiting her 8th house
- Mars conjunct her Descendant in the 7th house
- Venus moving through her 8th house, sextile Mercury and trine her natal Venus
- The Sun moving through her 7th house
- Saturn forming a sextile to Venus
- The North Node moving through her 5th house

Venus or Jupiter Aspecting House Rulers

Venus and Jupiter are considered the benefics in astrology, bringing opportunities and ease wherever they transit or make aspects. When either of these planets is activating the ruler of the 5th, 7th, or 8th house—or moving through these houses—they create windows of possibility for love, connection, and deepening relationships.

For both Carl and Carolyn, Venus and Jupiter were making key aspects: Carl had Venus opposing his natal Sun and Jupiter opposing Pluto, while Carolyn had Venus transiting her 8th house, sextile Mercury and trine her natal Venus, with Jupiter also aspecting her chart. These transits don't guarantee a relationship, but they set the stage for positive encounters by opening doors and adding a sense of attraction, luck, and emotional fulfillment to the moment.

Aspects to the Ascendant/Descendant Axis and Meeting Someone

The Ascendant/Descendant axis represents the dynamic between self and others, with the Ascendant reflecting personal identity and our approach to life and the Descendant indicating how we relate to and attract others. When significant transits or natal aspects activate this axis, they can play a major role in us meeting someone important.

Personal Planets (Sun, Moon, Mercury, Venus, Mars) Aspecting the Ascendant/Descendant Axis

When a personal planet is conjunct, opposing, or making a strong aspect to the Ascendant/Descendant axis, it can make relationships feel central to your personal growth. These aspects indicate that partnerships—romantic or otherwise—are tied to your sense of self and how you navigate the world. With transits, they often mark periods when you're more socially visible, attractive, or naturally drawing others to you.

Outer Planets (Jupiter, Saturn, Uranus, Neptune, Pluto) in Transit

Transiting outer planets aspecting your Ascendant or Descendant can mark significant shifts in relationships.

- Jupiter crossing the Descendant can bring relationship opportunities or an expansion of social and romantic possibilities.
- Saturn crossing the Descendant may bring commitment, maturity, or a reality check in relationships.
- Uranus can bring sudden, unexpected connections.
- Neptune can introduce idealized romance or confusion in relationships, but it can also open the door to soul-level connection.
- Pluto often signals deeply transformative connections that challenge and reshape how you relate to others.

In Carl and Carolyn's charts, we saw key transits affecting the Descendant, such as Mars conjunct Carolyn's Descendant and the Sun moving through her 7th house, signaling an active period for connection. When planets activate this axis, they can indicate timing and conditions that can make meeting someone more likely, even if it happens unexpectedly. But I don't recommend depending on this alone to determine the best timing for two reasons:

- The rulers of the relationship houses should also be experiencing some transit energy. In this example, the ruler of Carolyn's 8th house (Mars) is transiting her Descendant.

- Using the house cusps as your only means of timing something isn't always dependable given the time of birth may be off or not available at all.

House Rulers Transiting the Relationship Houses

As you track transits, pay attention to when the rulers of your 5th, 7th, or 8th house move through any of the relationship houses, as these periods often highlight relational growth, shifts, or new opportunities.

- When the rulers of your 5th, 7th, or 8th house move through the relationship houses, they activate those themes in a personal and significant way. This can indicate a period when romance, commitment, or intimacy becomes more of a focus, whether through meeting someone new, deepening an existing connection, or reevaluating what you want in relationships.
- In Carl's chart, the ruler of his 7th house (Mercury) was opposing his natal Moon, activating emotional self-reflection in relationships. His 8th house ruler (the Sun) was trine his Mercury and Descendant, further emphasizing communication and connections. With Saturn transiting his 5th house, there was a serious tone to dating—he was ready for a long-term relationship.
- For Carolyn, the ruler of her 7th house (Mercury) was transiting her 8th house, which intensified the potential for deeper connections. Mars (her 8th house ruler) was conjunct her Descendant, making relationships highly active at the time. Additionally, Venus, the planet of attraction, was transiting her 8th house while forming a sextile to Mercury and a trine to her natal Venus—all of which indicated a period ripe for significant relationship developments.
- When your relationship house rulers move through the 5th, 7th, or 8th house, pay attention! These transits often set the stage for romantic connections, deep emotional experiences, or new commitments. Whether you're actively seeking a relationship or not, these periods can reveal valuable insights about love, attraction, and intimacy in your life.

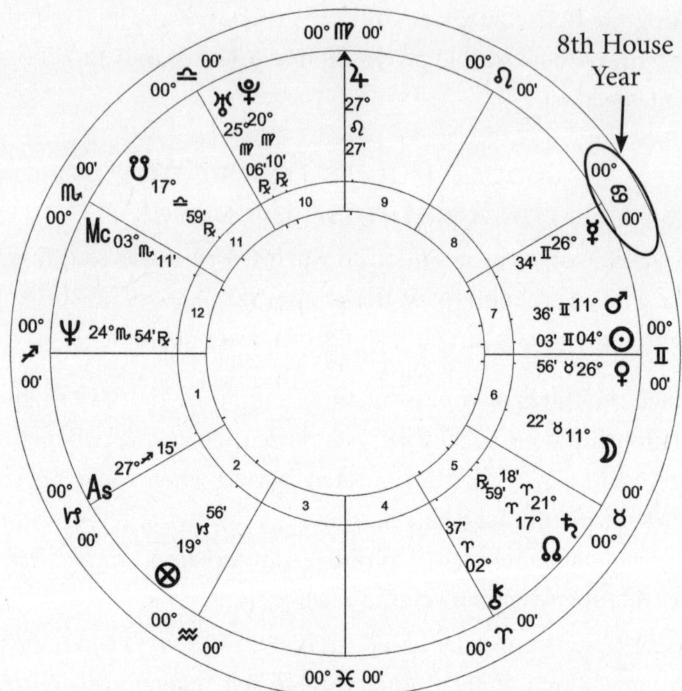

Chart 13: Carl's Chart, Whole Sign Houses, Profection Year

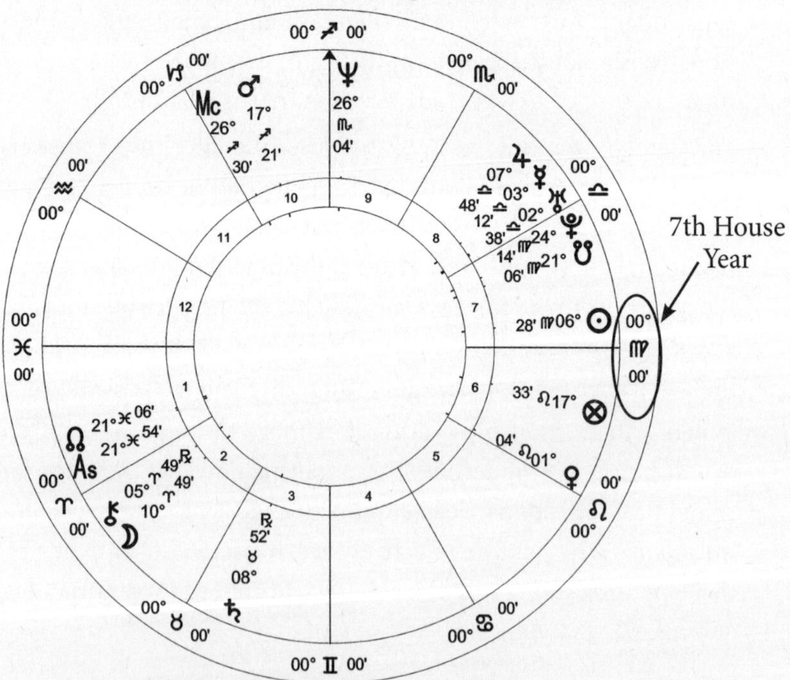

Chart 14: Carolyn's Chart, Whole Sign Houses, Profection Year

Annual Profections

Profections help pinpoint when the relationship areas of your life (and which planetary rulers) are active each year.

For example, when they met, both Carl and Carolyn were in relationship house profection years, which we can determine by first using Whole Sign houses to calculate their charts (charts 13 and 14). Using the annual profections wheel on page 273, we see that Carolyn was in a 7th house year (30 years old) and Carl in an 8th house year (31 years old). So Carl was in a Moon year (since the Moon rules his 8th house) and Carolyn was in a Mercury year (since Mercury rules her 7th house). This means aspects to Carl's natal Moon and transits involving the Moon took on added importance, while the same applied to Carolyn's Mercury. Not only were they both in relationship-focused profection years, but their lord of the year was experiencing significant transits, and the transiting time lords were making key aspects, further emphasizing relationship themes. (Remember, the planet in charge of the house you move into on your birthday becomes the lord of the year.)

To use this technique for timing, look at the ruler of your profected house—where it's placed in your natal chart and what transits it's receiving. If you're in a 7th house year and Venus is your 7th house ruler, then Venus transits and returns will be especially important for relationship timing.

Another way to work with profections is to track the movement of your natal relationship house rulers and use the timing of when the relationship ruler moves through your annual profected house. For example, if Mercury rules your 7th house and you're in a 9th house profection year, then the period when Mercury transits your 9th house could serve as a key timing indicator—especially when it aligns with other significant transits or timing techniques.

In the annual profections wheel, you can easily track which house is activated and use this insight to work with the energy of the year, making intentional choices in love and partnerships.

Secondary Progressions

With our example couple, they were each having significant transits and profections at the time of meeting, but we also see great potential in their progressed charts, which indicate they were ready to welcome a significant long-term, committed relationship.

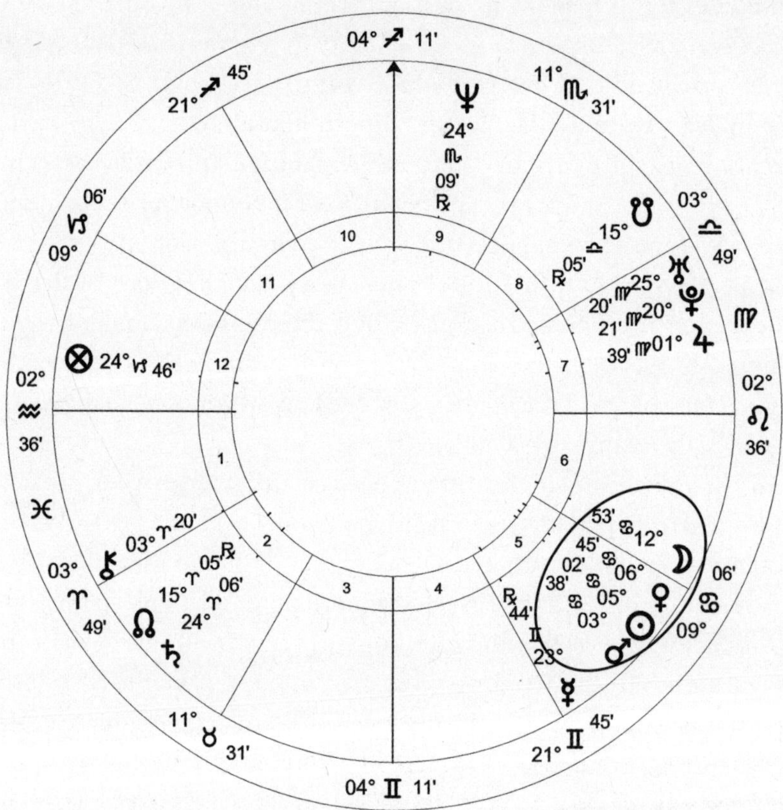

Chart 15: Carl's Progressed Chart at Time of Meeting

In Carl's progressed chart at the time of meeting Carolyn (chart 15), his progressed Sun was sitting between Venus and Mars, and those planets along with the Moon were all sitting in his natal 7th house (not pictured here). He was also in a progressed New Moon phase, which perfected in his progressed 5th house of romance but was happening in his natal 7th house. Progressed Mercury (ruler of Carl's natal 7th house) was moving away from a sextile to his natal Saturn (planet of commitment) and toward a sextile to his progressed Saturn.

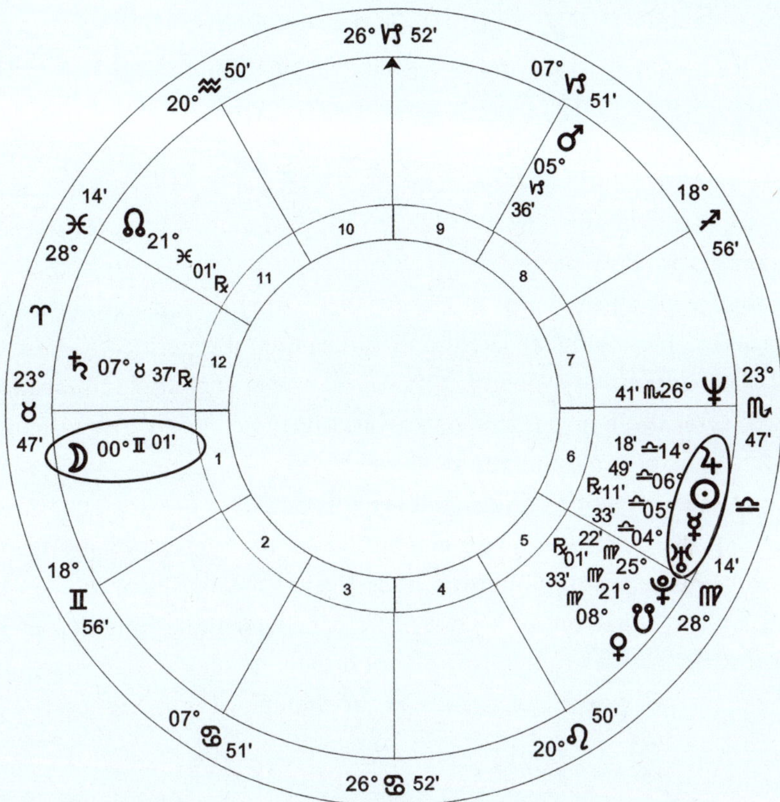

Chart 16: Carolyn's Progressed Chart at Time of Meeting

In Carolyn's progressed chart at the time of meeting Carl (chart 16), she had the progressed Sun conjunct the natal ruler of her 7th house of committed relationships (Mercury), and they were both in her natal 7th house as well (not pictured here). The progressed Moon had *just* changed signs the day before, when it moved into Gemini, the sign on Carolyn's natal 7th house. The progressed Moon in Gemini was getting ready to trine all the progressed and natal planets in Carolyn's natal 7th house. Progressed Venus was trine her natal Saturn. She was not in a progressed New Moon phase but had just gone through her progressed lunar phase return.

Summary: The Importance of Timing

As you've seen, timing plays a crucial role in relationships, and in this appendix we have explored the various astrological tools—transits, progressions, and profections—that help us understand when significant connections are more likely to happen. We've seen how planetary movements activate different areas of life, creating windows of opportunity for romance, commitment, and deeper intimacy. By tracking these cycles, you can align your efforts with the times when your relationship houses are most active, increasing the likelihood of meaningful experiences.

Looking at Carl and Carolyn's charts, we saw how multiple connections between transits, house rulers, and profections lined up to create the timing for their meeting. But you don't need every single piece to align perfectly to meet someone significant. Even just a couple of well-timed transits in an important profection year can be enough to bring a special someone into your life. If your relationship houses aren't obviously connected, that doesn't mean you're out of luck; it just means your timing might follow a different rhythm. Astrology isn't all about fate; it's about awareness—and using that awareness to put yourself in the right place at the right time.

To Write to the Author

If you wish to contact the author or would like more information about this book, please write to the author in care of Llewellyn Worldwide Ltd. and we will forward your request. Both the author and the publisher appreciate hearing from you and learning of your enjoyment of this book and how it has helped you. Llewellyn Worldwide Ltd. cannot guarantee that every letter written to the author can be answered, but all will be forwarded. Please write to:

Tracy Quinlan
℅ Llewellyn Worldwide
2143 Wooddale Drive
Woodbury, MN 55125-2989

Please enclose a self-addressed stamped envelope for reply,
or $1.00 to cover costs. If outside the U.S.A., enclose
an international postal reply coupon.

Many of Llewellyn's authors have websites with additional
information and resources. For more information,
please visit our website at https://www.llewellyn.com.